S0-AIL-248

Tradition and Revolt
in Latin America
and other essays

Institute of
Latin American Studies,
Columbia University

R. A. Humphreys

Tradition and Revolt in Latin America
and other essays

Columbia University Press
New York
1969

Published in Great Britain
by Weidenfeld and Nicolson

Copyright © 1969 by R. A. Humphreys
Library of Congress Catalog Card Number: 69-12966
Printed in Great Britain

LIBRARY
FLORIDA STATE UNIVERSITY
TALLAHASSEE, FLORIDA

The Institute of Latin American Studies of Columbia University was established in 1961 in response to a national, public, and educational need for a better understanding of the nations of Latin America and a more knowledgeable basis for inter-American relations. The major objectives of the Institute are to prepare a limited number of North Americans for scholarly and professional careers in the field of Latin American studies, to advance our knowledge of Latin America through an active program of research in the social sciences and the humanities, and to improve public knowledge through publication of a series of books and monographs on Latin America. Most of these volumes are the result of research by the faculty, by graduate students, and by visiting scholars to the Institute. The series also includes translations from Portuguese and Spanish of important contemporary books by Latin American scholars and occasional contributions by scholars of Latin America from other institutions in the United States and abroad. The faculty of the Institute are particularly proud to be able to include in this series the United States edition of *Tradition and Revolt in Latin America* by R. A. Humphreys. Professor Humphreys is a most distinguished British historian. He is Professor of Latin American History at Queens College, University of London, and he is the director of the Institute of Latin American Studies of the University of London.

In these essays on Latin America written in the last fifteen years, we feel that Professor Humphreys brings a British and a European perspective on Latin American history and society which is at once penetrating and profound and which will be especially enlighting to the North American student of Latin America.

The Institute of Latin American Studies is grateful to the Ford Foundation for financial assistance which has made this publication program possible.

Foreword

Most of the lectures and articles included in this volume were written in the last fifteen years. For permission to reprint them here I wish to thank the Athlone Press of the University of London, the Councils of the British Academy and of the Royal Historical Society, the editors of *History* and of the *Law Quarterly Review*, the Hispanic and Luso-Brazilian Councils, Messrs Eyre and Spottiswoode, and University College London. I should like to express my acknowledgements also to the Comité International des Sciences Historiques and to the editor of the *Hispanic American Historical Review*. Except for some small emendations and excisions the texts remain unaltered. But a few additional notes have been placed within square brackets.

To my wife, who has put these essays together, I owe more than I can say.   R.A.H.

Contents

Maps

I

Tradition and Revolt in Latin America*

In one of the most famous of his essays Montaigne discusses the New World. 'Our world,' he says – it is Florio's translation – 'hath of late discovered another . . . no lesse-large, fully-peopled, all-things-yeelding, and mighty in strength than ours; nevertheless so new and infantine, that he is yet to learne his A B C.' It was 'an unpolluted, harmelesse, infant world'; yet in this world great civilizations had existed. 'Nor Grece, nor Rome, nor Aegipt, can (bee it in profit, or difficultie or nobility) equall or compare sundrie and divers of their workes.' He condemns the conquest: 'the richest, the fairest and the best part of the world topsiturvied, ruined and defaced'. And, meditating on the rise and fall of civilizations, he looks into the future: 'if wee conclude aright of our end . . . this late-world shall but come to light when ours shall fall into darknesse.'[1]

I quote this passage for three reasons. Here, not fifty years after the conquest, is the familiar parallel between a corrupt Europe and an innocent America: the 'unpolluted, harmelesse, infant world'. Here – and this also is a theme constantly to be met with – is the idea of a young continent for which destiny holds high things in store: 'this late-world shall but come to light when ours shall fall into darknesse.' And here, finally, is the realization, not common in sixteenth-century Europe, nor indeed still later, that the New World had a past as well as a future, that native civiliza-

* [The Creighton Lecture in History, University of London, 1964. (Athlone Press, London, 1965.)]

[1] 'Of Coaches.' *The Essayes of Michael Lord of Montaigne* (translated by John Florio, 3 vols., Oxford, 1904–6), iii, 157–67. *Cf.* 'Of the Caniballes', *ibid.*, i, 245, 250, 255, and on Montaigne and the New World see Gilbert Chinard, *L'Exotisme Américain dans la Littérature Française au xvie siècle* (Paris, 1911), pp. 193–218, Antonello Gerbi, *Viejas Polémicas sobre el Nuevo Mundo* (3rd ed., Lima, 1946), pp. 84, 129, 176–7, and Pedro Henríquez-Ureña, *Literary Currents in Hispanic America* (Cambridge, Mass., 1946), pp. 23–5.

tions had there existed – Montaigne refers to their 'proud pompe and glorious magnificence' – which ought to be examined and compared with the civilizations of the Old World.

Few Europeans realized this, few, at least, who had not seen for themselves the great pre-conquest empires or their ruins.[1] Who the Indians were, whence they came, their innocence, their savagery, their rationality, whether they could be taught to live like Christian labourers in Castille, these questions much excited the European mind.[2] But save by a few of the chroniclers – Sahagún most notably – the character of the civilizations which they had established was little regarded. Robertson, in the eighteenth century, made one of the first serious attempts at understanding, and even Robertson did not get very far.[3] But though Europe in general failed to grasp the full significance of all that had been found, we can still sense the awed surprise which the Spaniards felt when first they gazed on the island city of Tenochtitlán, on whose ruins Mexico City was so soon to arise. 'We were amazed,' wrote that stout old soldier, Bernal Díaz del Castillo, as he looked back in his old age, 'and said that it was like the enchantments they tell of in the legend of Amadis, on account of the great towers and temples and buildings rising from the water, and all built of masonry. And some of our soldiers even asked whether the things that we saw were not a dream?'[4]

Like a dream they were soon to be. The native civilizations vanished before the white man with guns and horse and armour. But the Indian remained. The conquest, it is true, took a terrible toll of human life, by the sword, barbarity, famine and disease. But despite the great and prolonged decline in the numbers of the

[1] Henríquez-Ureña, *op. cit.*, pp. 20, 65.

[2] See Lewis Hanke, *The First Social Experiments in America* (Cambridge, Mass., 1935), pp. 3–25, and his *The Spanish Struggle for Justice in the Conquest of America* (Philadelphia, 1949), pp. 10–13, 40–1.

[3] See below, 'William Robertson and his *History of America*', pp. 28–30.

[4] Bernal Díaz del Castillo, *Historia Verdadera de la Conquista de la Nueva España* (ed. Genaro García, 2 vols., Mexico, 1904), i, 266; *The True History of the Conquest of New Spain* (translated by A. P. Maudslay, 5 vols., Hakluyt Society, 2nd series, Nos. 23, 24, 25, 30, 40, London, 1908–16), ii, 37. I have substituted 'temples' for 'cues', which is the word used by Díaz and retained by Maudslay. The Spaniards, says Acosta, used to call 'temples' by 'this word Cu, which word might be taken from the Ilanders of Santo Domingo, or of Cuba, as many other wordes that are in use, the which are neyther from Spaine nor from any other language now usuall among the Indians'. José de Acosta, *The Natural and Moral History of the Indies* (translated by Edward Grimston, 2 vols., Hakluyt Society, 1st series, Nos. 60, 61, London, 1880), ii, 327.

aboriginal peoples in Mexico[1] and in other parts of Spanish America also, it was not in Catholic and Spanish America but in what it is convenient, though inaccurate, to call Protestant and Anglo-Saxon America that the Indian was to suffer the same fate as the bison. 'It is to be admired,' says Daniel Denton in his *Brief Description of New York* in 1670, 'how strangely' the Indians 'have decreast by the Hand of God, since the English first setling of those parts . . . and it hath been generally observed, that where the English come to settle, a Divine Hand makes way for them, by removing or cutting off the Indians either by Wars one with the other, or by some raging mortal Disease.'[2] Where the Spaniards came to settle, it was not so. On the contrary, where the native populations were densest, there the seats of Spanish power were strongest.

Sudden, violent, unforseen, the Spanish conquest of America in the sixteenth century was the first great revolution on which modern Hispanic America is founded. The conquest gave rise to new Hispanic-American societies, moulded, in the infinite variety of the American environment, by the intimate contact of European with Indian, and soon, also, in some areas, with African culture. A 'new mestizo world was created for Spain, and, in Brazil, for Portugal'.[3] In Spanish America, though not in Portuguese America, it was, from the first, a world of cities, almost indeed of city states. Already before the sixteenth century closed most of what are today the capital cities of Spanish America, and many others also, dotted the map, like Roman coloniae in Britain, outposts of empire, centres of civilization in the wilderness. Architecture in Spanish America was always the first of the arts, and there is nothing in the United States to compare with the vanishing

[1] Sherburne F. Cook and Lesley Byrd Simpson estimated in 1948 that the aboriginal population of central Mexico in 1607 was less than a fifth of what it had been in 1519. *The Population of Central Mexico in the Sixteenth Century* (Ibero-Americana, 31, Berkeley, Cal., 1948). More recent work indicates that the pre-Conquest population was denser and the decline sharper even than this estimate suggests. Sherburne F. Cook and Woodrow Borah, *The Indian Population of Central Mexico, 1531–1610* (Ibero-Americana, 44, Berkeley, 1960), and Woodrow Borah and Sherburne F. Cook, *The Aboriginal Population of Central Mexico on the Eve of the Spanish Conquest* (Ibero-Americana, 45, Berkeley, 1963).

[2] Daniel Denton, *A Brief Description of New York, formerly called New Netherlands* (London, 1670), reprinted in *Gowans' Bibliotheca Americana* I (New York, 1845), pp. 6–7.

[3] W. L. Schurz, *This New World. The Civilization of Latin America* (London, 1956), p. 299.

splendour of these colonial cities. Separated by vast distances and empty spaces, they were, they still are, the outward and visible sign of Spain in America.[1]

More than a century divides the first Spanish settlement from the first English settlement in America, and it is tempting to compare the two types of colonization, one the product of medieval and renaissance Europe, the other of post-reformation England. 'The primary plan of the English colonist,' it is said, 'was to live on the land, and to derive his support from its cultivation. The primary plan of the Spanish colonist was to live in the town, and to derive his support from the labour of the Indians and of such other persons as found themselves compelled by unfavourable circumstances to turn to agriculture, or the work of the mines.'[2] Again, the Spaniards went to the New World in the classic phrase of Bernal Díaz, 'to serve God and his Majesty, to give light to those in darkness, and also to get rich'.[3] The Spaniard, says Prescott, was 'ever a Crusader'.[4] It is a cherished view, also, that the New England puritans, at least, left these shores in order to worship as they pleased, though not indeed to carry the gospel to new lands. But not all New Englanders were moved by motives of religion. Cotton Mather relates that when a minister was exhorting the people of a settlement to the north-east of Boston to hold fast to those religious principles whose preservation, he asserted, 'was the main end of planting this wilderness', he was interrupted by a member of the congregation who said: ' "Sir, you are mistaken: you think you are preaching to the people at the Bay; our *main end* was to *catch fish*." '[5] And if some Englishmen sailed to America to catch fish, not all Spaniards went there as soldiers or administrators, still less as missionaries. There were farmers in Spanish America as well as in English America, and in both areas,

[1] On the colonial city see C. H. Haring, *The Spanish Empire in America* (New York, 1947), pp. 158–78, and J. H. Parry's essay, *The Cities of the Conquistadores* (London, 1961).

[2] Bernard Moses, *South America on the Eve of Emancipation* (New York and London, 1908), p. 77.

[3] Díaz del Castillo, *Historia Verdadera*, ii, 485.

[4] W. H. Prescott, *History of the Conquest of Peru* (5th ed., 3 vols., London, 1857), ii, 153.

[5] Cotton Mather, *Magnalia Christi Americana* (1702, ed. Thomas Robbins, 2 vols., Hartford, 1853), i, 66. See a similar story in Professor C. C. Griffin's stimulating essay, 'Unidad y Variedad en la Historia Americana', in *Ensayos sobre la Historia del Nuevo Mundo* (Mexico, 1951), p. 107. There is an English version in Lewis Hanke, ed., *Do the Americas Have a Common History?* (New York, 1964).

it may be suspected, the majority of immigrants principally hoped, if not to get rich, at least to secure a competence.

But Spanish and English colonization did in fact result in differing structures of society: differing social structures, differing economic structures, differing political structures, though the differences, of course, were less marked in the colonies of exploitation than in those of settlement.[1] 'I came to get gold,' Cortés had said on his arrival in Hispaniola in 1504, 'not to till the soil like a peasant.'[2] Small properties there were in Spanish America. The Indian village and Indian communal agriculture survived. From time to time the crown tried to promote settlement on 'moderate' amounts of land, which Spaniards would work for themselves.[3] But neither the Spanish nor the Indian heritage, nor, indeed, the Spanish American environment itself, favoured the development of the kind of small farm economy which grew up in New England, for example. The Spanish disdain for manual work; the prestige traditionally attaching to land-ownership and stock-raising in Spain; the sheer amount of land available; its attractiveness as an investment; the presence of native Indian labour; urgent problems of food supply: all were factors which tended to encourage the growth of great estates. Much work remains to be done on the formation of these estates. The task which M. François Chevalier has performed for Mexico needs to be performed elsewhere. Conditions varied greatly from colony to colony, and from area to area within the same colony. The fact remains that almost everywhere in Spanish America, from New Spain to Chile, the great estate, the hacienda, the ranch, became as much a dominant feature of the colonial landscape as the planned and powerful city. By the eighteenth century it was buttressed by entail, and, when in ecclesiastical hands, by mortmain. Immense properties, for example, were owned by the Society of Jesus; and the sale of these properties to private individuals did something, no doubt, to mitigate colonial resentment when the Jesuits were expelled from the Spanish dominions in 1767.

[1] A distinction, as the late Richard Pares pointed out, much more real economically than the more popular distinction between the mainland colonies in North America and the West Indian colonies. *The Historian's Business and Other Essays* (Oxford, 1961), p. 56.

[2] Hanke, *The Spanish Struggle for Justice*, p. 71.

[3] François Chevalier, *La Formation des Grands Domaines au Mexique* (Paris, 1952), p. 61. For the colonization plans of Las Casas see Hanke, *The Spanish Struggle for Justice*, pp. 54–71.

The rise of the great estate and of the landed gentry, some of whose members hastened to purchase titles of nobility in Spain, was accompanied by the formation of a semi-servile Indian and mestizo peasantry. The crown had a genuine concern for the welfare of the Indian. He might be subject to various forms of labour service, but he was a free man, not a slave. Landowners were forbidden to attach Indians to their properties. They were forbidden to encroach on Indian lands.[1] In fact they did both, and, by advancing money and goods to labourers and tenants, tied the peon to the soil by an inescapable burden of debt.[2] Debt servitude of this kind was fully established in Mexico by the end of the seventeenth century, and some Indians, no doubt, were better off as debt peons than as members of the Indian communities.[3] A hundred years later, Humboldt, who knew something about peasants in Europe, thought that the lot of the Mexican agricultural labourer was perhaps happier than that of his North European counterpart.[4] In Chile, on the other hand, the secretary to the *consulado* of Santiago declared that the *inquilino*, or peasant, was 'subject to almost all the disabilities of a feudal system without enjoying any of its advantages'.[5] And Humboldt, it should be added, had no illusions about the 'extreme misery' in which most Mexican Indians lived.[6]

The landed gentry were, for the most part, creoles – Spaniards, that is, born in America, or persons who liked to think of themselves as Spaniards: legal whiteness could be purchased as well as inherited. They were divided from the Indian peon and, beneath him, the negro slave by a hierarchy of castes and classes. But creoles were also divided from Spaniards. In law there was no distinction between them. But it existed in practice. The greater merchants, representing the monopolistic houses of Seville and

[1] Chevalier, *op. cit.*, p. 369; Haring, *op. cit.*, pp. 68, 257.

[2] Chevalier, *op. cit.*, pp. 366–77; Silvio Zavala, 'Orígenes Coloniales del Peonaje en México', *El Trimestre Económico*, x (1944), 711–48, and see also his *New Viewpoints on the Spanish Colonization of America* (Philadelphia, 1943), pp. 98–9.

[3] Woodrow Borah, *New Spain's Century of Depression* (Ibero-Americana, 35, Berkeley, Cal., 1951), p. 42; Chevalier, *op. cit.*, pp. 384–6.

[4] Alexander von Humboldt, *Essai Politique sur la Royaume de la Nouvelle-Espagne* (5 vols., Paris, 1811), i, 421, iii, 7.

[5] Hernán Ramírez Necochea, *Antecedentes Económicos de la Independencia de Chile* (Santiago de Chile, 1959), p. 91.

[6] *Essai Politique*, i, 428 ff. For debt servitude in Peru in the early eighteenth century see the report of Jorge Juan and Antonio de Ulloa, *Noticias Secretas de América* (Buenos Aires, 1953), pp. 209 ff.

Cádiz, were usually Spaniards. So were the civil servants. Spaniards born in America had little or no share in the government of their homelands. It was no part of Spanish policy to create a creole administrative class, still less to endow the creoles with political responsibilities. The colonial aristocracy of landowners and lawyers was left, as Bolívar bitterly complained, without knowledge of public affairs and with no experience of their conduct;[1] and between the Spaniard born in America and the Spaniard born in Spain the gulf of resentment, envy and contempt constantly widened and deepened.

In the eighteenth century there were signs of a slow erosion of this social structure,[2] though there were signs, too, that social tensions were becoming more acute.[3] This was the result of the Bourbon administrative and economic reforms, which weakened the traditional order, and of the new economic prosperity which most of the colonies came to enjoy. The advent of 'enlightened despotism' in Spain, and the transmission to Spanish America of the ideas of the eighteenth-century enlightenment in general, were reflected also in a new spirit of criticism and enquiry directed to the advancement of useful knowledge and the improvement of existing conditions. These ideas were to be handed on to a later age and to form the basis of a new tradition. But only a few eighteenth-century reformers were also revolutionaries. Revolts, of course, occurred, of Indians, of negroes, even of creoles. But these were revolts against specific abuses or specific measures, not against the king or the crown. A traditional loyalty held the vast imperial structure together. Humboldt, with his usual acuteness, noted that towards the end of the century creoles began to call themselves, not Spaniards, but Americans;[4] and there were other evidences of a growing creole self-consciousness within the

[1] Contestación de un Americano Meridional a un Caballero de esta Isla, Kingston, 6 Sept. 1815. Simón Bolívar, *Obras Completas* (ed. Vicente Lecuna and Esther Barret de Nazaris, 2 vols., Habana, 1947), i, 165, 166. The creoles enjoyed a measure of representation in the *cabildos*, or town councils, and city government was reinvigorated in the eighteenth century. But a share in the management of a city ward provided little training for the government of independent states.

[2] L. N. McAlister, 'Social Structure and Social Change in New Spain', *Hispanic American Historical Review*, xliii (1963), 370.

[3] *Cf.* the denunciations of the mestizos and others by creoles and of creoles by European-born Spaniards. Eduardo Arcila Farías, *Economía Colonial de Venezuela* (Mexico, 1946), pp. 370–1; Catalina Sierra, *El Nacimiento de México* (Mexico, 1960), p. 75.

[4] *Essai Politique*, ii, 3.

several regions of the empire. But it was not till the crown fell into captivity and the armies of Napoleon over-ran the peninsula that the bonds between Spanish America and Spain were severed.

The fall of the empire is the second great revolution on wh' ı modern Hispanic America is founded. Like the conquest, it was written in blood. And like the conquest, it has been shrouded in myth. 'The War of Independence,' declared Alberdi, 'endowed us with a ridiculous and disgraceful mania for the heroic.'[1] And while, on the one hand, heroes and demigods were made to dominate the stage, on the other, the revolutions of the first quarter of the nineteenth century were seen as great popular movements leading to the triumph of the idea of liberty as against the defenders of a dark colonial past.[2]

Heroism, of course, there was, and not on one side only. But though much was said of the sovereignty of the people, the revolutions which transformed into independent states the Hispanic-American societies that had been evolving since the conquest were 'popular' revolutions only in a very restricted sense. They did not represent the sudden release of the resentments of a native people, or even of a large cross-section of a colonial population, against a European oppressor. Nor were they essentially democratic. On the contrary, most of them began, quite simply, as the revolt of one Spanish minority against another Spanish minority, of creoles, in the language of the day, against *peninsulares*. Their aim was self-government for creoles, not necessarily for the mixed races, for Indians, and for negroes, who, together, made up four-fifths of the population of Spanish America. And with the political emancipation of creoles was coupled their economic emancipation, the destruction, that is, of the commercial monopoly of Spain and the opening of the ports of the continent to the trade of the world.

But revolutions are not made in a day. Nor is it easy to control them. Conflicts of interests quickly appeared, and divergencies also of ideas and aims – between capital cities and provincial cities, for example, between conservatives and radicals, and between the reforming ideals of the 'age of the enlightenment' and its revolu-

[1] José Luis Romero, *A History of Argentine Political Thought* (translated by T. F. McGann, Stanford, Cal., 1963), p. 148.

[2] Silvio Zavala, *The Political Philosophy of the Conquest of America* (translated by Teener Hall, Mexico, 1953), p. 15.

tionary ideals.[1] Creoles fought Spaniards. But Spanish Americans also fought each other. And while rebels and royalists alike appealed to, and exploited, the illiterate masses, the struggle once begun released incalculable forces, was waged with ruthless violence, and left desolation in its wake. A few areas – Paraguay was one – escaped comparatively lightly. Coastal cities, such as Buenos Aires and Valparaiso, grew and flourished on the new currents of foreign trade. But, though the extent of the damage varied from region to region, in general the economic life of Spanish America was disrupted and the prosperity which had marked the closing years of the colonial period destroyed. Trade routes were abandoned, mines deserted, crops and livestock laid waste. The labour supply was dislocated, capital put to flight.[2]

As the economic life of Spanish America was disrupted, so also political stability was undermined. The crown had been the symbol of a political control which extended to almost every aspect of colonial life. Naturally it was not always obeyed. But it supplied a unifying, cohesive force, and, in theory at least, it was invariably respected. Its disappearance left a vacuum. This the creoles had expected to fill with a new republican authority, safeguarded in written instruments of government. Instead, as Lord Acton remarked, the habits of subordination departed with the Spaniard.[3] The wars themselves encouraged the military not the civilian virtues; and, while generals who had commanded armies aspired to govern countries, the consequences of that lack of experience in self-government which, with whatever limitations, the English colonies in North America had enjoyed became fully apparent. 'Until our countrymen,' wrote Bolívar, in his famous Jamaica Letter in 1815, 'acquire the political talents and virtues which distinguish our brothers of the north, entirely popular systems, far from working to our advantage, will, I greatly fear, come to

[1] Rivadavia represents one set of ideas in Buenos Aires, Mariano Moreno (who translated the *Contrat Social* in 1810) the other. For Bolívar's strictures on what has been called 'Jacobin anarchy' in Venezuela see his Manifesto of Cartagena, 15 Dec. 1812, and his Address to the Congress of Angostura, 15 Feb. 1819. *Obras Completas*, i, 41–5, ii, 1138–9. See also V. A. Belaunde, *Bolívar and the Political Thought of the Spanish American Revolution* (Baltimore, 1938), pp. 124–37.

[2] See Charles C. Griffin, 'Economic and Social Aspects of the Era of Independence', *Hispanic American Historical Review*, xxix (1949), 170–87, a pioneering article elaborated and, in some respects, modified in his *Los Temas Sociales y Económicos en la Epoca de la Independencia* (Caracas, 1962).

[3] *Historical Essays and Studies* (London, 1908), p. 145.

be our ruin.'[1] His disillusion and despair as, fifteen years later, he neared his tragic end, he summed up in a still more famous phrase: 'For us America is ungovernable. He who serves a revolution ploughs the sea.'[2]

The social results of the revolutions are more difficult to estimate. This also is a field of enquiry in which much work remains to be done. But the clash of race and class was clearly marked during the wars of independence. In Mexico the great Indian and mestizo rebellions led by Hidalgo and Morelos were revolts of the dispossessed against the possessing classes. The elements of racial war were plainly visible in Venezuela, and, in what Sarmiento described as the warfare of the countryside against the town, a conflict of cultures was equally evident in Argentina.[3] Heirs to the traditions of the eighteenth-century enlightenment, many of the revolutionary leaders, notably Bolívar and San Martín, Santander in Colombia, O'Higgins in Chile, and Rivadavia in Buenos Aires, were concerned with social and humanitarian, as well as with political and economic, reform.[4] And though their efforts were not always successful, it is obvious that some social consequences of great importance did flow from the revolutions. Negro slavery and the slave trade were in most countries restricted or abolished, in contrast to what happened in the old Portuguese colony of Brazil. The legal disabilities affecting the mulattos and other inferior castes were removed. New men, creoles and mestizos, rose by the revolutions to enter the ranks of the ruling class. And the all-pervading influence of the church, hitherto an arm, or at least an ally, of the state, was weakened.

The relation of the social classes to one another, already changing in the late eighteenth century, was thus further modified by the revolutions. But the hierarchial structure of society remained intact. Apart from the wild Indian tribes of the interior the whole population of Spanish America in 1825 was no greater than that of England, Wales and Scotland at the time of the first Reform Bill. The Indians were by far the largest element, and after them the

[1] *Obras Completas*, i, 168.

[2] Bolívar to General Flores, 9 Nov. 1830, *ibid.*, ii, 959.

[3] D. F. Sarmiento, *Life in the Argentine Republic in the Days of the Tyrants, or Civilization and Barbarism* (translated by Mrs Horace Mann, New York, 1961), pp. 33, 58–9, 63.

[4] See C. C. Griffin, 'The Enlightenment and Latin American Independence', in A. P. Whitaker, ed., *Latin America and the Enlightenment* (2nd ed., Ithaca, N.Y., 1961), pp. 131–4, and his *Temas Sociales*, pp. 23–6.

mestizos. But the coming of independence meant little or nothing to the Mexican peon, the Peruvian Indian or the Chilean *inquilino*, and the social and economic power of a small territorial aristocracy was in no way diminished. 'The distinctively Mexican economy,' Professor Woodrow Borah observes, 'was already organized on the basis of latifundia and debt peonage' at the end of the seventeenth century.[1] It was still so organized at the end of the nineteenth century. There were differences, certainly. New blood had again entered the ranks of the landed gentry. The agricultural labourer was probably still worse off at the end of the century than he was at the beginning. And the great estates, now 'little principalities',[2] had become more numerous. In Chile O'Higgins had attempted to abolish entail. In Chile, however, it was not the entailed estates that disappeared, but O'Higgins.[3] The *inquilinos* continued to be tied to the soil as serfs, and the great estates retained their pre-eminence until well after the middle of the century. In Venezuela, where the colonial aristocracy had been reduced both in numbers and importance, nevertheless its style of life remained, and the great estates passed into the hands of a new creole and mestizo oligarchy.[4] As for Argentina, a neglected peripheral region of the empire till after the middle of the eighteenth century, there land had endowed its holder with social rather than economic power. It was to give both in the nineteenth century, and political power also; and it was in the nineteenth century that the great estates were built up. 'We are all descendants of tradesmen or of ranchers,' says a character in a well-known Argentine novel: ' – this we know very well. But everyone tries to forget it, and the one who is furthest from his grandfather – who might have been a country storekeeper, a clerk, a shoemaker, or a shepherd – is the most aristocratic.'[5]

The conventional picture of Latin America in the half century after the establishment of political independence is that of a

[1] *New Spain's Century of Depression*, p. 44.

[2] Lesley Byrd Simpson, *Many Mexicos* (Berkeley, Cal., 1952), p. 230.

[3] Entail was not abolished in Chile till the eighteen-fifties. But the great estates remained intact for many years later. *Cf.* the interesting study of Jean Borde y Mario Góngora, *Evolución de la Propriedad Rural en el Valle del Puangue* (2 vols., Santiago de Chile, 1956), i, 58–60, 89–91.

[4] Guillermo Morón, *A History of Venezuela* (edited and translated by John Street, London, 1964), pp. 154–5; David Bushnell, *The Santander Regime in Gran Colombia* (Newark, Del., 1954), p. 277.

[5] Romero, *op. cit.*, p. 183.

continent of disorder, in which anarchy was tempered only by despotism and despotism only by revolution. Already by 1830 the faith in the future which had animated so many of the great revolutionary leaders had been dimmed – like those visions of El Dorado which had captivated the imaginations of the British merchants. 'I blush to say it,' wrote Bolívar, 'but independence is the sole good which we have gained at the cost of everything else.'[1] 'The labour and the blood given for the independence of America,' San Martín declared, twelve years later, 'have been, if not wasted, at any rate unfortunately spent in most of the new states.'[2] And the opinion expressed by Hegel to his students in Berlin, that in South America 'the republics depend only on military force; their whole history is a continued revolution',[3] was to become a widespread belief in Europe.

It cannot be denied that there was much truth in this picture. But it was not the whole truth. It did not hold for Brazil, for example. Portuguese America, of course, differed markedly from Spanish America, and the differences were nowhere more strikingly illustrated than in the manner in which the two great colonial areas won their independence. What was violently achieved in Spanish America was peacefully achieved in Portuguese America. There was no sudden break with the colonial past, no prolonged and devastating civil war. The heir to the crown of Portugal himself became the emperor of Brazil, endowed the country with its constitution, and secured its entry into the family of nations. And the throne thus peacefully established was to survive for more than sixty-five years. Nor did this picture of chronic instability hold for Chile. Chile, like Brazil, had its domestic disorders, most serious in Chile in the eighteen-twenties and in Brazil in the eighteen-thirties. But Chile, like Brazil, early succeeded in establishing stable political institutions; and these rested, in both countries, on the support of a landed aristocracy, which in Chile, at least, was remarkably successful in assimilating new elements.[4]

But the empire of Brazil and the 'aristocratic republic' of Chile

[1] Mensaje al Congreso Constituyente de la República de Colombia, 20 Jan. 1830. *Obras Completas*, ii, 1275.

[2] San Martín to Joaquín Prieto, 30 Aug. 1842. *San Martín. Su Correspondencia (1823–1850)* (Madrid, 1919), p. 222.

[3] c.1830. G. W. F. Hegel, *Lectures on the Philosophy of History* (translated by J. Sibree, London, 1861), p. 87.

[4] Fredrick B. Pike, 'Aspects of Class Relations in Chile, 1850–1960', *Hispanic American Historical Review*, xliii (1963), 14–33.

were exceptional. In Mexico, in the thirty years before the great civil wars of the middle of the century began, the executive office changed hands forty-six times. Argentina fell under the long dictatorship of Rosas and still had to face war between Buenos Aires and the provinces before the country could enter on the full and natural development of its economic life in 1862. And not till the end of the nineteenth century did Uruguay shake off its turbulent past. There were, of course, enlightened despots and unenlightened despots, liberal revolutions and illiberal revolutions. But for many years, and over large parts of Spanish America, it was the law of force, not the force of law, that held most governments in power; and, since force could only be met by force, revolution became an essential element in the political system. Venezuela is said to have experienced fifty-two major revolutions, in all, in the first century of its independent life, and Bolivia more than sixty – by 1952, indeed, more than a hundred and sixty.[1]

Yet few of these nineteenth-century revolutions led to any fundamental changes in the structure of society or the sources of social and economic power. In Mexico the great movement of the *Reforma* in the eighteen-fifties stripped the church of much of its temporal power; in the name of nineteenth-century liberalism it transferred ecclesiastical estates, often unbroken, into the hands of lay landlords; and, in the name of nineteenth-century individualism, it tried, without much success, to substitute private for collective ownership of land in the Indian villages. But what other revolutionary movement resembled this? In general, the revolutionary tradition in politics was combined with a conservative tradition in society. What invites the attention of the historian in Latin America, indeed, is not so much the instability of politics as the extraordinary stability of social institutions. The landed gentry, it is true, were less successful in resisting political, personal, or military pressures in Mexico than in Chile, or in Bolivia than in Peru. As politicians they failed again and again. But they preserved their way of life. One dictator succeeded another; in some countries a mestizo oligarchy gradually replaced a creole oligarchy; but the great estate remained at the basis of the social and economic system.

[1] *Cf.* D. F. Munro, *The Five Republics of Central America* (New York, 1918), p. 187, and F. B. Pike, ed., *Freedom and Reform in Latin America* (Notre Dame, Indiana, 1959), pp. 27, 51, 260.

Not only did the great estate remain at the basis of the social and economic system; its importance was to be enhanced. In the last quarter of the nineteenth century, as in the first, a great transformation, this time an economic transformation, took place in Latin America. Its connections with the outside world were revolutionized. Foreign capital flowed in, to build the docks and the railways, to operate the banks and the insurance companies, and to modernize the plantations and the mines. Latin American foodstuffs and raw materials flowed out, in ever greater quantities, to supply the expanding populations and industries of Europe and North America. And with the migration of capital and technology there came also a migration of people, though this, mostly from southern Europe, was principally directed to two countries, Argentina and Brazil, the 'pioneer hinterlands' of South America.

Of the changes which resulted Argentina provides the most remarkable example. In 1862, when the political unity of Argentina was at last assured, the country contained only fifty miles of railway. Less than four hundred square miles of land were under cultivation. A 'nomadic centaur', the gaucho, the Argentine cowboy, roamed the plains. The prairie Indians were unsubdued. Sheep counted for more than cattle. And the whole population was under two million. It was still under two million in 1869. But now the face of the country began to be changed. The immigrant and immigrant capital, the railway network, wire-fencing, the refrigerator and the refrigerator ship, these were the instruments of a pastoral, an agrarian and a commercial revolution which, within a very few years, raised land values to extraordinary heights and transformed a backward frontier area into one of the great granaries and stockyards of the world. The gaucho became a legend – or a peon. The immigrant became a labourer or a tenant farmer. But only rarely did he become a landowner. The great estate had been the rule when the country was purely pastoral. It remained the rule when arable had been added to pasture.[1] The pampas, the immense grass-covered plains, contained the richest agricultural land. But much of the good public land on the pampas had already been transferred to private hands before the great influx of European immigrants, and the steep rise in land values,

---

[1] Isaiah Bowman, *The Pioneer Fringe* (New York, 1931), p. 303. The average holding in Buenos Aires Province in 1840 was 40,339 acres. Carl C. Taylor, *Rural Life in Argentina* (Baton Rouge, 1948), p. 177.

began. 'In the rural districts,' Lord Bryce noted in 1910, 'there are two classes only – landlords, often with vast domains, and labourers, the native labourers settled, the Italians to some extent migratory.' Estancias of sixty thousand acres, he added, were not uncommon; and some, indeed, were very much larger still.[1]

It was difficult for the labourer or the tenant farmer on the Argentine pampa to become the owner of the land he worked. But the soil was virgin. There were no existing small proprietors, no Indian village communities, to be deprived of their traditional holdings to swell the great estates, as happened to some extent, for example, in the highlands of Bolivia and in Peru,[2] and as happened also in Mexico. The Indians of the Argentine pampa were nomadic, not sedentary Indians, or, at the most, only semi-settled. They were much dreaded, though perhaps they had much to dread, and their fate was similar to that of the plains Indians in the United States. The campaign of General Roca against them in 1879 marked the beginning of their end.

In Mexico – my second example – a very different situation prevailed. The modernization of Mexico in the late nineteenth century was as impressive to the foreign observer as the transformation of Argentina. Railways, ports and telegraphs were built. The mining industry was reconstructed. The shattered finances of the country were restored. Banditry was suppressed. And, as in Argentina, the public lands were distributed. But in Mexico, where the Indian was a major element in the population, the rape of the Indian villages accompanied the alienation of the public domain. At the end of the long dictatorship of Porfirio Díaz – the longest and most efficient in Mexican history – not only had millions of acres of the public lands been sold to a few individuals and companies for a few million dollars, but the landed estate had swallowed the landowning village. Most Mexicans lived off the land. But few indeed were the villages which retained any

[1] James Bryce, *South America. Observations and Impressions* (New York, 1920), pp. 331, 341; Taylor, *op. cit.,* pp. 176–7, 185; M. A. Cárcano, *Evolución Histórica del Régimen de la Tierra Pública, 1810–1916* (2nd ed., Buenos Aires, 1925), p. 344; Mark Jefferson, *Peopling the Argentine Pampa* (New York, 1930), pp. 162, 167. Jefferson and Taylor both describe agricultural colonization in the provinces of Santa Fe and Entre Ríos between 1853 and 1895.

[2] For the decrease in Indian community holdings on the Bolivian altiplano see G. M. McBride, *The Agrarian Indian Communities of Highland Bolivia* (New York, 1921), pp. 10–11, 26–7, and, for the formation of 'oligarquías latifundistas' in Peru, Emilio Romero, *Historia Económica del Perú* (Buenos Aires, 1949), pp. 282–5.

land whatever. The rural inhabitants who held no individual property were 'probably more numerous than they had been at any previous time in the history of the country'.[1] Agricultural wages had remained almost stationary for over a hundred years. And while the dominance of the great estates had never been more complete, a high proportion of the labourers who worked them was tied to the soil in debt peonage.[2]

The result, in 1910, was revolution, a revolution which began mildly enough, but which attained such cataclysmic proportions that by 1920 the population of Mexico had fallen by more than three quarters of a million. The Mexican Revolution, in the words of Daniel Cosío Villegas, 'totally swept away not only the political regime of Porfirio Díaz but all of Porfirian society, that is, the social classes or groups together with their ideas, tastes and manners. Not only the commanders-in-chief of the army but their officers and all the soldiers disappeared without exception. Landholders, urban and especially agricultural, were almost entirely replaced by new ones. Not one of the great newspapers survived. Only two of about fifty banks continued into the new regime. Official bureaucracy – federal, state and municipal – was wholly reformed.'[3]

This was not the conventional Latin American revolution. It was a social as well as a political and economic revolution. Though it had affinities with the great Indian rising of a hundred years earlier, nothing like it had occurred before in the history of the Americas. And nothing like it was to occur again, at least till the decade of the nineteen-fifties.

But if Mexico provided the only example in Latin America of social change by revolution in the first half of the twentieth century,[4] evolutionary social change took place both there and elsewhere. Hitherto the relation of Latin America to the rest of the world had been that of the farm to the factory, of the rancher and miner to the manufacturer. In Latin America itself, moreover, there had been little or no countervailing power in industry or

[1] G. M. McBride, *The Land Systems of Mexico* (New York, 1923), p. 155.

[2] Helen Phipps, *Some Aspects of the Agrarian Question in Mexico* (Austin, Texas, 1925), pp. 106–28; E. N. Simpson, *The Ejido, Mexico's Way Out* (Chapel Hill, N.C., 1937), pp. 27–42.

[3] Daniel Cosío Villegas, *Change in Latin America: the Mexican and Cuban Revolutions* (Lincoln, Nebraska, 1961), pp. 24–5.

[4] Save, perhaps, for a revolution of a very different kind, the Peronista revolution in Argentina.

population to the hacienda and the ranch, except, indeed, where the mine challenged the farm, as, in Chile, the desert north challenged the agricultural centre and south. But, in the twentieth century, the Industrial Revolution, which had already transformed western Europe and the United States, began to make its appearance in Latin America also. And though its progress was slow, its consequences – and those of the increased commercialization of economic life – were familiar: the more rapid growth of the cities, a drift from the countryside to the towns, the rise of a new financial and commercial middle class, of an urban proletariat, of an artisan class, and of organized labour.[1]

Today the population of Latin America is already greater than than that of the United States, and it is growing fast – faster, indeed, than that of any other major area of the world. There are steel-mills on the Orinoco and air-fields in the jungle. Large-scale commercial farms have replaced the traditional form of the hacienda in the coastal valleys of Peru. The capital cities grow by leaps and bounds. But much in the rural landscape remains the same. The middle class is still small. The Indians, in some countries, still form a society within a society. Perhaps half the population of the Andean and Indian republics cannot speak Spanish. And not merely there, but everywhere, rich and poor live in worlds apart.

But the traditional organization of society in Latin America has been challenged: not only what was bad in it, but what was good; not only the tyranny of the great estate, but, at its best, the old paternal relation between *patrón* and peasant. It was violently challenged in Mexico in 1910; it was violently challenged again in Bolivia in 1952, and in Cuba in 1959; and it is directly and indirectly challenged elsewhere. This is not simply one more expression of the tradition of revolt at work in Latin America, though of that, too, examples enough can be found: it is a revolt against tradition.

[1] The Chilean peasants were already deserting the great estates for the towns in the later nineteenth century, and Chile's urban population rose from 27 per cent of the whole in 1875 to 43 per cent in 1902 and 60 per cent in 1952. The rural population of Argentina decreased from roughly 66 per cent of the total in 1869 to 57 per cent in 1895, 43 per cent in 1914 and 25 per cent in 1947. On the rise of the cities and changes in the classes see F. B. Pike, ed., *Freedom and Reform in Latin America*, pp. 180–7, John J. Johnson, *Political Change in Latin America. The Emergence of the Middle Sectors* (Stanford, Cal., 1958), and Federico Debuyst, *Las Clases Sociales en América Latina* (Freiburg, 1962).

2

William Robertson and his
*History of America**

There are two classic histories of the Spanish conquest of America in the English language. The one is the splendid narrative of Prescott, written more than a century ago, but still unrivalled. The other, equally celebrated in its day, but now almost forgotten, is William Robertson's *History of America*, published at London in two volumes on 28 May 1777.[1]

Robertson died three years before Prescott was born. In 1759, when, as a thirty-seven-year-old Scottish Presbyterian clergyman, he was as yet barely known outside his beloved Edinburgh, he had enchanted the literary world of England with a *History of Scotland during the Reigns of Queen Mary and of King James VI*, which is properly to be regarded as a major contribution to the new historiography of the eighteenth century. Ten years later – he was now Historiographer Royal in Scotland and principal of the University of Edinburgh – he had capped this success with a yet more resounding triumph, a *History of the Reign of the Emperor Charles V*, which was read all the way from Paris to St Petersburg and brought him European fame. His third great history, the *History of America,* was his most distinguished achievement. It arose, naturally and inevitably, from his European subject. And, in origin at least, it was no more than a by-product of his work on Charles v.

Prescott, sixty years later, trod a similar path. Prescott made his name with a *History of the Reign of Ferdinand and Isabella*, and Spain was his first and his last love. But as *Charles V* had led Robertson, so *Ferdinand and Isabella* led Prescott from Europe to America; and

* [The first Canning House Annual Lecture, delivered on 11 June 1954. (London, The Hispanic and Luso-Brazilian Councils, 1954.)]

[1] All citations are to the fifth and definitive edition (3 vols., London, 1788). This contains such corrections and additions as Robertson thought necessary.

Prescott was to tell in detail the story which Robertson told in out-line. 'The most poetic subject ever offered to the pen of the historian,' he calls it.[1] 'A perfect epic,' he says a little later, 'and as full of incident as any tale of chivalry.'[2] And, again, when his *Conquest of Mexico* was nearly finished: 'The story', he writes, 'is so full of marvels, perilous adventures, curious manners, scenery, etc., that it is more like a romance than a history, and yet every page is substantiated by abundance of original testimony.'[3]

But Prescott, with far richer resources at his disposal than Robertson could command, never forgot what Robertson had done before him. In his two great American histories and else-where he is generous with his praise of the 'illustrious historian of America' – such is his phrase.[4] 'It is very absurd,' he says in one of his letters, 'to consider the pennyweight of commendation that might be conceded to my efforts as any deduction from the solid worth of Robertson.'[5] And hidden in his private journals there lies a warning note. 'Beware of Robertson,' he writes. 'Never glance at him till after subject moulded in my mind and thrown into language.'[6] So, across the years, one great historian of the New World saluted another.

Prescott was a product of the nineteenth-century 'flowering of New England', Robertson of the eighteenth-century 'awakening of Scotland'. He was born in 1721,[7] two years before Adam Smith. A studious and rather awkward lad, brought up, as his friend Dr Alexander Carlyle says, never to dance, to attend the theatre,

---

[1] Rollo Ogden, *William Hickling Prescott* (Boston and New York, 1904), p. 137.

[2] Roger Wolcott, ed., *The Correspondence of William Hickling Prescott, 1833–1847* (Boston and New York, 1925), p. 99.

[3] *Ibid.*, p. 328.

[4] *History of the Conquest of Peru* (5th ed., 3 vols., London, 1857), i, 226.

[5] Wolcott, *op. cit.*, p. 421. [6] Ogden, *op. cit.*, p. 154.

[7] Robertson's papers are in the Robertson-Macdonald Papers in the National Library of Scotland, to whose courtesy I am indebted for the privilege of examining them. The classic 'life' is the stately memoir by Dugald Stewart, written in 1796, and reprinted in his *Biographical Memoirs, of Adam Smith, LL.D., of William Robertson, D.D., and of Thomas Reid, D.D.* (Edinburgh, 1811). See also George Gleig, *Some Account of the Life and Writings of William Robertson, D.D., F.R.S.E.* (1812), reprinted in vol. i of the *Works of William Robertson* (12 vols., Edinburgh, 1822); Henry, Lord Brougham, *Lives of Men of Letters and Science who flourished in the time of George III* (London, 1845); H. G. Graham, *Scottish Men of Letters in the Eighteenth Century* (London, 1901); and the article by Thomas Seccombe in the *Dictionary of National Biography*. The best study of Robertson as a historian is in J. B. Black, *The Art of History* (London, 1926). [See also D. B. Horn, 'Principal William Robertson, D.D., Historian', *University of Edinburgh Journal* (Autumn, 1956), pp. 155–68.]

or to play cards.[1] he entered the University of Edinburgh at the mature age of twelve, was licensed to preach before he was twenty-two,[2] and soon afterwards was presented to the small living of Gladsmuir, no great distance from the capital. Here he remained for fourteen years, active in the affairs of his parish; riding into Edinburgh to consult the shelves of the Advocates' Library or to attend the sessions of the General Assembly of the Scottish Church; looking after six sisters and one younger brother – the sisters, as Brougham, his great-nephew, noted many years later, always addressed their brother as 'Sir';[3] marrying his cousin; and in, or about, 1753, beginning his first great history.

What turned his thoughts to the historian's trade can only be conjectured. Classical rather than historical studies had attracted him first.[4] But his father before him had shown an eager interest in the tragic events of Queen Mary's reign, and in the Advocates' Library in Edinburgh his friend David Hume was hard at work on his *History of England*. Hume's first volume was published – to fall exceedingly flat – in 1754, and the second, which, as he said, helped to 'buoy up' the first,[5] in 1756. Two years later, in 1758, Robertson's own *History of Scotland* was finished, and at the same time he moved from his country parish to an Edinburgh church. He had already made a local name both as a preacher and as a rising statesman in the ecclesiastical politics of Scotland. But the day after his book was published, on 1 February 1759, he awoke to find himself famous. The first edition – 1,250 copies[6] – was sold out in a month. 'The town will have it,' reported David Hume, then in London, 'that you was educated at Oxford; thinking it impossible for a mere untravel'd Scotchman to produce such language.'[7] Horace Walpole was profuse in compliments. Lord Chesterfield and Lord Lyttleton were equally flattering. And,

[1] 'A Comparison of two Eminent Characters attempted after the manner of Plutarch', Lee Papers, Alexander Carlyle, Miscellaneous Transcripts, MS. 3464, National Library of Scotland.

[2] Hew Scott, *Fasti Ecclesiae Scoticanae* (rev. ed., 8 vols., Edinburgh, 1915–50), i, 41.

[3] Henry, Lord Brougham, *The Life and Times of Henry Lord Brougham. Written by himself* (3 vols., London, 1871), i, 35.

[4] His incomplete translation of the meditations of Marcus Aurelius, dated 21 Jan. 1742, is in the Robertson-Macdonald Papers.

[5] G. Birkbeck Hill, *Letters of David Hume to William Strahan* (Oxford, 1888), p. xxviii.

[6] Hume to Robertson, 8 Feb. 1759. Robertson-Macdonald Papers.

[7] *Ibid.*

what is perhaps the most impressive tribute of all, Gibbon later confessed that 'the perfect composition, the nervous language, the well-turned periods of Dr Robertson, inflamed me to the ambitious hope that I might one day tread in his footsteps'.[1]

Such was the beginning; and so soon as the *History of Scotland* was off the press, Robertson turned his thoughts to a new work. The choice which he made was momentous, for on it depended his future *History of America*. His friends and admirers urged all manner of subjects upon him, ranging from a history of Greece to a history of England; and he himself was at first doubtful. But already in writing his history of sixteenth-century Scotland he had begun to feel the spell of sixteenth-century Europe. This was the period, as he says, at which 'the powers of Europe were formed into one great political system'.[2] It was the age of the reformation in Germany, of the renaissance in Italy, of the conquest of the New World; and, bestriding the first half of this century, was the king of Spain who was in a manner emperor of Europe, Charles v.[3] The reign of the emperor Charles v! This, then, was Robertson's choice; and by the summer of 1761 he had made such progress with the book that he had begun to think that another two years would see the end.[4]

In the event, *Charles V* took him, not two years more, but seven. For, apart from the great difficulties of the work, he found himself more and more immersed in public affairs, though perhaps he was all the better historian for that. His *History of Scotland* had attracted the notice of Lord Bute, the friend and confidant of the young George III, and soon to become prime minister. Bute was a patron of literature as well as of Scotsmen. Did he not give a pension to Dr Johnson? And not only Bute, but apparently George III also, had come to the conclusion that Robertson ought to undertake a history of England once his *Charles V* was finished. Every encouragement would be given to him, he was told, and every source of information which government could command would be

[1] G. B. Hill, ed., *The Memoirs of the Life of Edward Gibbon* (London, 1900), p. 122.
[2] Preface to *The History of the Reign of the Emperor Charles the Fifth. Cf. The History of Scotland*, i, 70–73, in *The Works of William Robertson* (8 vols., Oxford, 1825).
[3] *Cf.* Robertson to Walpole, 20 Feb. 1759, and Walpole to Robertson, 4 March 1759. W. S. Lewis, ed., *The Yale Edition of Horace Walpole's Correspondence*, xv (London, 1952), 45–6, 48–51.
[4] Stewart, *Memoirs*, p. 206. He still thought so in Jan. 1762, when he declared that he had got through more than a half of *Charles V*. Robertson to Edmonstone, 4 Jan. 1762. National Library of Scotland, MS. 1005, f. 5.

made available. But, obviously, he would need to devote his full time to the task, and, obviously also, since he declined to exchange life in Edinburgh for some comfortable Anglican sinecure, a more ample provision than the royal chaplaincy, which he had already been given, would have to be found for him in Scotland.[1] When, therefore, in 1762, the Principalship of the University of Edinburgh fell vacant and Robertson was appointed to the post, the circumstances seemed providential. Bute took great credit for the result. Pray let Dr Robertson know, he wrote, before the election was announced, 'that, from the minute I first fixed on him for our great undertaking, I determined to assist him in obtaining the Principal's chair either in Edinburgh or Glasgow; for that, being *otium cum dignitate*, suited extremely my views'.[2] And it was certainly Bute, with the same object in mind, who revived in Robertson's favour in the following year the office of Historiographer Royal in Scotland, after it had been in abeyance for more than a quarter of a century.[3]

The salary was only £200 a year but, combined with his other emoluments, though all of these were small,[4] it raised Robertson from comparative poverty to comparative affluence. And though the appointment carried with it, as Robertson fully recognized, an implied engagement to write a history of England once the history of the reign of Charles v was off the stocks,[5] Bute, the author of this scheme, fell from power in 1763 and disappeared from political life altogether in 1765. No one else shared his enthusiasm. And, fortunately for the future *History of America*, the projected history of England sank into oblivion. On the other hand, though the post of historiographer was certainly a sinecure, that of principal as certainly was not. For thirty-one years Robertson reigned over the university. As principal, moreover, he

[1] Cathcart to Robertson, 20 July, 7, 21 Aug. 1761. Robertson-Macdonald Papers. Stewart, *Memoirs*, pp. 202–8.

[2] Bute to Baron Mure, 27 Feb. 1762. *Selections from the Family Papers preserved at Caldwell* (2 parts in 3 vols., Maitland Club, Glasgow, 1854), II (i), 146. See also Cathcart to Robertson, 4 April 1763, where Cathcart explains that Bute looked upon the principalship as part of the provision which he intended for Robertson. Robertson-Macdonald Papers.

[3] *Cf.* Denys Hay, 'The Historiographers Royal in England and Scotland', *Scottish Historical Review*, xxx (1951), 15–29.

[4] £138 odd as a minister of Edinburgh, £111 and a house as principal, and £49 as one of H.M.'s chaplains. Robertson to Bute, 9 April 1763. N. S. Jucker, *The Jenkinson Papers, 1760–1766* (London, 1949), pp. 136–9.

[5] Robertson to Baron Mure, 19 March 1765. *Caldwell Papers*, II (ii), 23.

obtained, in effect, a permanent seat in that 'ecclesiastical parliament of Scotland', the General Assembly of the Scottish Church, and, until his retirement from it in 1780, he reigned over that body also, directing, says Brougham, the ecclesiastical affairs of Scotland 'with unexampled success'.[1] And as Gibbon, in a famous phrase, records his indebtedness to the captain of the Hampshire grenadiers, so of Robertson it may well be thought that the manager of the Church of Scotland and the principal of the University of Edinburgh were by no means useless to the historian of the Spanish empire.

At last, and in despite of Robertson's other avocations, *Charles V* was finished. It was published on 9 March 1769, and was translated into French, sheet by sheet, as it passed through the press. For the copyright the author was paid the then enormous sum of £3,500 and was to receive, besides, another £500 if a second edition should be called for.[2] And the success was prodigious. Like the *History of Scotland, Charles V* has failed to withstand the assaults of time. But it passed through edition after edition before it finally became outmoded. As late as 1855 Prescott was quite content to write a new conclusion to the book, and to appear, as he says, like a little urchin holding on to the coat-tails of Robertson's 'strapping giant'.[3] And in England, at least, no one attempted to treat the period on a comparable scale until the beginning of the present century.[4]

Much the most remarkable part of the book, however, was not the detailed history of Charles's reign, but a long introduction which Robertson called a *View of the Progress of Society in Europe, from the Subversion of the Roman Empire to the Beginning of the Sixteenth Century*. This, as Professor Black has observed, was a 'philosophical essay', a 'kind of physiological analysis of the developing structure of European civilization',[5] the like of which no historian had attempted before. Gibbon refers to it with respect in his own great history, and, what is more, pays it the compli-

---

[1] Brougham, *Lives*, p. 267. *Cf*. W. L. Mathieson, *The Awakening of Scotland* (Glasgow, 1910), p. 170, and Graham, *Scottish Men of Letters*, p. 87.

[2] W. Strahan to Robertson, 27 May 1768. Robertson-Macdonald Papers. The figure usually given is £4,500.

[3] George Ticknor, *Life of William Hickling Prescott* (London, 1864), p. 434.

[4] See E. F. Henderson, 'Two Lives of the Emperor Charles V', *American Historical Review*, ix (1903), 23–35.

[5] Black, *The Art of History*, p. 129.

ment of paraphrasing, without acknowledgment, more than one passage.[1] And it was reprinted, in a new Italian translation, as late as 1951.[2]

Notable also, though for another reason, was a passage in Robertson's preface. 'Every intelligent reader,' he says, 'will observe one omission in my work, the reason of which it is necessary to explain. I have given no account of the conquests of Mexico and Peru, or of the establishment of the Spanish colonies in the continent and islands of America. The history of these events I originally intended to have related at considerable length.' But, he continues, 'upon a nearer and more attentive consideration of this part of my plan, I found that the discovery of the new world; the state of society among its ancient inhabitants; their character, manners, and arts; the genius of the European settlements in its various provinces, together with the influence of these upon the systems of policy or commerce in Europe, were subjects so splendid and important, that a superficial view of them could afford little satisfaction. . . .' These, therefore, he concluded, he had reserved 'for a separate history; which, if the performance now offered to the public shall receive its approbation, I purpose to undertake'.

This then, was the beginning of Robertson's American history. It appeared eight years later, less than a twelve-month after the English colonies in North America had declared their independence; and it is Robertson's masterpiece. But it was not the book which he had intended to write. He had proposed to describe the rise not only of the Spanish empire in America but of the British and Portuguese empires also; and he had meant to publish no part of his work until the whole should have been completed. The revolt of the English colonies changed his mind. 'It is lucky,' he wrote in 1775, 'that my American History was not finished before this event. How many plausible theories, that I should have been entitled to form, are contradicted by what has now happened!'[3] Not all historians have been so fortunate; and, true Scot that he was, Robertson preferred to postpone his discussion of the British colonies until he should know what was going to happen to them.

[1] For one example see J. W. Oliver, 'William Robertson and Edward Gibbon', *Scottish Historical Review*, xxvi (1947), 86, and, for another, Michael Joyce, *Edward Gibbon* (London, 1953), pp. 133–4.

[2] Edited with an introduction by Giorgio Falco (Giulio Einaudi Editore, 1951).

[3] Stewart, *Memoirs*, p. 246.

He would wait, he said, 'with the solicitude of a good citizen, until the ferment subside, and regular government be re-established, and then I shall return to this part of my work. . . .'[1] But the ferment did not subside and Robertson did not return. Nor did he have the energy to take up the Portuguese side of his story or the history of the European settlements in the West Indies. 'As I had written between two and three hundred pages of *excellent* History of the British Colonies in North America,' he complained in 1784, 'I long flattered myself that the war might terminate so favourably for G. Britain, that I might go on with my work. But alas! America is now lost to the Empire and to me, and what would have been a good introduction to the settlement of British Colonies, will suit very ill the establishment of Independent States.'[2] The pages, however, were found among his papers after his death. They comprised the histories of Virginia and New England and were printed by his son in 1796 as Books IX and X of the *History*. As for the histories of the West Indies and Brazil, it was left for Bryan Edwards to take up, in part, the one and Robert Southey the other.

Strictly speaking, therefore, the *History of America,* as Robertson gave it to the world, was a history of Spanish America. More particularly, it was a history of Spanish America in the great age of discovery and conquest, 'the most splendid portion', as he calls it, 'of the American story'.[3] As a prelude to discovery, however, he traced the course of European exploration from ancient times to the fifteenth century, when, as he says, 'the glory of leading the way . . . was reserved for Portugal'.[4] And, as a conclusion to the story of the conquest, he appended a remarkable chapter, Book VIII, in which he analysed the nature and effects of Spanish colonization in the New World and discussed also contemporary imperial reforms. He was at pains, moreover, to examine, so far as he could, the indigenous cultures of Mexico and Peru, and in what he called a 'View of America when first discovered, and of the manners and policy of its most uncivilized inhabitants', he showed, as Professor Black has pointed out, a quite unusual awareness of the relation between geography and history,[5] and no sympathy at

---

[1] Preface to the *History of America*.
[2] Robertson to (?), 8 March 1784. British Museum, Add. MSS., 35,350, f. 70 ff.
[3] Preface to the *History of America*.   [4] *History of America*, i, 56.
[5] Black, *Art of History*, pp. 137–8.

all with the legend of the 'noble savage'. Whatever Rousseau's opinions might be, Robertson was under no illusion that 'the most perfect state of man' was, as he dryly observed, 'the least civilized'.[1]

In all this Robertson broke fresh ground. Englishmen, when his book appeared, knew even less about Spanish America than they do now – if that is possible. The man of letters might have dipped into one or another translation of early Spanish chronicles and histories and into one or another collection of voyages. The merchant was familiar with the transatlantic commerce of Cádiz and Lisbon, and with the profits and hazards of the contraband trade, and he long retained memories of the famous *Asiento*, or contract to supply slaves to Spanish America, of the South Sea Company, and of the South Sea Bubble. Grub Street provided some indifferent manuals, of which the most informative – despite its author's capacity, if Boswell is to be believed, for drinking thirteen bottles of port at a sitting – was *A Concise History of the Spanish America,* published by Dr John Campbell in 1741.[2] And one work of real merit, *An Account of the European Settlements in America,* which Robertson himself praises, and which is attributed to Edmund Burke, appeared in 1757. Travellers' accounts, moreover, such as the celebrated *Voyage to South America* of the two young Spanish naval officers, Juan and Ulloa, were eagerly read.[3] And when the Abbé Raynal's *Histoire philosophique et politique des établissements et du commerce des européens dans les deux Indes* came out in English dress in 1776, it proved so popular that fourteen editions were called for by the end of the century.[4]

But Raynal's famous 'philosophic history' – dreary enough reading now – contained as much fiction as fact. The literature of travel was all too meagre. And, as Robertson himself observed, Spain, 'with an excess of caution', had 'uniformly thrown a veil over her transactions in America'.[5] The wealth of the Indies was legendary; and from the days of Elizabeth to those of George III successive British governments had attempted to take a bite at the

[1] *History of America,* ii, 58.
[2] See also Richard Rolt, *A New and Accurate History of South-America . . .* (London, 1756), and *An Account of the Spanish Settlements in America* (Edinburgh, 1762), which unblushingly plagiarizes both Campbell and Rolt.
[3] London, 1758, 1760, 1772, and later editions.
[4] See Dallas D. Irvine, 'The Abbé Raynal and British Humanitarianism', *Journal of Modern History,* iii (1931), 576–7.
[5] Preface to the *History of America.*

Spanish American cherry. But of the history or institutions of Spain's empire in America little was known; and to an Englishman, nourished in Elizabethan and Cromwellian traditions, what was known was usually thought to be discreditable to Spain.[1]

Robertson lifted the veil. 'The longer I reflect on the nature of historical composition,' he wrote, 'the more I am convinced that ... scrupulous accuracy is necessary.'[2] It is impressive to notice his close scrutiny of his sources and the judgements which he passes on the early Spanish chroniclers and historians: on Garcilaso de la Vega, for example, who, he remarks, is unable to distinguish between 'what is fabulous, what is probable, and what is true'; on Herrera and Solís; on Cieza de León; and on Bernal Díaz del Castillo, whose account, he says, 'bears all the marks of authenticity, and is accompanied with such a pleasant *naïveté*, with such interesting details, with such amusing vanity, and yet so pardonable in an old soldier who had been (as he boasts) in a hundred and nineteen battles, as renders his book one of the most singular that is to be found in any language'.[3]

Impressive also was his eagerness to seek out first-hand evidence. 'Emboldened,' he says, 'by a hint' from Gibbon, he printed a catalogue, or bibliography, of the Spanish books and manuscripts which he had consulted and collected – a notable departure from eighteenth-century practice. It contained most of what was of importance to his subject then in print, and the Advocates' Library in Edinburgh, which refused to buy his Spanish collection for £100 odd in 1781, must often have repented of its folly.[4] In Spain the archives of Simancas were closed to him. The great Arabic scholar, Gayangos, was one of the first persons to be allowed to use them, on Prescott's behalf, nearly seventy years later, and his description of what he found makes amusing reading.[5] But Robertson was able to procure copies of other Spanish manuscripts through the good offices of the Rev. Robert Waddilove, then the chaplain to the British embassy in Madrid

[1] But not always. See *An Account of the European Settlements in America,* cited above.

[2] Preface to the *History of America*.

[3] *History of America*, iii, 368; ii, 477. Compare Prescott's later observations.

[4] Robertson offered 253 volumes which he had collected from Spain, together with 16 volumes of manuscripts. Robertson-Macdonald Papers.

[5] Gayangos to Prescott, 1 Aug. 1844. Wolcott, *Correspondence of William Hickling Prescott,* pp. 488–9.

and later dean of Ripon. He instituted a search in the Imperial Library at Vienna for the first letter sent by Cortés to Charles v from New Spain[1] – it is still lost – and discovered instead a copy of the famous letter written by the town-council of Vera Cruz and a copy also of Cortés's account of his expedition to Honduras. To support his theory that the American Indians were probably descended from the 'rude' tribes of Tartary, and to prove how easily man might have passed from the old world to the new, he secured from St Petersburg a translation of the manuscript journal of the expedition which had been sent in 1768 to continue the progress of Russian exploration off the north-eastern shores of Asia; and this helped to confirm Robertson in an opinion, soon shown to be correct, that Asia and America were only separated by a narrow strait.[2] He prepared a questionnaire, which was sent to a number of Spaniards who had lived in the New World, asking for information on various colonial institutions and practices, on the population of Spanish America, the royal revenues, and the like,[3] and he addressed a further set of queries both to Spaniards and to non-Spaniards, dealing with the customs and habits of the American Indians.[4] Finally, he consulted, among others, the surviving members of the French scientific expedition which had been sent to measure an arc of the meridian at Quito in 1735.

The result was the first modern history of Spanish America. Contemporaries, Gibbon and Burke, for example, were fascinated by Robertson's account of the Indian aboriginals. But, not surprisingly, this is the part of his work which has worn the least well. So far as the pre-conquest cultures of Mexico and Peru are concerned, it is only necessary to compare Robertson's pages with those of Prescott to see the bareness of his ground; and in some respects at least, though certainly not in all, the gulf between Prescott and the modern ethnologist and archaeologist is not less wide than the gulf between Robertson and Prescott. Not, indeed, till 1839 did John Lloyd Stephens and Frederick Catherwood begin their explorations of the ruined cities of Central America which were to result in the discovery of the civilization of the

---

[1] Robertson to Sir R. M. Keith, 14 Oct. 1776. British Museum, Add. MSS., 35,511, f. 21.
[2] *History of America,* ii, 37–45, 431–9.
[3] Robertson-Macdonald Papers.   [4] *Ibid.*

Mayas. Compelled to rely almost wholly on literary sources alone, and these inadequate, Robertson, as Prescott wrote to Stephens, 'underestimated everything in the New World. It was little understood then,' adds Prescott, 'and distrust which had a knowing air at least was the safer side for the historian.'[1]

Yet Robertson's discussion of the American Indian was far more considered and careful than was common among his contemporaries. The *philosophes* had discovered the American Indian. Rousseau, though he had not created the legend of the 'noble savage', had greatly strengthened it by his glowing descriptions of the virtuous simplicity of primitive life.[2] Rousseau, it is true, knew nothing of the American Indian, and indeed barely mentioned him. But Buffon had surveyed the world from China to Peru, and Buffon had found him. The animals of South America, he had noted, were different from, and smaller than, those of the Old World. There were no elephants and rhinoceroses, for example, no lions and tigers, and no giraffes. The domestic creatures transported from Europe had diminished in size. The men had no beards; their constitutions were feeble. And, putting these matters together, Buffon had arrived at the conclusion that the greater part of the New World was a young continent where nature had not yet 'had time to establish all her plans', and where man himself was only an animal of the first rank.[3] Finally, de Pauw, the notorious de Pauw, rejecting this theory of the youthfulness or immaturity of the New World, had maintained that America was not young but degenerate, and had included in one ferocious condemnation its climate, its fauna, and its native inhabitants.[4] Where Rousseau had seen the 'noble savage', de Pauw found the 'ignoble savage'.

But the *philosophes*, as Robertson complained, 'too impatient to inquire', hastened to decide, and 'began to erect systems, when they should have been searching for facts';[5] and it was facts that Robertson wanted. There is, it is true, much of Buffon in his pages, though nothing at all of Rousseau. But he was careful to

---

[1] Wolcott, *op. cit.*, p. 211.

[2] *Discours sur l'origine et les fondements de l'inégalité* (1754).

[3] *Histoire naturelle*, iii (Paris, 1749), 511; ix (1761), 102–14. *Cf.* Gilbert Chinard, *L'Homme contre la nature* (Paris, 1949), pp. 15–24, and Antonello Gerbi, *Viejas polémicas sobre el Nuevo Mundo* (Lima, 1946), pp. 11–36. As Chinard points out (p. 34), Buffon, in 1774, modified his views on the debility of the American Indian.

[4] *Recherches philosophiques sur les Américains* (1768–9).

[5] *History of America*, ii, 56.

test the opinions and information which he had collected and collated by the experience of scientists, missionaries, and administrators who had had first-hand knowledge of various parts of the Americas. Were the bodily constitutions of the Indians, he inquired, as vigorous and robust as those of the inhabitants of similar climates in the ancient continent? Was the absence of a beard natural to the Indian? Was he defective in animal passions, the passion of love for example? What was his attitude in regard to parental affection or filial duty? What ideas did he have of property? And what conception did he entertain of a future life? What was the genius and what the structure of the Indian languages? Moreover, did European animals which propagated in America improve or degenerate? Were animals which were common to both continents greater or smaller in size? And other questions of a like kind.[1]

'If, in advanced years,' Adam Ferguson had written, 'we would form a just notion of our progress from the cradle, we must have recourse to the nursery.'[2] Robertson went to the nursery. 'That state of primaeval simplicity, which was known in our continent only by the fanciful description of poets,' he remarked, 'really existed in the other.'[3] And whatever its errors and inconsistencies, his analysis of primitive Indian life must be regarded as one of the earliest critical inquiries into the subject.[4] Though Buffon, moreover, had realized the significance of Russian discoveries in the sea of Kamchatka,[5] it was left for Robertson to demonstrate the probability that man first reached the New World by way of the Bering Strait. His conclusion failed, alas, to check that 'extravagance of conjecture', as he called it, which found the origin of the American Indian in the hills of Wales or the lost ten tribes of Israel.[6] But informed opinion has long supported it.

If time has done much to destroy the value of Robertson's

---

[1] See Robertson's queries in the Robertson-Macdonald Papers, together with replies from Godin le Jeune, Bougainville, and, in North America, Gideon Hawley, George Croghan, etc.

[2] *An Essay on the History of Civil Society* (6th ed., London, 1793), p. 134. On Robertson and Ferguson see Friedrich Meinecke, *Die Entstehung des Historismus* (2 vols., Berlin, 1936), i, 260.

[3] *History of America*, ii, 51.

[4] Chinard's remarks upon this point (*op. cit.*, pp. 41–2) seem to me to be singularly unjust.

[5] *Histoire naturelle*, iii (Paris, 1749), 515.

[6] *History of America*, ii, 28.

chapters both on the aboriginal Indians and on the higher cultures of Mexico and Peru, it has also done much to vindicate an attitude of mind which shocked and distressed some of his contemporary critics,[1] namely, his refusal to accept what has come to be called the 'black legend'. And here again Robertson differed widely from the fashionable doctrines of Raynal, de Pauw, and others of the *philosophes*. 'I am satisfied,' he wrote, 'that upon a more minute scrutiny' into the 'early operations' of the Spaniards in the New World, 'however reprehensible the actions of individuals may appear, the conduct of the nation will be placed in a more favourable light.'[2] He did not disguise the acts of cruelty and perfidy, the licentiousness, the tyranny, and the rapacity, which stain the annals of the conquest.[3] He noted the terrible toll of human life taken in Hispaniola and Puerto Rico by the sword, by barbarity, by famine, and by disease.[4] Of Mexico he remarked that 'in almost every district of the Mexican empire, the progress of the Spanish arms' was 'marked with blood, and with deeds so atrocious, as disgrace the enterprising valour that conducted them to success'.[5] The agreement made between Pizarro and his associates, which was to result in the conquest of Peru, moved him to the biting comment that 'in name of the Prince of Peace' they 'ratified a contract of which plunder and bloodshed were the objects'.[6] And the execution of the Inca, Atahualpa, he characterized as an action 'the most criminal and atrocious that stains the Spanish name, amidst all the deeds of violence committed in carrying on the conquest of the New World'.[7]

On the other hand, Robertson declined to take at their face value the sweeping charges made against the sixteenth-century Spaniards by one of the greatest of them all – Las Casas.[8] He perceived the strange mixture of motives mingling in their breasts: 'religious enthusiasm', he says, united with the spirit of adventure, and both with avarice.[9] He was lost in admiration at their 'fortitude and perseverance'.[10] Of the march which Cortés made to Honduras, he remarks that what Cortés suffered 'from famine, from the

---

[1] *Cf.* Bryan Edwards, *The History, Civil and Commercial, of the British Colonies in the West Indies* (3rd ed., 3 vols., London, 1801), i, 105.
[2] Preface to the *History of America*.
[3] *Cf. History of America*, i, 205, 254; iii, 99, 143, 256.
[4] *Ibid.*, i, 186, 258–60, 262, 266, 304; iii, 252.
[5] *History of America*, ii, 404.   [6] *Ibid.*, iii, 5.   [7] *Ibid.*, 43.
[8] *Ibid.*, ii, 496; iii, 102.   [9] *Ibid.*, ii, 242, 260–1.   [10] *Ibid.*, iii, 84.

hostility of the natives, from the climate, and from hardships of every species, has nothing in history parallel to it, but what occurs in the adventures of the other discoverers and conquerors of the New World'.[1] Above all, though his description of the 'bustling, indefatigable activity' of Las Casas was certainly unhappy, Robertson insisted on the devoted labours of the missionary orders, on the humanity of the crown, and on the royal concern for the welfare of the native Indians.[2] And he rightly remarked that 'in no code of laws is greater solicitude displayed, or precautions multiplied with more prudent concern for the preservation, the security, and the happiness of the subject, than we discover in the collection of the Spanish laws for the Indies'.[3]

Robertson's narrative ends with the civil wars in Peru. It begins with Columbus and ends, as Prescott was to end his own fine history, with the conciliatory mission of that great ecclesiastical statesman, Pedro de la Gasca. It deals only briefly with events outside the major theatres of Spanish operations, and it touches only lightly on such matters as the territorial organization of the colonies and the beginnings of royal government. Discovery and conquest, not colonization, are its main themes.

But Robertson was not content with this alone. The Spanish crown, he observed, 'having acquired a species of dominion formerly unknown', formed 'a plan for exercising it, to which nothing similar occurs in the history of human affairs'.[4] The successors of Ferdinand and Isabella were 'the universal proprietors' of the territories which their subjects had conquered. 'It is true,' he continued, 'that when towns were built, and formed into bodies corporate, the citizens were permitted to elect their own magistrates, who governed them by laws which the community enacted. Even in the most despotic states, this feeble spark of liberty is not extinguished. But in the cities of Spanish America, this jurisdiction is merely municipal. . . . No political power originates from the people. All centres in the crown, and in the officers of its nomination.'[5]

---

[1] *Ibid.*, ii, 497–8.

[2] *Ibid.*, i, 251, 305–36; iii, 103, 255–8. For a modern view see Lewis Hanke, *The Spanish Struggle for Justice in the Conquest of America* (Philadelphia, 1949).

[3] *History of America*, iii, 288.

[4] *Ibid.*, 261. For medieval precedents of Spanish colonization see Charles Verlinden, *Précédents médiévaux de la colonie en Amérique* (Mexico, 1954).

[5] *History of America*, iii, 261–2.

His narrative ended, Robertson appended, therefore, in Book VIII, a review of Spanish colonial policy and administration from the sixteenth century to the Bourbon reforms of his own time, and surveyed also the internal development of the colonies during this period and their economic impact upon Spain and Europe. Here he examined the effects of the flow of American treasure upon Spanish commerce and industry, pointed out the disproportion between Spain's economic capacities and her colonies' economic needs,[1] discussed the rise of the contraband trade, and concluded with an account of contemporary imperial reorganization. The chapter, as Burke remarked, threw 'quite a new light' on the state of Spanish America;[2] as an example of Robertson's analytical powers it deserves to be compared with his famous introduction to the *History of the Reign of the Emperor Charles V*; and for the modern historian it retains its value after the lapse of nearly a hundred and eighty years.

Inevitably, of course, Robertson sometimes fell into errors of fact, though these, like the obvious *lacunae* in his work, were more often a reflection of deficiencies in the sources of his information than of carelessness in himself. Prescott, after all, was able to draw on a far greater corpus of materials, both printed and unprinted. Sometimes, also, Robertson's critical sense in the use of his authorities failed him. But the outstanding impression created by the *History of America* is one of general truthfulness and fairmindedness. It was a pioneer history, and destined to be superseded as the archives were opened and new documents brought to light. But, as a pioneer history, it was good history, and, what is more, it is extremely good reading.

The display of Robertson's skill as a narrative historian in the *History of America* is, indeed, superb. And here, surely, he is the 'master-artist' that Gibbon called him. As Brougham says in another connexion, and as Professor Black very properly repeats, 'the things described are presented in the clearest light, and with the most vivid, natural and unambitious colouring, without exaggeration, apparently without effort'.[3] The march of Cortés across the mountains to what is now Mexico City, Pizarro's seizure of

---

[1] *History of America*, iii, 319.
[2] Burke to Robertson, 9 June 1777. Robertson-Macdonald Papers. Stewart, *Memoirs*, p. 234.
[3] Brougham, *Lives*, p. 281; Black, *Art of History*, p. 123.

Atahualpa, the 'romantic history of Pedro de Gasca', are all magnificently told. It is easy to understand why Robertson's account of Balboa's first sight of the Pacific, 'stretching in endless prospect before him', should have remained in the mind of Keats to inspire the four famous lines on 'stout Cortez' and all his men 'silent, upon a peak in Darien', though Robertson would certainly have been shocked at the confusion between Cortés and Balboa. As for the plain, unadorned description of the landfall of Columbus on 12 October 1492, Lord Wellesley confessed that he shed tears when he read it, and that it broke his rest at night.[1] And, despite some small inaccuracies,[2] it remains the most moving account of the discovery of America in the English language.

In modern Spain, as in Spanish America, the great merits of Robertson's book have long been recognized,[3] and, in the eighteenth century, so distinguished a statesman, economist, and historian as the Conde de Campomanes read it with admiration.[4] Campomanes was president of the Royal Academy of History at Madrid, and the Academy, in August 1777, unanimously elected Robertson as a corresponding member. But though the *History of America* was quickly translated into French, German, and Italian, a Spanish translation had long to wait. The Academy, indeed, undertook the task, entrusting it to one of its own members, Ramón de Guevara. Progress was rapid, and in December 1777 Campomanes was able to report not only that the translation was exact but that it was no whit inferior to the original in elegance and purity of style. But the Academy was not content with this alone. Further to enhance the value of Robertson's work, it proposed to enrich the Spanish edition with additional notes and with corrections and amplifications; and for this purpose the Academy sought and obtained, in January 1778, a royal order requiring the officials of the Council of the Indies to supply it with the documentary materials and information it required.[5]

[1] Brougham, *Lives,* p. 295.

[2] *Cf.* Black, *op. cit.,* pp. 124–6, who follows Brougham in comparing Robertson's narrative with Washington Irving's.

[3] *Cf.* B. Sánchez Alonso, *Fuentes de la Historia española e hispano-americana* (2nd ed., 2 vols., Madrid, 1927), i, 271, and Diego Barros Arana, *Historia Jeneral de Chile* (16 vols., Santiago de Chile, 1884–1902), vii, 508–9.

[4] Rodrígues Campomanes to Robertson, 23 Sept. 1777. Robertson-Macdonald Papers.

[5] See C. Fernández Duro, 'D. Juan Bautista Múñoz. Censura por la Academia de su "Historia del Nuevo Mundo" ', *Boletín de la Real Academia de la Historia,* xlii(1903),

But Robertson had already been warned that he should not be too 'solicitous' about the Spanish version of his book, that Campomanes had many enemies, and that, if the whole of the *History of America* were translated, the work would be prohibited or burnt.[1] And barely had the Academy begun its researches when the blow fell. The history was now violently assailed as offensive to the honour of Spaniards, a *precursor de fatalidades*, and a source of corruption to the 'youth of Spain' and to the 'unwary reader' everywhere.[2] Its publication in Spanish was forbidden, and a royal decree of 23 December 1778 prohibited its introduction into Spanish America and the Philippines.

Nevertheless, Robertson's book was read in Spanish America[3] as everywhere else; and in Spain itself the commotion to which it had given rise had a fortunate outcome. The Cosmographer of the Indies, Juan Bautista Múñoz, no friend to Campomanes, now insisted that Spaniards must write their own history of their empire overseas, and from the original records. The crown approved his proposal that he himself should write it and that he should be given the fullest access to the documentary sources. Taking a leaf out of the Academy's book, Múñoz began to inspect and ransack the Spanish archives; and though his own history never got beyond the year 1500, the materials which he collected were later to be of immense benefit to Prescott, and, what is more, his activities resulted in the bringing together of the records relating to America and their concentration in the old home of the *Casa de Contratación*, the Spanish India House, at Seville. Robertson's *History of America* played its part, therefore, in however

---

pp. 6–15, and J. Torre Revello, *El Libro, La Imprenta y el Periodismo en América durante la Dominación Española* (Buenos Aires, 1904), pp. 77–80, and docs. 87 and 88.

[1] Waddilove to Robertson, 3 Nov. 1777. Robertson–Macdonald Papers.

[2] 'Examen de la Historia de America, escrita por el Doctor Guillermo Robertson . . . traducida del Yngles por dⁿ. Ramon de Guebara . . . Y conclusion de este asunto, prohibiendo S.M. la impresion y publicacion de este obra en España y sus Dominios'. British Museum, Add. MSS., 17,633, catalogued as 'Discurso qᵉ. sirve de Prologo á la Histᵃ. de America, del Dr. Robertson con reflexiones'. See also an undated but apparently later denunciation, 'Noticia . . . de algunos reparos que ha encontrado el Ministro de Marina dn. Juan Antono. Enriquez en la Historia de America escrita en Ingles por el Doctor Robertson'. Archivo General de Indias, Indiferente General, Legajo 1706. I am indebted for this last reference to my friend Dr John Lynch.

[3] *Cf.* Torre Revello, *op. cit.*, pp. 121–4, and, for an example of the confiscation of the book by the colonial authorities, see *ibid.*, pp. 80–1, and Barros Arana, *loc. cit.*

indirect a manner, in the foundation in 1784–5 of the great Archivo General de Indias.[1]

The *History of America* set the crown on Robertson's fame. To the fifth edition, printed in 1788, he made some few additions and corrections, noticing also, generally with disapproval, the strictures passed upon him by the Abbé Clavigero – a 'weak and credulous bigot', in Robertson's opinion.[2] And in 1791, at the age of seventy, he produced one more book – a *Historical Disquisition concerning the Knowledge which the Ancients had of India,* which illustrated, once again, his lively curiosity and his versatility. But the *History of America* was his last great work. He died on 11 June 1793. Brougham, in later days, recalled the charm of his voice and the sweetness of his mouth, the cocked hat which he always wore, even in the country, his courtly manners, and his stately gait; and Henry Cockburn remembered, also, the sparkle of his eye, his large projecting chin, the small hearing-trumpet which was fastened by a black ribbon to his coat, and his rather large wig, powdered and curled. The final portrait is Alexander Carlyle's. 'To begin with Robertson, whom you shall see no more', he wrote to a friend in 1796. 'In one word, he appeared more respectable when he was dying than ever he did even when living. He was calm and collected, and even placid, and even gay. My poor wife had a desire to see him, and went on purpose, but when she saw him, from a window, leaning on his daughter, with his tottering frame, and directing the gardener how to dress some flower-beds, her sensibility threw her into a paroxysm of grief. . . . His house, for three weeks before he died, was really an anticipation of heaven.'[3]

---

[1] Torre Revello, *op. cit.,* pp. 81–3; Antonio Ballesteros Beretta, 'Don Juan Bautista Muñoz. Dos Facetas Científicas', *Revista de Indias,* Año II, Núm. 3 (1941), 10–13. I am indebted to Professor Lewis Hanke for a copy of the 'Carta de Súplica' of Muñoz to the crown, dated 8 June 1779, from the Biblioteca de la Real Academia de la Historia in Madrid.

[2] Robertson to Eliock, 3 April 1782. National Library of Scotland, MS. 1036, f. 106. Clavigero's *Storia Antica del Messica* appeared in 1780–1 and was translated into English in 1787.

[3] Brougham, *Lives,* p. 316; Henry Cockburn, *Memorials of his Time* (Edinburgh, 1856), p. 48; J. H. Burton, ed., *Autobiography of the Rev. Dr Alexander Carlyle* (Edinburgh and London, 1860), p. 549.

3
William Hickling Prescott:
The Man and the Historian*

'There is only one way to look at life,' wrote Henry Adams to the young Henry Cabot Lodge in 1872,' and that is the practical way. . . . Sentiment is very attractive and I like it as well as most people, but nothing in the way of action is worth much which is not practically sound. The question is whether the historico-literary line is practically worth following, not whether it will amuse or improve you. Can you make it *pay*? either in money, reputation, or any other solid value. Now if you will think for a moment,' Adams continued, 'of the most respectable and respected products of our town of Boston, I think you will see at once that this profession does pay. No one has done better and won more in any business or pursuit, than has been acquired by men like Prescott, Motley, Frank Parkman, Bancroft, and so on in historical writing; none of them men of extraordinary gifts, or who would have been likely to do very much in the world if they had chosen differently. What they did can be done by others.'[1]

That is a revealing letter. It says something of Henry Adams and something of Boston, and, incidentally, it passes a judgement on William Hickling Prescott, with which Prescott – a man of singular modesty as well as of singular charm – would have been the first to agree. Whether he would also have agreed with the very worldly advice which Adams gave to Lodge on the reasons why a talented young man should choose to follow 'the historico-literary line' is another question.

The Boston mind, of course, in Prescott's day, as in Adams's, was not indifferent to 'money, reputation, or any other solid value'. And Prescott, though he had been born not at Boston but at

---

* [A lecture delivered at Canning House on 28 Jan. 1959, the 100th anniversary of Prescott's death. (London, The Hispanic and Luso-Brazilian Councils, 1959.)]
[1] W. C. Ford, ed., *Letters of Henry Adams (1858–1891)* (London, 1930), p. 228.

Salem, in 1796, was very much a Boston man.[1] A New England gentleman, moreover, however well-to-do, was not expected to pass a life of idleness and pleasure. And Prescott was very much a New Englander and a gentleman. His grandfather was old Colonel William Prescott of Bunker Hill fame. His father was Judge Prescott, who had amassed a comfortable fortune at the Massachusetts bar. He himself had not only been born of the right stock; he had been sent to one of the best schools – that of Dr Gardiner, the Rector of Trinity Church; he had gone to the right university – indeed, for a Bostonian, the only university – Harvard; he held the right opinions – federalist, in the language of the day, or, in more modern terms, conservative; and he belonged to the right church – Unitarian. And in the normal course of events the young man should have become, like his father, a successful lawyer and a respected man of affairs. Nothing in his bright and happy boyhood and early youth foreshadowed any different future, except, perhaps, a love of reading and of telling stories. And both at school and college he seems to have aimed at acquiring no more than that ordinary stock of learning which would enable him to do himself and his family credit.

But an accident which happened in his second, or junior, year at Harvard changed his whole life. Leaving the dining hall one day, he was struck in the left eye by a crust of bread and was instantly and permanently blinded. Nevertheless, he was able to complete his college course, graduated with moderate distinction

[1] The biography of Prescott written by his life-long friend, George Ticknor, *Life of William Hickling Prescott* (Boston, 1864), is a classic. Rollo Ogden's delightful *William Hickling Prescott* (Boston and New York, 1904) contains much supplementary information drawn from Prescott's journals and manuscripts, and there is a further 'life' by H. T. Peck, *William Hickling Prescott* (New York, 1905). See also the article by R. B. Merriman in the *Dictionary of American Biography*, xv (1935), and S. T. Williams, *The Spanish Background of American Literature* (2 vols., New Haven, 1955). Roger Wolcott, ed., *The Correspondence of William Hickling Prescott, 1833–1847* (Boston and New York, 1925), draws upon the great collection of Prescott's papers now in the custody of the Massachusetts Historical Society. It has been supplemented by C. L. Penney, ed., *Prescott: Unpublished Letters to Gayangos in the Library of the Hispanic Society of America* (New York, 1927). William Charvat and Michael Kraus, *William Hickling Prescott. Representative Selections, with Introduction, Bibliography, and Notes* (New York, 1943), contains much useful bibliographical information, together with an assessment of Prescott as an historian. [See also the Prescott Memorial number of the *Hispanic American Historical Review* (xxxix, no. 1, Feb. 1959), in which this lecture was first printed, together with C. Harvey Gardiner's *William Hickling Prescott. An annotated bibliography of published works* (Washington, D.C., 1958), and *The Literary Memoranda of William Hickling Prescott* (2 vols., Norman, Oklahoma, 1961).]

– the family marked the occasion by giving a dinner for five hundred in a tent – and began to read law in his father's office. Then
in January 1815 acute rheumatism attacked his right eye and other
parts of his body also, and for weeks he lay in darkness. Recover-
ing, he sailed for the Azores to stay with his maternal grandfather,
Thomas Hickling, who was the American consul in the island of
St Michael's. The visit gave him his one glimpse of the kind of
tropical scenery he was later so vividly to describe.[1] But on
1 November darkness again fell, and for three months he was shut
up in a single room, walking backwards and forwards, throwing
out his elbows to feel the walls, and – for he was already beginning
to cultivate those powers of memory which were later to be his –
singing, reciting, and composing a Latin ode for one of his
friends.[2]

The light returning and his rheumatism lifting, he visited
England, where the specialists told him that there was no hope of
a permanent cure and that he must abandon all thought of his
profession – a sentence which he received with the utmost calm.
'Do not think that I feel any despondency,' he wrote to his
parents. 'My spirits are full as high as my pulse; fifteen degrees
above the proper temperament.'[3] He now bought his famous
noctograph or writing case – a frame with brass wires stretched
across it and holding a piece of carbon paper tightly clamped to a
piece of ordinary paper. Guided by the wires and using an ivory
stylus, he could write without having to try to read what he had
written, and without the lines running into one another, though
the resulting hieroglyphics were the despair of his friends and of
his future secretaries. The autumn saw him in Paris and the winter
in Italy, crossing without note, as Ticknor observes, the battle-
fields of Gonsalvo de Córdoba, but with a Horace and a Livy in
his travelling carriage and a shrewd eye for the contemporary
scene. On his way back to England in the following spring, however, he was again prostrated, and at mid-summer, 1817, he was
glad to leave Europe and England for Boston and home.

Home, yes, to a devoted family. But to what else? Prescott had
now turned twenty-one. Tall, handsome, and extremely enter-

[1] Van Wyck Brooks, *The Flowering of New England, 1815–1865* (London, 1936),
pp. 139–40.
[2] Ticknor, *Life of William Hickling Prescott*, pp. 34, 40–1, 122.
[3] Ogden, *William Hickling Prescott*, p. 40.

taining, he was everywhere a favourite. His light-heartedness was infectious, his smile irresistible. But what was he to do? 'I can't say that I like to be called blind . . . ,' he wrote, many years later. 'I have it is true but one eye, but that has done me some service, and with fair usage will I trust do me some more.'[1] But his journal records the careful examination he made of his habits and way of life in order to determine how best to preserve his halting sight[2] and to keep at bay the dreaded rheumatic attacks, and it records also how often all precaution was in vain. Fortunately, there was no need for him to earn his living, for it was increasingly obvious that all ordinary careers were closed to him. But in Prescott the ancestral and New England virtues were too strong, he had too much force of character, too fine a sense of moral obligation, too ardent and gallant a nature, to allow his physical disabilities to serve as an excuse for idleness. For a while he was content to watch and weigh himself. Then, in 1820, the year also of his most happy marriage, he made up his mind. His life should be given to literature.

It was a courageous choice. For Prescott knew that only by the most rigorous self-discipline could he preserve his health and his sight. And he knew also that he must depend much upon the sight of others. But literature was his natural bent. There were friends to encourage and help him – George Ticknor, for example, the new professor of the French and Spanish languages at Harvard, who had only recently returned from Göttingen and Europe with incredible stories of German scholarship and a library of Spanish books the like of which Boston had not seen before. And, fortunately, he could afford to employ a secretary. He began to do so regularly in 1824. Meanwhile, he had laid down for himself a course of study. It is best given in his own words. 'I am now twenty-six years of age, nearly,' he wrote in 1822. 'By the time I am thirty, God willing, I propose, with what stock I have already on hand, to be a very well-read English scholar; to be acquainted with the classical and useful authors, prose and poetry, in Latin, French, and Italian, and especially in history. . . . The two following years, 31–32, I may hope to learn German, and to have read the classical German writers; and the translations, if my eye continues

---

[1] Prescott to Thomas Aspinwall, 15 May 1845. Wolcott, *Correspondence of William Hickling Prescott*, p. 538.

[2] Ogden, *op. cit.,* pp. 42–4.

weak, of the Greek. And this is enough for general discipline.'[1]

Enough, indeed. But the programme was carried out, except that German proved too difficult a language to master for a man who could only use his one eye with great caution and for short periods at a time. Reluctantly, Prescott substituted Spanish for German. Ticknor's Harvard lectures on Spanish literature, read over to Prescott in the evenings, seem to have been the origin of this momentous change. But it was made without enthusiasm. 'I am battling with the Spaniards this winter,' he wrote in 1824, 'but I have not the heart for it that I had for the Italians.' And in view of what was to come, his further comment was indeed ironic. 'I doubt whether there are many valuable things that the key of knowledge will unlock in that language!'[2]

All of this was preliminary. Prescott was fast becoming a man of letters. Working hard – *never* put up with a smaller average than seven hours intellectual occupation *per diem*'[3] was one of his resolutions – he was writing as well as reading and noting. 'State with confidence what I know to be true,' he observes in October 1824; 'Never introduce what is irrelevant or superfluous or unconnected for the sake of crowding in more facts,' he remarks in July 1828 [4] – both admirable maxims. And, beginning in 1821, each year till 1833 he contributed what he called his 'annual peppercorn' to the *North American Review*[5] – the 'old North', which was the American equivalent of the *Edinburgh* and of the *Quarterly*.

But he had yet to discover his all-absorbing field of study. History had always attracted him – history, that is, as a branch of literature, history in the grand manner of Robertson or Gibbon. An American history, a Roman history, a history of Italian literature, he considered them all. But, more and more, he began to feel the lure of Spain. Unexpected riches opened before him in the language which he had at first been tempted to underrate. And as he reflected on the course of Spanish history between the Arab invasion of the peninsula and the consolidation of the monarchy under Charles v, suddenly his mind took fire. Here was the age of Ferdinand and Isabella; here the age which contained 'the germs of

[1] Ogden, *op. cit.*, p. 49; Ticknor, *op. cit.*, p. 68.
[2] Ticknor, *op. cit.*, p. 72; Ogden, *op. cit.*, p. 54.
[3] Ogden, *op. cit.*, p. 55.
[4] *Ibid.*, pp. 56–7.
[5] *Ibid.*, p. 63.

the modern system of European politics'. It was full of brilliant episodes and striking events – the conquest of Granada, the exploits of the Great Captain, Gonsalvo de Córdoba, in Italy, 'the discovery of a new world, my own country,' the establishment of the Inquisition. 'Untried ground,' he noted, early in January 1826, 'and in my opinion a rich one.' But could he rise to the subject? Was he not more at home in literary history, particularly Italian literary history? He hesitated painfully. Then, on 19 January, he entered in his journal: 'I subscribe to the History of the Reign of Ferdinand and Isabella.'[1] He was twenty-nine, and he had found his theme.

Ten years of almost unremitting toil followed. At first, while he read widely in the literature of English and European history in order to lay a firm foundation for his work, doubts continued to assail him, as well they might, for at this time he was deprived almost entirely of the use of his eye. But, soon, books and manuscripts arrived from Spain. The subject began to unfold in his imagination. And by the summer of 1828 all hesitation had vanished. Six hours a day his secretary would read to him in a darkened room while Prescott made notes on his noctograph, and then, sitting alone, he would 'digest' what he had heard.[2] Presently, in October 1829, he began to compose, 'ripening' a chapter in his mind during his early morning rides or on his walks, and striving never to write until he should know exactly what he wanted to say. Later, at the height of his powers, he could retain in his memory as much as sixty or seventy pages of future print without putting a single word on paper, and he could amend and correct what lay in his mind just as if he had the manuscript in front of him.[3] Yet, all the while, Prescott had to force himself to work. He hated early rising, but always rose early, and his servant had instructions to take away the bedclothes if he did not get up so soon as he was called.[4] He hated having to begin a new chapter. And he was always making bets with his secretary that he would get through a certain amount of writing by a given time and imposing penalties on himself if he failed.

At last, in June 1836, the *History of the Reign of Ferdinand and*

---

[1] Ticknor, *op. cit.,* pp. 75–6.
[2] *Ibid.,* p. 87.
[3] *Ibid.,* pp. 149–50; Ogden, *op. cit.,* pp. 188–9.
[4] Ticknor, *op. cit.,* p. 126.

Isabella was finished. Few people in Boston, or anywhere else, knew that young Mr Prescott had been writing a book. Indeed, says Ticknor, 'most of his friends thought that he led rather an idle, unprofitable life, but attributed it to his infirmity, and pardoned or overlooked it as a misfortune, rather than as anything discreditable'.[1] And Prescott himself, having finished the book, was in two minds whether to publish it. He need never have doubted. 'Their Catholic Majesties,' as he called it, appeared on Christmas day, 1837, to captivate all Boston and to win for the author the respect and admiration of the scholarly world not only in America but in England and Europe.

The book was not a masterpiece of historical interpretation. It was not a penetrating analysis of a great historical period. And it did not provide that 'thorough view of the literary and social, as well as the political condition of Spain' which Prescott seemed to think that it provided.[2] Literature indeed he discussed, and at length. He was accustomed to writing on literature in the pages of the *North American Review*. But Prescott never ranked his critical and literary essays highly, and there is no reason to dissent from his judgement. His comment, when a collected edition came out, was characteristic. 'My portrait,' he wrote, 'is to be prefixed thereto – which they consider, I suppose, putting a good face on the matter.'[3] As for social, constitutional, and economic history, it cannot be denied that Prescott's interest in these matters in *Ferdinand and Isabella* was of a very limited kind.[4] It was the politics, the personalities, the conflicts of wills and of arms, that fascinated Prescott. History, as he saw it, was a story, full, as he says, of 'picturesque delineations of incident' and 'dramatic exhibitions of character'.[5] And this is what *The Reign of Ferdinand and Isabella* was – a narrative history, splendidly conceived and solidly based. 'Much new material has been discovered,' wrote one of the greatest of Prescott's successors in the field of Spanish history, Roger Merriman, in 1918, '... and the fashions of historical writing have greatly changed; but Prescott's work still remains

[1] *Ibid.,* p. 154.
[2] Prescott to Obadiah Rich, 22 July 1835. Wolcott, *Correspondence,* p. 5.
[3] Ogden, *op. cit.,* p. 67.
[4] 'The author,' wrote Theodore Parker, in a stricture often quoted, 'seems to know nothing of the philosophy of history, and little even, of political economy.' F. P. Cobbe, ed., *The Collected Works of Theodore Parker,* x (London, 1865), 116.
[5] Ticknor, *op. cit.,* p. 103.

the standard authority on the reign of the Catholic Kings'. And testifying to the 'profound learning' and 'unfailing honesty' of Prescott's writing, Merriman added: 'Such errors as he made were due to lack of material, and to a really noble inability to comprehend a policy of treachery or deceit.'[1]

Ferdinand and Isabella was the story of the rise of Spain from 'chaos', as Prescott puts it, 'not to the first class only, but to the first place, in the scale of European powers.'[2] In it he had traced the unification of the country and the consolidation of its monarchy, and he had traced also the progress of maritime discovery and the foundation of the first great European empire overseas. And as he closed his survey of what he believed to be 'the most glorious epoch' in Spanish history,[3] the future was already calling. 'Scarcely was Ferdinand's reign brought to a close,' he wrote, 'before Magellan completed (1520), what that monarch had projected, the circumnavigation of the southern continent; the victorious banners of Cortes had already (1518) penetrated into the golden realms of Montezuma; and Pizarro, a very few years later (1524), following up the lead of Balboa, embarked on the enterprise which ended in the downfall of the splendid dynasty of the Incas.'[4]

Here was the theme of Prescott's next and greatest books – *The Conquest of Mexico* and *The Conquest of Peru*. And it was exactly suited to his talents. His comments are revealing. 'An epic in prose,' he notes in his journal.[5] 'As full of incident as any tale of chivalry,' he tells his publisher.[6] 'More like a romance than a history,' he says a little later,[7] and, again, it is, he writes, 'as brilliant a subject, with adventures as daring and wonderful as ever occupied the pen of a historian.'[8]

Yet for some time after he had 'knocked their Catholic highnesses on the head' – his own phrase – Prescott hesitated. He even thought of writing a life of Molière. But his heart, as he well knew, was elsewhere. What deterred him was the problem of sources.

[1] R. B. Merriman, *The Rise of the Spanish Empire in the Old World and the New*, i (New York, 1918), xii.
[2] *History of the Reign of Ferdinand and Isabella* (8th ed., 3 vols., London, 1857), iii, 385, 440.
[3] *History of the Reign of Ferdinand and Isabella*, iii, 448.
[4] *Idem.*
[5] Ogden, *op. cit.*, p. 137.
[6] Prescott to Richard Bentley, 10 Oct. 1839. Wolcott, *Correspondence*, p. 99.
[7] Prescott to Richard Bentley, 31 Dec. 1842. *Ibid.*, p. 328.
[8] Prescott to Thomas Aspinwall, 1 April 1843. *Ibid.*, p. 345.

'Your manuscripts,' he wrote, 'is the only staple for the historic web – at least the only one to make the stuff which will stand the wear and tear of old Father Time.'[1] Could he get them?

His doubts were soon dispelled. Obadiah Rich, a bibliophile and bibliographer, who, after serving as an American consul in Spain and in the Balearic Islands, became a bookseller in London, had collected materials for *Ferdinand and Isabella*. *Ferdinand and Isabella* brought the friendship of the great Arabic scholar, Pascual de Gayangos, who later catalogued the Spanish manuscripts in the British Museum. It brought the friendship of the Spanish minister to the United States, Ángel Calderón de la Barca, who was shortly to be transferred to Mexico. It brought election to the Royal Academy of History in Madrid. All doors were opened. The Academy placed its great resources at Prescott's disposal and allowed him to employ copyists, and here he could consult the immense collection of documentary materials which the celebrated Cosmographer of the Indies, Juan Bautista Muñoz, had brought together in preparation for that history of the new world which Charles III had commissioned him to write, and of which one volume only appeared.[2] The ageing president of the Academy, Martín Fernández de Navarrete, who had long been engaged in compiling and editing, with loving care, the records of Spanish maritime discovery in America,[3] made available his own fine collection of manuscripts. The representative of the family Cortés opened his private archives. Everywhere Prescott found willing helpers. In the end he came to possess an unrivalled corpus of materials – 8,000 folio pages of manuscripts from Spain alone, enriched with further gleanings from public and private archives in Mexico, France, England, Italy and Sicily.

Prescott records that he began his 'scattered reading' on *The Conquest of Mexico* in May 1838, and began 'to read in earnest' in April 1839.[4] Meanwhile he was dismayed to learn that 'the most popular of American authors', Washington Irving, was

[1] Ogden, *op. cit.*, p. 132.

[2] On Muñoz see Antonio Ballesteros Beretta, 'Don Juan Bautista Muñoz. Dos Facetas Científicas', *Revista de Indias*, Año II, Núm. 3 (1941), pp. 5–37; 'Don Juan Bautista Muñoz. La Creación del Archivo General de Indias', *ibid.*, Núm. 4, pp. 55–95; 'Don Juan Bautista Muñoz. La Historia del Nuevo Mundo', *ibid.*, Año III, Núm. 10 (1942), pp. 589–660.

[3] *Colección de los Viajes y Descubrimientos, que hicieron por mar los españoles desde fines del siglo xv* (5 vols., Madrid, 1825–37).

[4] Ogden, *op. cit.*, pp. 135–6.

engaged on the same subject. Twice already Irving had crossed Prescott's path. In 1828, two years after Prescott had begun his work on *Ferdinand and Isabella*, Irving had published his *Life and Voyages of Christopher Columbus*. This was the author of Rip Van Winkle in a new role. Southey, reading the book for John Murray, had remarked that it displayed 'neither much power of mind nor much knowledge' but that it presented 'a most remarkable portion of history in a popular form' and was 'therefore likely to succeed'.[1] It was in fact chiefly based, with very inadequate acknowledgements, on Navarrete's collection of voyages. But the story was romantically told in Irving's characteristic style; only with the years were its pretensions to independent scholarship exposed;[2] and succeed it did. It was followed in 1829 by *The Conquest of Granada*, fiction rather than history, indeed, but, once again, Prescott's ground, and Prescott, though he paid a handsome tribute to Irving in the preface to *Ferdinand and Isabella*, had been 'sorely troubled'.[3] But in 1838 the boot was on the other leg. For Irving, once he knew of Prescott's plans, impulsively, but also wisely as well as generously, withdrew from the field, taking, as he said, to 'planting cabbages most desperately'.[4]

Thenceforth all was plain, or relatively plain, sailing. The introductory section to *The Conquest of Mexico*, which dealt with what Prescott called 'the moonshine period of the old Aztecs', was hard labour and cost him two years.[5] But by the middle of 1841 he was 'in full march' with Cortés across the mountains.[6] And by August 1843, the book was finished. *The Conquest of Peru*, which came next, was even more rapidly completed. The first words were written in August 1844, and the last in November 1846. But despite this heavenly speed, Prescott enjoyed the work less. The first chapter, in which he began his discussion of the civilization of the Incas, was, he complained, 'a perfectly painful task, as painful as ever I performed at school'.[7] For the rest, the history of the conquest of Peru lacked, he felt, that dramatic inevitability which the conquest

---

[1] S. T. Williams, *The Life of Washington Irving* (2 vols., New York, 1935), i, 322.
[2] *Ibid.*, ii, 296–308.
[3] Prescott to Jared Sparks, 1 Feb. 1841. Wolcott, *Correspondence,* p. 204.
[4] Williams, *op. cit.,* ii, 105.
[5] Ogden, *op. cit.,* p. 137; Prescott to Angel Calderón de la Barca, 29 June 1841. Wolcott, *Correspondence,* p. 229.
[6] Prescott to Angel Calderón de la Barca, 29 June 1841. *Ibid.,* p. 230.
[7] Ticknor, *op. cit.,* p. 258.

of Mexico possessed. It had less of a unity. And besides, while Cortés had all the character of a hero, Prescott could only express the wish that Pizarro had been 'more of a gentleman and less of a bandit'.[1]

But, like its predecessor, the book was a magnificent achievement. Both in the Peruvian and in the Mexican story, Robertson, in the eighteenth century, had covered the same ground; and for Robertson Prescott had a great respect.[2] But the plan of Robertson's famous *History of America* allowed, as Prescott said, 'only an outline of the Mexican campaigns' and a 'masterly sketch' of the conquest of Peru.[3] Prescott provided the detailed narrative. And it is the measure of his success that after more than a hundred years there is still no narrative history of the Spanish conquest of America to equal his.

Like Robertson, of course, Prescott was greatly hampered in his discussion of the native civilizations of America by the novelty of the subject. His literary sources, it is true, were far more extensive than those available to Robertson. He could read Sahagún, for example, as Robertson could not.[4] He reaped the benefit, moreover, of Humboldt's researches, for Humboldt had spent nearly five years in Spanish America, exploring, collecting, and describing, and every subject, from archaeology to mineralogy, had been grist to Humboldt's mill.[5] And he could draw both on the magnificent collection of the *Antiquities of Mexico*, which Lord Kingsborough had published, hoping to prove that the American Indians were really Jews,[6] and on the great folios of the *Antiquités Mexicains,* printed at Paris in 1834, which contained, as indeed did Kingsborough's volumes, reports of the archaeological expedi-

[1] Prescott to Pascual de Gayangos, 28 Sept. 1845. Wolcott, *Correspondence*, p. 553.

[2] See above, 'William Robertson and his *History of America*', p. 19.

[3] Prescott to Robert Walsh, 23 Dec. 1843. Wolcott, *Correspondence*, p. 421; Preface to the *History of the Conquest of Peru*.

[4] Bernardino de Sahagún's *Historia General de las Cosas de Nueva España* was first published at Mexico City in 1829–30. See, on Sahagún, Luis Nicolau d'Olwer, *Fray Bernardino de Sahagún* (1499–1590) (Mexico City, 1952).

[5] See, in particular, his *Vues des Cordillères, et Monumens des Peuples Indigènes de l' Amérique* (Paris, 1810), and the *Essai Politique sur le Royaume de la Nouvelle Espagne* (5 vols., Paris, 1811). Cf. Prescott to Alexander von Humboldt, 23 Dec. 1843. Wolcott, *Correspondence*, p. 422.

[6] *Antiquities of Mexico, comprising Facsimiles of Ancient Mexican Paintings and Hieroglyphics . . . together with the Monuments of New Spain by M. Dupaix* (9 vols., London, 1830–48). The first seven volumes appeared in 1830.

47

tions which Captain Guillaume Dupaix, a discharged French officer, had led to various sites in Mexico.[1]

But the archaeological evidence at Prescott's disposal was all too scanty. In the 'shadowy field' which he was now exploring,[2] he could derive little help from contemporary studies in anthropology and ethnology. These sciences were in their infancy.[3] And though, since Robertson's day, much more information had become available to illustrate the character of the native Indian societies which the Spaniards had found in the Valley of Mexico, the most remarkable of all pre-conquest civilizations – that of the Maya – was still unknown. Two or three Mayan sites had been cursorily examined,[4] and, even as Prescott wrote, John Lloyd Stephens and Frederick Catherwood were uncovering in the jungles of Central America and on the limestone plains of Yucatán the lost cities of the Maya world.[5] But it was long before these discoveries were followed up. Prescott saw quite clearly – and the conclusions of Stephens confirmed his own[6] – that the ruins of such cities at Mitla, Palenque and Uxmal argued, as he said, 'a higher civilization than anything yet found on the American continent'.[7] Like Stephens, he strongly distrusted the great antiquity commonly ascribed to them.[8] And he was inclined to think that they were Toltec in origin.[9] But beyond this he could not go. Of the inscriptions at Palenque he remarked that 'the language of the race' who devised them, and 'the race itself', were unknown. And

---

[1] *Antiquités Mexicains. Relation des trois expéditions du Capitaine Dupaix, ordonnés en 1805, 1806, et 1807, pour la recherche des antiquités du pays, notamment celles de Mitla et la Palenque* . . . (2 vols. and atlas, Paris, 1834).

[2] Prescott to Alexander von Humboldt, 23 Dec. 1843. Wolcott, *Correspondence*, p. 422.

[3] See T. A. Joyce's introduction to *The Conquest of Mexico* (2 vols., London, Chatto and Windus, 1922), pp. xix–xxiv.

[4] Palenque, Uxmal and Copán. See V. W. von Hagen, *Maya Explorer. John Lloyd Stephens and the Lost Cities of Central America and Yucatan* (Norman, Oklahoma, 1948), pp. 62, 72–4, 151–5, and *Frederick Catherwood, Archt.* (New York, 1950), p. 153.

[5] J. L. Stephens, *Incidents of Travel in Central America, Chiapas, and Yucatan* (2 vols., New York, 1841); *Incidents of Travel in Yucatan* (2 vols., New York, 1843); Frederick Catherwood, *Views of Ancient Monuments in Central America, Chiapas, and Yucatan* (London and New York, 1844).

[6] *History of the Conquest of Mexico* (8th ed., 3 vols., London, 1860), iii, 302.

[7] *Ibid.*, iii, 332; i, 10.

[8] *Ibid.*, iii, 337; Prescott to John Lloyd Stephens, March 1841. Wolcott, *Correspondence*, p. 211.

[9] *Conquest of Mexico*, iii, 339; i, 10.

he doubted whether their 'mysterious import' would ever be revealed.[1]

Yet whatever the limitations set by the then boundaries of knowledge, Prescott's account of pre-conquest Mexico and pre-conquest Peru, read in the light of what had gone before, was a remarkable achievement; and, seen in the light of what has come after, it appears more impressive still. A later generation, it is true, found Prescott's colours exaggerated and his sources suspect. Prescott, for example, follows Cortés and Bernal Díaz del Castillo in describing the 'barbaric splendour' of Montezuma's household, the state in which the 'emperor' dined, the retinue which attended him, the dishes which he ate, the Cholula earthenware on which they were served, the golden goblets from which he drank;[2] and Prescott's description was still further elaborated by H. H. Bancroft in 1875.[3] But to the pioneer ethnologists of the school of Lewis H. Morgan, the so-called 'social evolutionists', this picture was absurd. Morgan had lived and worked among the Iroquois. He knew an Indian when he saw one, and none that he had met remotely resembled Montezuma. The explanation was plain. The picture of ancient Mexico as drawn by the first Europeans was delusive and fictitious. The halls of Montezuma were nothing more than a 'joint-tenement house of the aboriginal American model, owned by a large number of related families, and occupied by them as joint-proprietors'. The dinner which Montezuma ate was simply 'the usual single daily meal of a communal household, prepared in a common cook-house from common stores, and divided, Indian fashion, from the kettle'. All that the Spaniards found in Mexico, wrote Morgan, was a 'simple confederacy of three Indian tribes, the counterpart of which was found in all parts of America'.[4] And while Montezuma, under Morgan's hand, was reduced to the stature of some early Pontiac or primitive Tecumseh, Prescott himself was dismissed as a romantic who had allowed his critical judgement to be warped by the picturesque tales of the conquistadores and others.

These are ancient controversies. The terms of discussion have

---

[1] *Ibid.*, iii, 336.
[2] *Ibid.*, ii, 105–11.
[3] *Native Races of the Pacific States of North America*, ii (New York, 1875), 174–8.
[4] Lewis H. Morgan, 'Montezuma's Dinner', *North American Review*, cxxii (April 1876), 265–308, reprinted, New York, Labor News Co., 1950. For Morgan see B. J. Stern, *Lewis Henry Morgan. Social Evolutionist* (Chicago, 1931).

long since changed and the world of American archaeology has been revolutionized. But Prescott's scholarship has been vindicated and his reputation rehabilitated. Prescott, of course, had been fully alive to the 'proneness to exaggerate, which was natural', he says, to the early conquistadores.[1] He was always careful to test and weigh the credibility of his Spanish sources. But it never occurred to him to reject their testimony out of hand. Like the Spaniards, no doubt, he was constrained to describe the political organization of semi-civilized indigenous societies in terms of European institutions, though he was well aware of the dangers which such analogies entailed;[2] and to illustrate the development of these societies he made use of classical, oriental and Egyptian parallels which carried greater conviction in the eighteen-forties than they do in the nineteen-fifties. But Prescott's description of the pre-Colombian civilizations of the New World was the most penetrating appraisal that had yet been made. And though much has been discovered since his day, though there were fields into which he could not enter, it approached far closer to the truth than his later nineteenth-century detractors were disposed to allow.[3]

But all of this, of course, was merely preliminary to Prescott's main purpose – to tell the story of the conquest itself; and, however much these introductory surveys may need to be revised and amplified, from the moment when the Europeans first set foot on American soil Prescott was on firm ground. And he built to last. Such is his mastery of his materials that even his descriptions of landscape and seascape leave the impression that Prescott had seen it all himself. And so he had, in his vivid imagination and through the eyes of others. 'I want to dip my pencil in your colours,' he writes to Fanny Calderón de la Barca, the charming Scottish wife of the first Spanish minister to Mexico – 'the colours of truth, gently touched with fancy, at least feeling'.[4] And as her enchanting

---

[1] *Conquest of Mexico*, ii, 111.

[2] *Ibid.*, i, 23.

[3] *Cf.* T. A. Joyce's introduction to the Chatto and Windus edition of *The Conquest of Mexico,* already cited, and P. A. Means, 'A Re-Examination of Prescott's Account of Early Peru', *New England Quarterly*, iv (Oct. 1931), 645–62. See also Charvat and Kraus, *op. cit.,* pp. cxxii–cxxvi, and Williams, *The Spanish Background of American Literature*, ii, 114–15.

[4] Prescott to Fanny Calderón de la Barca, 28 July 1841. Wolcott, *Correspondence,* p. 240.

Life in Mexico shows,[1] no one who had Fanny for a correspondent
could ask for more.

Prescott's style, it is true, was a little magniloquent. His grass is
'verdant' rather than green. His 'monarchs' are 'sagacious' and his
'soldiery' 'licentious'. He was even capable of referring to 'the
feathered tribes' when he meant birds. He himself was aware of
this weakness. 'Finished text of chap. 1, Book 3rd,' he notes in
1841. 'Full of the picturesque – reads very like Miss Porter –
rather boarding-schoolish finery.'[2] And 'boarding-schoolish finery'
some of it is. Prescott prefers 'gales' to 'winds' and 'groves' to
'woods', and when insects appear he cannot refrain from painting
them with 'enamelled wings', glistening 'like diamonds in the
bright sun of the tropics'. But there is good, plain, homespun stuff
too – the Prescott of the letters and journals, and, whatever his
love of the conventional ornament and the rhetorical word, sooner
or later every reader succumbs to the spell he weaves. For Prescott
was an artist. The easy flow of his narrative, its admirable clarity,
never reveal the enormous pains which he had taken to master the
difficulties of construction and to ensure, both in *The Conquest of
Mexico* and in *The Conquest of Peru*, that his book should be a whole
in which every part was exactly right.

They never conceal, either, the absolute integrity both of the
man and of his writing. For though Prescott trod enchanted
ground, no one was less capable of sacrificing truth to effect. His
passion for accuracy was unquenchable. And while he sought to
establish his narrative, as he says, 'on as broad a basis as possible of
contemporary evidence',[3] he sought also to see the sixteenth
century through sixteenth-century eyes. He burkes no awkward
facts. 'Never shrink from the truth . . . ,' he notes in his private
journals. 'I spoke fearlessly in "F[erdinand] and I[sabella]". Do so
now.'[4] But the historian, he thought, gained nothing 'by throwing
about hard names . . . like Southey and others of that plain spoken
school'.[5] And the Spanish conquistadores, those 'antique heroes
whose great deeds were so nearly allied to great crimes',[6] were to

---

[1] First published, with a preface by Prescott, in 1843.
[2] Ogden, *op. cit.*, p. 139. [3] Preface to *The Conquest of Mexico*.
[4] Williams, *Spanish Background*, ii, 105; Ogden, *op. cit.*, p. 117.
[5] Prescott to Pascual de Gayangos, 16 Aug. 1856. C. L. Penney, ed., *Prescott:
Unpublished Letters to Gayangos,* p. 124.
[6] Prescott to Martín Fernández de Navarrete, 9 June 1844. Wolcott, *Correspondence*,
p. 436.

be judged not by the standards of the nineteenth century but by those of their own times. So, he remarks, after describing the massacre at Cholula, 'It is far from my intention to vindicate the cruel deeds of the old Conquerors. Let them lie heavy on their heads. They were an iron race, who periled life and fortune in the cause; and as they made little account of danger and suffering for themselves, they had little sympathy to spare for their unfortunate enemies. But, to judge them fairly, we must not do it by the lights of our own age. We must carry ourselves back to theirs.'[1]

And Prescott, in his fine imagination, had lived with the Spaniards. He knew their sixteenth-century world in all its violence and vitality. Side by side with the 'capricious cruelty of the conqueror' and the 'cupidity of the colonist',[2] he saw also the courage which 'no danger could appal', the lure of the unknown which charmed the Spanish mind, the sense of high adventure.[3] And more than this, even amid the 'coarse and covetous spirit' which marked, he says, 'the adventurers of Peru',[4] he recognized something else. 'One might have supposed,' he writes of Pizarro and his men as they prepared to seize the Inca, 'one might have supposed them a company of martyrs, about to lay down their lives in defence of their faith, instead of a licentious band of adventurers, meditating one of the most atrocious acts of perfidy on the record of history! Yet, whatever were the vices of the Castilian cavalier, hypocrisy was not among the number. He felt that he was battling for the Cross, and under this conviction, exalted as it was at such a moment as this into the predominant impulse, he was blind to the baser motives which mingled with the enterprise.'[5] For the Spaniard, Prescott says again, 'was ever a Crusader. He was, in the sixteenth century, what *Coeur de Lion* and his brave knights were in the twelfth, with this difference; the cavalier of that day fought for the Cross and for glory, while gold and the Cross were the watchwords of the Spaniards.'[6]

The New World was conquered in the name of the Cross of Christ as well as in a search for gold.[7] This dual motive is the

---

[1] *Conquest of Mexico*, ii, 30.
[2] *History of The Conquest of Peru* (5th ed., 3 vols., London, 1857), i, 223.
[3] *Ibid.*, i, 182–3.
[4] *Ibid.*, ii, 117.
[5] *History of the Conquest of Peru*, ii, 55–6.
[6] *Ibid.*, ii, 153. Cf. *Conquest of Mexico*, iii, 297.
[7] Cf. *Conquest of Peru*, i, 226–7; ii, 50, 355; *Conquest of Mexico*, i, 229; iii, 54, 62, 297.

paradox, or rather it is one of the paradoxes, the seemingly contradictory impulses, in the mind of the sixteenth-century Spaniard. Prescott recognized it fully, as he recognized also the contrast between the humane intentions of the crown and the 'practical licence', as he says, of the colonists.[1] His view of history was not profound. As Theodore Parker observed, in a famous comment, he was fond of referring events to Providence 'which other men would be content to ascribing to human agency'.[2] But, like Lady Bertram of Mansfield Park, if Prescott did not think deeply, he always thought justly. His writings, as Stirling Maxwell remarked in 1859, reflect that 'calm good sense' which 'directed every action of his life'.[3] *The Conquest of Mexico* and *The Conquest of Peru* do not present the total picture of the action of Spain in America in the first half of the sixteenth century. They need to be supplemented by studies of a different kind, in administration, in economic life, in political thought. But they must always remain two of the great adventure stories of history, and stories which, at every point, are solidly tied to established fact.

'Of late years,' wrote Prescott in April 1846, 'I have had a fair use of my eyes. But I fear I am not to count on this for the future. The sight has grown much dimmer, and I have at times pain which warns me not to press the matter further. So I complete "Peru" as I began "Ferdinand and Isabella". But I shall not abandon the historian's career. For how can I?'[4] He had, indeed, long been collecting materials for what was to be his last important book – the *History of the Reign of Philip the Second*. He had been thinking about it as early as 1833.[5] The idea constantly recurred to him, and in December 1841 his journal records: 'I have had the satisfaction to learn from that accomplished scholar, Gayangos, that he will undertake the collection of manuscripts for me relating to Philip the Second's history, so far as it can be effected in Paris and London.'[6]

From that moment the work went merrily forward. In 1842

---

[1] *Conquest of Mexico*, i, 230. Cf. *ibid.*, iii, 217; *Conquest of Peru*, i, 223; ii, 174-5, 355; iii, 50-3.
[2] *Works*, x, 153.
[3] W. Stirling Maxwell, *William Hickling Prescott: a memorial sketch* (London, 1859), p. 23.
[4] Prescott to Pascual de Gayangos, 30 April 1846. Wolcott, *Correspondence*, p. 594.
[5] Prescott to Obadiah Rich, 13 Aug. 1833. *Ibid.*, p. 2.
[6] Ticknor, *op. cit.*, p. 286.

Gayangos wrote that he had four copyists at work in the British Museum and another in Holland House.[1] From the British Museum he proceeded to the Public Record Office – a disgrace to the country, he writes. 'Not only it requires great favour to obtain admission; but when admitted the papers are only trusted into your hands after a succession of ridiculous formalities.' The papers themselves were in a lamentable state of confusion. No one could be employed as a copyist, copying being a perquisite of the clerks, who charged eight pence per folio of 72 words. And the office was only open from eleven to two.[2] The great collection of Sir Thomas Phillipps was also laid under requisition – a collection so large that the papers flowed into Sir Thomas's bedroom and even under his bed. And then Gayangos was off to Brussels, the Hague and Paris, and finally to Madrid and Simancas.

If the Public Record Office, or State Papers Office, as it was then called, was a disgrace, it is difficult to know what term to apply to Simancas. Gayangos was one of the first scholars ever to be admitted within its precincts. Visitors, he found, were forbidden to copy, to take extracts or notes, or even to make a summary of the documents they were allowed to examine. The confusion of the papers was appalling, and though in Simancas one could work four hours a day instead of three, as in London, the archives were closed every saint's day, of which, in Spain, there was a profusion.[3]

Gayangos, however, triumphed over all difficulties. Other friends assisted Prescott in Florence, Vienna and Berlin. And by 1847, when Prescott was ready to start, he had as noble a collection of manuscripts on his shelves as the heart could desire. But he had already had to resolve 'to relinquish *all* use of the eye' for the future in his studies, and to be content, as he records, if he 'could preserve it for the more vulgar purposes of life'.[4] The mere sight of his collection filled him 'with apprehension bordering on despair'.[5] He doubted much whether he would be able to produce anything more than a series of memoirs, and hardly had he begun to write, in July 1849, when his strength began to fail.

Urged by his friends, Prescott decided to try a change of scene, and this was the reason for his visit to England in 1850, 'the most

[1] Pascual de Gayangos to Prescott, 27 Jan. 1842. Wolcott, *Correspondence*, p. 280.
[2] Pascual de Gayangos to Prescott, 2 Feb. 1843. *Ibid.*, p. 335.
[3] Pascual de Gayangos to Prescott, 1 Aug. 1844. *Ibid.*, pp. 488–9.
[4] Ticknor, *op. cit.*, p. 281; Ogden, *op. cit.*, p. 156.
[5] Ticknor, *op. cit.*, p. 282.

brilliant visit ever made . . . ', as Ticknor says, 'by an American citizen not clothed with the prestige of official station'.[1] He met everyone and was invited everywhere. He stayed at Alnwick with the duke of Northumberland, at Inverary with the duke of Argyll, at Naworth and Castle Howard with the earl of Carlisle, and at Trentham with the duchess of Sutherland. He was presented at court. Oxford made him a Doctor of Civil Law. Lockhart, Hallam, Macaulay, Lyell, Ford, Milman, all welcomed him. 'Pray,' said Disraeli, 'are you related to the great American author – the author of the Spanish Histories?' 'I squeezed his arm,' says Prescott, 'telling him that I could not answer for the greatness, but I was the man himself.'[2]

The visit was short. But it did much to revive Prescott's spirits. And he had made a brief excursion to Brussels, Antwerp and Holland – Motley's country, for Motley, with Prescott's blessing, was hard at work on *The Rise of the Dutch Republic*. Still, he had to describe the revolt of the Netherlands himself, and so soon as he had returned to America he was back at work, enlarging his plans and resolving that he would treat the reign of Philip II *in extenso* and not in the more desultory manner that he had at first envisaged.[3] And by April 1852 the first volume was finished. The second was ready by August 1854, and Prescott then turned aside to prepare a new conclusion to Robertson's famous *History of the Reign of the Emperor Charles V* in the light of documents unknown to Robertson and dealing with Charles's life after his abdication. Soon, however, he was 'Philippizing' (his own word) again. 'Rebellion of the Moriscoes,' he records, in June 1857, 'making in all 289 pages – more than half a volume! As bad as Macaulay – without his merits to redeem it.' And, a few days later, 'Finished Battle of Lepanto. I hope it will smell of the ocean.'[4]

It does. The set pieces of *Philip II* show no decline in Prescott's dramatic powers. But the book was never to be completed. In February 1858, Prescott suffered a slight stroke. He carried on and managed to produce a conclusion to his third volume. He even started to work on the fourth, though he was not able to begin to write. 'As to not working, as you kindly recommend,' he wrote to

[1] Ticknor, *op. cit.*, p. 339.
[2] Ogden, *op. cit.*, p. 165.
[3] Ticknor, *op. cit.*, p. 346.
[4] Ogden, *op. cit.*, p. 225.

Gayangos in September 1858, 'to use Scott's words on a similar recommendation to him, "Molly, when she puts the kettle on, might as well say, Don't boil, kettle." But then I manage matters with more prudence, and make it a rule, one indeed that I have generally followed, never to sacrifice pleasure to business. But in truth long habit makes me find business – that is literary labour – the greatest pleasure.'[1] On 28 January 1859, however, Prescott suffered a second stroke and in a few hours was dead.

It is related of the great Spanish scholar, Navarrete, to whom Prescott had owed much, that 'on the evening that he died, finding himself alone in his bedroom after having received extreme unction, he managed to get up without being heard by anyone and tottered into his study. He was found there by his daughters and when they asked him what he was doing he replied that he was bidding farewell to his books.'[2] So, also, Prescott had expressed the wish that he might lie for a time in the library which he had built for himself. And, there, he, too, bade farewell to the books and manuscripts which had been the friends of his life.

[1] Prescott to Pascual de Gayangos, 14 Sept. 1858. Penney, *op. cit.,* pp. 140–1.
[2] Pascual de Gayangos to Prescott 15 Oct. 1844. Wolcott ,*Correspondence*, p. 509.

4

The Rule of Law and the American Revolution*

The American colonies of the seventeenth century were dependent communities legally subject to the authority of the English crown. The history of their constitutional development in the first half of the eighteenth century is essentially the history of the efforts of the colonial assemblies to establish their supremacy within the colonies and over the instruments of the royal prerogative. In their conflicts with the crown and its agents the colonies won repeated victories; and from parliament they had received support rather than opposition.[1] To what extent they were themselves subject to the authority of parliament was a question which had only indirectly arisen, and which, so long as that authority was exerted only in matters of general and external polity, troubled them little. But while the revolution settlement had defined in some important respects the limits of the royal prerogative – in itself a notable assertion of parliamentary supremacy – the two houses of parliament had continually strengthened their control over the executive authority of the crown. They had displayed increasing interest and activity in the affairs of the colonies. Above all, they had asserted more and more confidently that there was, in Lord Mansfield's words, 'no restriction to the legislative authority of Great Britain'.[2] It thus followed that in the moment of their victory over the instruments of the royal prerogative, the colonial assemblies found themselves threatened by the omnipotent claims of a distant legislature.

This establishment of the fact and theory of the absolute supremacy of the crown in parliament did not pass unnoticed or unchallenged in England. Legally and historically, as far as the

* [*Law Quarterly Review*, liii (1937), 80–98.]
[1] *Cf.* L. W. Labaree, *Royal Government in America* (New Haven, 1930), p. 34.
[2] 11 March 1766, *American Historical Review*, xvii (1912), 584.

colonies are concerned, the right of the crown in parliament, even before the revolution settlement, still less after, to legislate for the American dependencies cannot be denied.[1] But it was and is possible to contend that the extent of that right, and indeed of all legislative right, was limited by a law above parliament. Parliament itself, in the early eighteenth century, seems to have regarded its authority as at once finite and boundless. It passed the Act of Union with Scotland, with intent to establish a fundamental law beyond the authority of future statutes. Ten years later it defied the electorate and, with an assumption of unbounded authority, prolonged its life to seven years – not, indeed, without protests that such action was in excess of its legal powers. If parliament was inconsistent, legal and political theory were no less so. The seventeenth century belief in a controlling rule of law, above and beyond the authority of parliamentary statutes, died hard. It was still possible for the lawyers to refer to a law of nature, of reason, or of God, which limited the arbitrary rule of parliament.[2] But the doctrine, however respectable, was also vague. Not much can be made of Mansfield's declaration that an act of parliament could not alter the law of nations, or of his assertion that the Elizabethan Statute of Artificers was 'in restraint of natural right'.[3] In neither case was the validity of a statute impaired. And it was Mansfield who, during the debates on the repeal of the Stamp Act, protested that an appeal to the law of nature or of nations was irrelevant.[4] The weakness, yet persistence, of this higher law doctrine, exemplified both in the contradictory opinions of the judges and in formal commentaries, is admirably illustrated by Blackstone, who declared that the 'law of nature, being coeval with mankind and dictated by God himself, is of course superior in obligation to any other . . . no human laws are of any validity, if contrary to this'; and yet affirmed that the 'power of parliament is absolute and without control'. 'If the parliament will positively

---

[1] The arguments against are set forth by C. H. McIlwain, *The American Revolution* (New York, 1923), and refuted by R. L. Schuyler, *Parliament and the British Empire* (New York, 1929).

[2] *Cf.* an interesting discussion in C. K. Allen, *Law in the Making* (2nd ed. Oxford, 1930), pp. 264 ff.; F. T. Plucknett, 'Bonham's Case and Judicial Review', *Harvard Law Review*, xl (1926–7), 54.

[3] See C. H. McIlwain, *The High Court of Parliament* (New Haven, 1910), p. 329; E. Heckscher, *Mercantilism* (London, 1933), i, 316. For the contradictions of Holt in *Re City of London* v. *Wood,* see Plucknett, *op .cit.,* p. 55.

[4] *Parliamentary History*, xvi, 172.

enact a thing to be done which is unreasonable,' he wrote, 'I know of no power in the ordinary forms of the constitution, that is vested with authority to control it.'[1]

When the Commentaries were published, convention still demanded, in a formal treatise, a graceful deference to that law of nature which Locke had described as 'an eternal rule to all men, legislators as well as others',[2] and on which the British constitution was believed to have been founded. But grounded on the immutable laws of nature and reason, the constitution seemed to attain perfection at the moment when, by a happy coincidence, Blackstone attained a professor's chair. Or if, as some thought, it was indeed in 'a moving state',[3] they did not doubt that the sovereignty of parliament was its fly-wheel. The two houses were not inclined to admit that their legislative will could be contrary to substantial justice. They positively denied the existence of limitations upon that will. Alderman Beckford, indeed, during the debates on the Stamp Act, quoted the words of Chief Justice Coke in *Bonham's Case* on the right of the common law to control and adjudge void an Act against common right and reason,[4] and Lord Camden's protest is famous. 'The sovereign authority, the omnipotence of the legislature, my lords, is a favourite doctrine, but there are some things they cannot do. They cannot enact anything against the divine law. . . .' The Declaratory Act he condemned as 'absolutely illegal, contrary to the fundamental laws of nature, contrary to the fundamental laws of this constitution'.[5] But the reception of these views is illuminating. The supposition that there were things which parliament could not do was flatly contradicted by the lawyers, headed by Northington, Mansfield, Yorke and Wedderburn. Burke, who was to insist on the 'overruling plenitude' of parliamentary power, avowed the impossibility of fixing 'bounds' to the legislature.[6] Shelburne, who, on the contrary, was to ridicule the 'specious language of the supremacy of the British legislature', as yet admitted the power of parliament to be 'supreme'.[7] Pitt asserted its supremacy 'in every circumstance of

---

[1] *Commentaries on the Laws of England* (10th ed. 1797), i, 41, 162, 91.
[2] *Two Treatises of Government*, ii, s. 135.　　[3] *Parl. Hist.*, xvi, 197.
[4] *American Historical Review*, xvii, 568. The best discussion of this case is Plucknett, *op. cit.*
[5] *Parl. Hist.*, xvi, 168, 178.
[6] *Ibid.*, xvi, 170–7; *American Historical Review*, xvii, 566 ff.
[7] *Parl. Hist.*, xviii, 162; *Chatham Correspondence*, ii, 355.

government and legislation whatsoever',[1] and Camden himself seems soon to have retreated from his bold position.[2]

By the middle of the eighteenth century, then, not only had the two houses greatly extended their control over the executive authority of the crown, but the doctrine of the absolute legal sovereignty of the crown in parliament had been firmly established. Ridiculing Blackstone's reference to a law of nature, 'Let us avow . . .', wrote Bentham in 1776, 'steadily but calmly, what our Author hazards with anxiety and agitation, that the authority of the supreme body cannot, *unless where limited by express convention,* be said to have any assignable, any certain bounds. That to say there is any act they *cannot* do, – to speak of any thing of their's as being *illegal,* – as being *void*; – to speak of their exceeding their *authority* (whatever be the phrase) – their *power,* their *right,* – is, however common, an abuse of language.'[3] And however common such an abuse of language may still have been, any important criticism in England of this legal theory was to arise not from the old belief in a controlling rule of law, but from the feeling that Parliament imperfectly represented the sovereign will of the people. 'If omnipotence can, with any sense, be ascribed to a legislature,' wrote Richard Price in the year in which the *Fragment on Government* was published, 'it must be lodged where all legislative authority originates; that is, in the People.'[4]

Between the two houses of parliament thus wielding the weapon of omnipotence and omnicompetence, and the colonial assemblies lately victorious over the royal prerogative, conflict was bound to occur. For it was precisely this omnipotence and omnicompetence, which they resented in parliament, that the assemblies had been increasingly prone to arrogate to themselves. They had long striven for parliamentary powers as well as parliamentary forms. They had sought to free themselves from the shackles of royal instructions and judicial review, and to establish their superiority over the colonial executive and the colonial judiciary.[5] They had proved themselves increasingly intolerant of restraints upon their legislative will either within or without the colonies. Virginia affords an admirable example.

[1] *Ibid.,* ii, 366.   [2] *American Historical Review,* xvii, 585.
[3] *A Fragment on Government,* ed., F. C. Montague (Oxford, 1891), p. 218.
[4] *Observations on the Nature of Civil Liberty* (3rd. ed. 1776), p. 15.
[5] On the position of the colonial assemblies, see H. Hale Bellot, 'The Mainland Colonies in the Eighteenth Century', *History,* xvii (1933), 344–8.

'No man or body of men, however invested with power, have a right to do anything that is contrary to reason and justice,' declared the Virginia Committee of Correspondence in 1764, in protesting against the intention of parliament to tax the colonies. In the same letter the Committee urged its agent in England to secure an affirmation by the Privy Council of a judgement given by the General Court against one, the Rev. John Camm, who had carried his case to the council on appeal.[1] Under the Virginia Two-Penny Act of 1758 debts contracted in tobacco were permitted to be paid in currency at the rate of two pence a pound. The clergy, whose salaries were thus affected, protested, and in the next year the Privy Council disallowed the Act. Many of the clergy thereupon sued the tax collectors for the full market value of the tobacco. The collectors appealed to the law of 1758 as being valid when in 1759 the salaries for 1757–8 were due, and the Virginia courts, except in one instance, sustained them. Camm's case was the decisive one; and it was to the recent judgement against him that the Virginia Committee referred at the moment when it invoked the laws of reason and justice against parliament. But to these laws also Camm and the clergy in part appealed. The Act of 1758, they contended, was both beyond the competence of the legislature, in violation of the royal instructions, and also 'void in itself, being contrary to the principles of justice' and repugnant to reason. To these assertions the defendants, and the supporters of the assembly, retorted that the legislature could enact any law it thought fit, and that the alleged injustice was not 'pertinent' to the question, because the Virginian legislature was the judge of the justice of its own laws.[2] There were other lines of attack and defence, but these suffice here; and it plainly appears that it is one thing to affirm a rule of law against parliament, and quite another to affirm that same rule against the assembly. Old habits of expression may easily cloak new frames of mind. Not until 1773 did the colonies in general contend that they were 'free and distinct' states entirely independent of parliamentary authority. But it is not so much a question of a formal argument as of a state of mind. In the clash between the Virginian clergy, the assembly and the parliament, the

[1] [Letter to the Agent], 28 July 1764, *Virginia Magazine of History and Biography*, xii (1905), 13.
[2] A. P. Scott, 'The Constitutional Aspects of the "Parson's Cause" ', *Political Science Quarterly*, xxxi (1916), 560, 563, 571, 573.

interesting fact is not so much that a belief in a controlling rule of law survives in the colonies, and may be used legitimately both against the assembly and against the parliament, but that here it is also appealed to in support of a body which in reality contends that it is above the law, and which will brook no restraint upon its legislative will. The comment of Archdeacon Burnaby comes forcibly to mind. Of the Virginians he observed, They 'can scarcely bear the thought of being controuled by any superior power. Many of them consider the colonies as independent states, not connected with Great Britain, otherwise than by having the same common king, and being bound to her by natural affection'.[1]

Had this been all, and had the question been merely that of the absolutism of parliament or the absolutism of the colonial legislatures, it would have been relatively simple. But it was not merely that. These absolutisms were also unpopular absolutisms. It was idle, and indeed rather insulting, to bolster up the imperial and parliamentary case against the colonies by the argument that parliamentary authority was not unpopular because the colonists were virtually represented. The colonial idea of representation squared ill with this theory. A representative who should have said in Boston what Burke said in Bristol, 'I know nothing of Bristol but by the favours I have received and the virtues I have seen exerted in it', is scarcely to be imagined. The colonists thought of their representatives as agents. But the cry of 'No taxation without representation' was not therefore intended as an argument for parliamentary reform. James Otis declared that 'Besides the equity of an American representation in parliament, a thousand advantages would result from it';[2] and similar expressions can be garnered. But despite the equity, it required no great penetration to realize that the honour of voting with the minority in the House of Commons was doubtful or that the alternative of changing the whole basis of parliament was impossible. In any case the colonists contended that they already possessed 'compleat and adequate legislative authority' of their own,[3] competent at least for all pur-

[1] A. Burnaby, *Travels through the Middle Settlements in North America, 1759–60*, ed. R. R. Wilson (New York, 1904), p. 55.

[2] *The Rights of the British Colonies Asserted and Proved*, (1764), reprinted in C.F. Mullett, *Some Political Writings of James Otis* (Univ. of Missouri Studies, iv, Nos. 3 and 4, 1929), p. 71.

[3] The phrase is from Daniel Dulany's *Considerations on the Propriety of Imposing Taxes in the British Colonies, for the Purpose of Raising a Revenue, by Act of Parliament*, (1765).

poses of taxation. They were satisfied with their own institutions as they were. No taxation without representation, they held, was a principle of the British constitution; and they relied upon it not as a revolutionary or reforming argument, but as a conservative one.[1]

Conservative as the principle was, it nevertheless invited attention to the source of parliamentary authority. 'Right reason and the spirit of a free constitution,' wrote Otis, 'require that the representation of the whole people should be as equal as possible. A perfect equality of representation has been thought impracticable; perhaps the nature of human affairs will not admit of it. But it most certainly might and ought to be more equal than it is at present in any state.' 'To what purpose,' he complained, 'is it to ring everlasting changes to the colonies on the cases of Manchester, Birmingham and Sheffield, who return no members? If those now so considerable places are not represented, they ought to be.'[2]

But if parliament imperfectly represented the sovereign will of the people, if its authority might be questioned because it was unpopular as well as competitive, the imperfections of the colonial assemblies were only different in degree and not less obvious. Not all the colonists were satisfied with their institutions as they were. Almost everywhere the suffrage was limited. The distribution of seats was commonly unfair. Newly settled western areas were often either under-represented in the assembly or not represented at all.[3] '. . . Representation in proportion to the number of taxable inhabitants is the only principle which can at all times secure liberty, and make the voice of a majority of the people the law of the land,' declared the Pennsylvania Constitution of 1776;[4] and the idea that the will of the majority must rule, in part prevailed against both parliament and assemblies. There was thus a double conflict, a double opposition. The American revolution, it has been well said, was not merely a struggle for home rule; it involved the question who

[1] See A. C. McLaughlin, *The Foundations of American Constitutionalism* (New York, 1932), p. 59.
[2] *Considerations on Behalf of the Colonists in a Letter to a Noble Lord* (1765), Mullett, *op. cit.*, p. 110.
[3] *Cf.* Allan Nevins, *The American States During and After the Revolution, 1775–1789* (New York, 1924), pp. 10–14; A. E. McKinley, *The Suffrage Franchise in the Thirteen English Colonies in America* (Philadelphia, 1905), p. 487.
[4] S. E. Morison, ed., *Sources and Documents Illustrating the American Revolution* (Oxford, 1923), p. 168.

should rule at home.[1] Corresponding to obvious physiographical differences within the colonies were almost equally obvious differences in political ideas, economic interests and social outlook; and almost everywhere there accompanied the imperial struggle a conflict between tidewater and uplands, between eastern and western sections, between socially superior and economically depressed classes, of which the issue was an attempted democratization of politics. Like all great social movements in the United States, the American revolution was in part an upward surge of democracy. It represented an attempt to replace unpopular government both without and within the colonies by the uncontrolled will of the people.

Yet no very critical study of revolutionary literature is necessary to discover that here also is no adequate explanation of the motives which led to the rejection of the sovereign authority of the crown in parliament. When John Adams advocated that in the foundation of a new government it was necessary to 'realize the theories of the wisest writers, and invite the people to erect the whole building with their own hands, upon the broadest foundation', since 'the people were the source of all authority and original of all power', these, he affirms, were 'new, strange, and terrible doctrines to the greatest part' of those who heard them.[2] There was, in truth, little either strange or new in these doctrines. But if they did indeed appear so, it is because side by side with the exaltation of popular rights in revolutionary literature is evident a great mistrust of democracy. That men had natural rights, that to preserve these rights governments by compact and consent had been instituted among men, drawing their just powers from the consent of the governed, these, as Jefferson would say, were part of the 'harmonizing sentiments of the day', but it by no means followed that the will of the people should be absolute and supreme.

The American revolution, indeed, was carried through on the most conservative principles. The literature of the revolution is eminently a conservative literature, and to an uncommon degree a legal literature. From beginning to end the justification of the revolution is a legal justification. Combating the novel claims of

[1] C. L. Becker, *The History of Political Parties in the Province of New York, 1760–1776* (Madison, 1909), p. 22.

[2] *The Works of John Adams*, ed. C. F. Adams, iii (Boston, 1851), 16. Adams, however, plainly disapproved of the 'most democratical forms' to which his cousin, Samuel, leaned; *ibid.*, p. 18.

parliamentary absolutism the colonists based their case either on the principles of constitutional or of natural law, or of both. They appealed first to colonial charters, then to the rights of Englishmen and the nature of the English constitution; finally they cast off their rights as Englishmen to appeal to their rights as men; they turned from the nature of the constitution to nature's laws themselves.[1] And an appeal to the laws of nature and of nature's God was no mere rhetorical flourish. It was an appeal to the most sacred and fundamental of all laws.

These phrases and these appeals might, it is true, have no more than a verbal significance, and represent no more than a conventional usage of words hallowed by tradition and familiar through constant use. The law of nature, for example, implied very different degrees of obligation to Blackstone and to James Otis. What John Adams meant by the sovereignty of the people was something rather different from what Samuel Adams meant. In the name of reason and justice the Virginian clergy protested against the Virginian assembly; in the name of reason and justice the assembly protested against parliament. All these phrases, these appeals to precedents and principles, must be construed according to the different directions in which men's minds were intended. They could be invoked for widely different reasons, and their implications might be widely apart. 'You know,' said Samuel Adams, 'there is a charm in the word "constitutional".'[2]

But yet this atmosphere of legality is characteristic of the colonial climate of opinion. And it points the way to what was after all the most significant and interesting of the colonial arguments. Parliamentary authority might be rejected because it was competitive, or because it was unpopular. But it was to absolutism as such that many of the colonists passionately objected. They were compelled ultimately to deny the legal authority of parliament only because parliament itself denied that its authority was limited by a

---

[1] For the evolution of these arguments, see R. G. Adams, *Political Ideas of the American Revolution* (Durham, N.C., 1922); C. L. Becker, *The Declaration of Independence* (New York, 1922); and C. F. Mullett, *Fundamental Law and the American Revolution, 1760–1776* (New York, 1933).

[2] Quoted by V. L. Parrington, *The Colonial Mind, 1620–1800* (New York, 1927), p. 237. *Cf.* Jeremy Bentham's criticism: 'A great multitude of people are continually talking of the law of nature; and then they go on giving you their sentiments about what is right and what is wrong; and these sentiments, you are to understand, are so many chapters, and sections of the law of nature': *Principles of Morals and Legislation*, cap. ii.

c*

controlling rule of law. But in rejecting parliamentary absolutism they had no desire to erect the despotism of the people. They had no desire to exchange one absolutism for another. This claim to absolute power, John Quincy Adams maintained in 1831, was precisely the cause of the revolution. 'The pretence of an absolute, irresistible, despotic power [existing] in every government *somewhere*,' he declared, was 'incompatible with the first principle of natural right.'[1] Adams was the heir to a great tradition. To the claims of parliamentary omnipotence and omnicompetence the colonists replied that parliament itself was subject to a rule of law; to absolutism, of whatever predicated, whether of parliament or people, they could oppose not only charters and constitutional rights, but what was the very foundation of those rights, the fundamental law of God and nature, of which Locke had said that it was 'an eternal rule to all men, legislators as well as others', and of which even Blackstone had felt constrained to say, 'no human laws are of any validity, if contrary to this'.

What did this law of nature mean? How was it discovered? 'He who bids the law rule, may be deemed to bid God and Reason alone rule,' said Aristotle;[2] and from Aristotle to the eighteenth century the theory of the natural, or ideal law of human society continued to attract the thoughts of men. That the universe was a universe of law, devised by a divine architect, that merely by the use of his 'natural faculties' man could bring his life, his morals and his institutions into harmony with this natural and rational order, these were commonplaces of much of eighteenth century thought. To the eighteenth century *philosophes* it was evident that, merely by inspecting the nature of the universe around him and nature's voice within him, man could discover those laws of nature and of nature's God which were the only valid laws of politics and morals.[3] This may well be so, and it cannot be denied that the *philosophes* belonged to all countries, and that their writings were well enough known in America. Jefferson, no less than Diderot, was a *philosophe*.[4] But if these doctrines contributed to the colonial

[1] Quoted by B. F. Wright, *American Interpretations of Natural Law* (Cambridge, Mass., 1931), p. 170.　　　　[2] *Politics* (trs. Jowett), iii, cap. xvi, 5.

[3] See Carl L. Becker's two charming studies, *The Declaration of Independence* (New York, 1922) and *The Heavenly City of the Eighteenth-Century Philosophers* (New Haven, 1932), pp. 63, 65.

[4] *Cf.* H. M. Jones, on the importation of French literature into New York and Philadelphia, in *Studies in Philology*, xxviii, No. 4 (1931), 235, and *Modern Philology*, xxxii, No. 2 (1934), 157; Becker, *Heavenly City*, pp. 33–5.

climate of opinion, it was because the minds of the colonists were already predisposed to accept them. Theology, history, tradition, all alike confirmed them in their beliefs that men had natural rights, founded on the laws of God and nature, that to preserve these rights governments by compact and consent had been instituted amongst men, and that the eternal laws of nature, discoverable by human reason, were universally valid. It was the traditions of the political and ecclesiastical doctrines of England in the seventeenth century, perhaps refined by the rationalistic atmosphere of the eighteenth century, which survived in the colonies – the traditions of the civil war and revolution, and the tenets of Puritan theology, kept strong and vigorous by the teaching of the New England clergy.[1]

For the Puritan, like the philosopher, saw the universe as a universe of law. If political philosophers spoke of compacts, the Puritans spoke of covenants. They too believed in natural rights protected by unchallengeable law. They too affirmed the existence of a rational order of society, of a universe, indeed, governed according to the strictest legal principles. 'God proceeds legally,' said John Donne, the Anglican; and the Puritans saw that God had agreed with man in a covenant way; he himself was bound by his own laws. King of kings and lord of lords, he was yet 'a constitutional monarch'. 'The Divine Government,' they declared, was 'managed by fixed and steady rules.' 'God himself,' said that eminent New England divine, Jonathan Mayhew, 'does not govern in an absolutely arbitrary and despotic manner. The power of this Almighty King (I speak it not without caution and reverence); the power of this Almighty King is *limited by law*; not indeed, *by Acts of Parliament*, but by the eternal *laws* of truth, wisdom and equity; and the everlasting *tables* of right reason.'[2] The laws of God, then, were the eternal rules of right and reason; they were the natural and rational laws of human society; and they were revealed not merely in the universe around us. They were planted deep in the minds of men, and they were written for all to read in Holy Writ. The law of nature, that part of divine law fathomable by human reason, as reason searched the heart and the scriptures, was an

---

[1] See A. C. McLaughlin's admirable work, *The Foundations of American Constitutionalism* (New York, 1933), p. 68. If this essay only serves as an introduction to the works of Professors Becker and McLaughlin, it will have served its purpose.

[2] McLaughlin, *op. cit.*, pp. 73, 123, 129; A. M. Baldwin, *The New England Clergy and the American Revolution* (Durham, N.C., 1928), pp. 17 n., 18.

absolute law. No human law was of any validity if contrary to this.

Philosophy and theology alike, then, conducted the colonists to beliefs which they could only regard as self-evident truths. If the Divine Government was managed by fixed and steady rules, so much the more was human authority limited by known and established laws. If God himself was bound by His own laws, so much the more were earthly powers confined by their obligations. If the laws of nature and of nature's God were supreme, all other laws were declaratory, all other authority was partial. Governments existed to preserve those rights which God and nature had given to all, not to reduce them. ('No rational creature', observed Locke, of the contract on which society was based, 'can be supposed to change his condition with an intention to be worse.') The very definition of liberty was freedom from arbitrary rule. By compact, charter and consent human authority had been marked out. It followed, therefore, that any Act which transcended these limitations was null and void. 'The obligations of the law of Nature,' Locke had said, 'cease not in society . . . the law of Nature stands as an eternal rule to all men, legislators as well as others. The rules that they make for other men's actions must, as well as their own and other men's actions, be conformable to the law of Nature – *i.e.* to the will of God, of which that is a declaration. . . .'[1]

What reason and religion taught, history and experience supported. Colonial history, from the beginnings, was compact of charters and covenants in matters both civil and ecclesiastical; and at every turn the colonists were confronted with the spectacle of authority limited by law and agreement. Their own constitutions were 'fixed' either in colonial charters or, with some degree of permanence, in the commission and instructions of a governor. The legal spheres of royal and popular authority in the colonies were carefully separated and defined. Such Acts as colonial legislatures passed in excess of their powers were disallowed by the Privy Council in England. And when the colonists thought historically, they did not merely think in terms of Mayflower compacts, charters and covenants, but they thought of the great constitutional struggles of the seventeenth century, of the arguments which common lawyers used against prerogative, of the ideas for which their ancestors suffered, of the Great Rebellion and the Glorious Revolution, of Milton, and of Locke. History, indeed,

[1] *Second Treatise*, ss. 131, 135.

became philosophy teaching by examples. Aristotle, Cicero, Vattel, what Jefferson called the 'elementary books of public right' – and there were many of them – these were familiar enough to the colonists. But it was English ideas and English history of the seventeenth century which they particularly cherished. Had not Harrington pleaded for an empire of laws not of men? Had not Locke declared that the law of nature was an eternal rule to all men, legislators as well as others? Had not Coke – whatever the basis of his theory may have been – said that an Act against common right and reason was void, and that the common law might control acts of parliament? It may be difficult to 'pin Coke to a theory'; but what Coke said Hobart repeated and Holt endorsed.[1] There was nothing novel in the colonial belief in a controlling rule of law – though opinions about the nature of that law might differ. 'In the sixteenth and seventeenth centuries,' says Professor Allen, 'it would have required considerable audacity on the part of any lawyer to deny that the only ultimate, supreme authority lay in a law higher than any man-made ordinance – the eternal dictates of natural justice, reason or equity; or, in its theological aspect, the law of God.'[2] ' 'Tis hoped,' wrote James Otis, 'that it will not be considered as a new doctrine, that even the authority of the parliament of *Great-Britain* is circumscribed by certain bounds, which if exceeded their acts become those of meer *power* without *right*, and consequently void. The judges of England have declared in favour of these sentiments, which they expressly declare; that *acts of parliament against natural equity are void*. That *acts against the fundamental principles of the British constitution are void*. This doctrine is agreeable to the law of nature and nations, and to the divine dictates of natural and revealed religion.'[3]

This passage admirably sums up both the character and the sources of the colonial belief in a controlling rule of law. That law was valid against all absolutism, of the people as well as of Parliament. 'The same law of nature and reason,' said Otis, 'is equally obligatory on a *democracy*, an *aristocracy*, and a *monarchy*. Whenever the administrators, in any of these forms, deviate from truth,

---

[1] Allen, *op. cit.*, p. 266; Plucknett, *op. cit.*, pp. 45, 49, 54.
[2] Allen, *op. cit.*, p. 264. *Cf.* E. S. Corwin, 'The "Higher Law" Background of American Constitutional Law', *Harvard Law Review*, xlii (1928–9), 369–70, 372.
[3] *The Rights of the British Colonies Asserted and Proved* (1764), Appendix. A learned note referred the reader to Coke, Hobart and Holt. Mullett, *op. cit.*, pp. 95–6.

justice and equity, they verge towards tyranny, and are to be opposed. . . .'[1]

It is important to notice the partial identification of this law of nature with the British constitution. Reasonably enough, the colonists assumed that the teachings of this law would be reflected in the experience of man in society, that its light illumined the English common law, that in it the British constitution was founded, a constitution which was not only by far 'the best, now existing on earth',[2] but 'the best that ever existed among men'.[3] 'It is the glory of the British constitution,' declared the Assembly of Massachusetts Bay, 'that it hath its foundation in the law of God and Nature.'[4] But if the constitution was founded in the laws of God and nature, it was therefore rigid as those laws themselves. 'In all free states,' remarked the assembly, generalizing from its own experience, 'the constitution is fixed.' Further, 'The supreme legislative, in every free state,' it affirmed, 'derives its power from the constitution; by the fundamental rules of which it is bounded and circumscribed.' These rules ascertained and limited both sovereignty and obedience. And the assembly implied that there were certain essential rights so firmly founded 'in the law of God and Nature' that in fact they were beyond the reach of parliamentary statute.[5] 'To say the parliament is absolute and arbitrary, is a contradiction,' declared Otis in a famous passage. 'The parliament cannot make 2 and 2, 5; omnipotency cannot do it. The supreme power in a state, is *ius dicere* only; – *ius dare*, strictly speaking, belongs alone to God.'[6] An Act contrary to the constitution, contrary to the law of nature, ran his argument, was void; and it was the duty of the courts to declare it so. But, said Blackstone, no court may defeat the intent of the legislature.[7] There is revealed the measure of the difference between the colonial and English interpretations of the constitution.

The colonists, then, assumed that the law of nature was engrafted into the British constitution. The constitution contained a body of fundamental principles; it guaranteed a number of natural rights which no authority within the state could abrogate. But

[1] *Ibid.*, p. 55.
[2] *Ibid.*, p. 91.
[3] Stephen Hopkins, *The Rights of Colonies Examined* (1765).
[4] *Writings of Samuel Adams*, ed. H. A. Cushing, i (New York, 1904), 135.
[5] *Ibid.*, pp. 134, 185, 190. See also McIlwain, *The American Revolution*, pp. 148–55.
[6] Mullett, *op. cit.*, p. 78.   [7] *Commentaries*, i, 91.

what if, despite the constitution, despite basic common law, what if there should be a difference of opinion about these rights, for they were nowhere very precisely stated? What if parliament should refuse to admit that its legislative will was subject to a higher law? In that case it might prove impracticable for men who held such contradictory ideas of right to live together in the same society. But this was a conclusion from which the colonists shrunk. And since all their petition was for the laws of England, it seemed, indeed, a monstrous conclusion. It was to avoid this conclusion that Otis, that most brilliant and pathetic of colonial writers, enmeshed himself in contradictions. Now denouncing absolutism, now declaring that 'the power of parliament is uncontroulable, but by themselves, and we must obey', now that an Act against reason and equity was void, now that parliament might 'abrogate and annihilate all colony or subordinate legislation', the unhappy man could only point the way to arguments he hesitated to follow.[1] But 'what is important', says Professor Mullett, 'is Otis's state of mind. Like the majority of his sympathizers he was able to be vastly illogical, even unhistorical, and yet justify his whole point of view and the inconsistencies themselves.'[2]

Only reluctantly did the colonists come to the conclusion that it was hopeless to contend that there were limits to parliamentary authority, and that therefore they must deny all parliamentary authority. It was at this point that the American revolution, properly speaking, began. 'Whatever difficulty may occur in tracing the line,' wrote John Dickinson as late as 1774, 'yet we contend, that by the laws of God, and by the laws of the constitution, a line there must be' beyond which parliamentary authority 'cannot extend'.[3] Dickinson and others had long laboured hard to establish that line by distinguishing between those powers which were proper to parliamentary authority and those which were not. But in vain. 'A new party,' he complained, had arisen in England, which sought to 'erect a new sovereignty over the colonies inconsistent with liberty or freedom.'[4] That 'new sovereignty', later to receive its systematic definition at the hands of Austin, was consistently attacked by the colonists in the belief that sovereignty

---

[1] Mullett, *op. cit.*, pp. 73, 139.
[2] *Ibid.*, p. 10.
[3] *A New Essay on the Constitutional Power of Great Britain Over the Colonies in America* (1774).
[4] Quoted by R. G. Adams, *Political Ideas of the American Revolution*, p. 82 n.

was not absolute or arbitrary, but limited and divided. Constitutional and juridical theory failing them, they were compelled ultimately to fall back upon the laws of nature and of nature's God alone. In their name they declared their independence, and rejected the authority of parliament as that of a body foreign to their constitution and unacknowledged by their laws.

For totally different reasons men of widely divergent views had combined to secure an immediate common end. Independence was achieved through a temporary alliance of mutually conflicting principles. In part it represented an attempt to transfer the sovereign attributes of parliament to the legislatures of the several colonies; in part it was an effort to replace unpopular by popular sovereignty; in part it was a denial of any theory of absolute sovereignty in the name of an overruling law. Independence achieved, the work of reconstruction, of replacing one form of government by another, made clear this hostility of principles. United in resistance men became aware that they were yet divided in opinion. 'An *elective despotism*,' wrote Jefferson in his *Notes on Virginia*, 'was not the government we fought for, but one which should not only be founded on free principles, but in which the powers of government should be so divided and balanced among several bodies of magistracy, as that no one could transcend their legal limits, without being effectually checked and restrained by the others.'[1] But it was precisely such a despotism that many now feared; and the struggle over the new state governments, and the experience of their working under the weak union of the Confederation, confirmed or inspired in many an American mind an invincible distrust of democracy. In part, no doubt, this was a distrust born of turbulence, and the fear of the subversion of all government. Gerry, in the Federal Convention, confessed that 'he had been too republican heretofore; he was still, however, republican, but had been taught by experience the danger of the levelling spirit'.[2] The bright democratic faith of some was dimmed. The Federal Constitution was in part a remarkably successful effort on the part of the propertied classes to stop revolution at a point at which it became dangerous for themselves.[3]

[1] *The Writings of Thomas Jefferson*, ed. P. L. Ford, iii, 224 (1782).
[2] Quoted by C. E. Merriam, *A History of American Political Theories* (New York, 1926), p. 99.
[3] *Cf.* D. W. Brogan, *The American Political System* (1933), p. 16.

That there is much truth in this judgement cannot be denied. But it is not the whole truth. If, as Acton said, 'the authors of the most celebrated Democracy in history esteemed that the most formidable dangers which menaced the stability of their work were the very principles of Democracy itself',[1] they cannot therefore be dismissed simply as reactionaries. For the very *fons et origo* of the revolution had been the belief in a controlling rule of law, a mistrust of absolutism as such. That the people were the source of political authority, that they had rights anterior to all government, these were doctrines on which few would dare to take issue. 'British liberties,' said John Adams, were 'not the grants of princes or parliaments, but original rights, conditions of original contracts, coequal with prerogative, and coeval with government.'[2] In founding a new government, he declared, it was necessary to 'realize the theories of the wisest writers, and invite the people to erect the whole building with their own hands, upon the broadest foundation'.[3] If these, as he avers, were 'new, strange and terrible doctrines to the greatest part' of those who heard him, 'not a very small number heard them with apparent pleasure'. On these principles at least John Adams and his great rival, Thomas Jefferson, were agreed; never throughout their lives did Adams or Jefferson deny them. But not therefore were democratic governments omnipotent and absolute.

Jefferson, indeed, had leanings towards absolutism. The faith in the 'steady and rational character of the American people' burned clearly within him. The dead, he felt, had no right to control the living. Every constitution and every law ought naturally to expire at the end of nineteen years. 'After all,' he declared, 'it is my principle that the will of the majority should always prevail.'[4] But yet, he was to say in his Inaugural, that will, to be rightful, must be reasonable. And perhaps Jefferson would not have endorsed all majority wills. Natural rights and bills of rights were close to his heart. After all, it was not an elective despotism he had fought for, 'but one which should not only be founded on free principles, but in which the powers of government should be . . . divided and balanced'.

---

[1] *Historical Essays and Studies* (1908), p. 129.
[2] Adams, *Works*, iii, 463 (1765).
[3] *Ibid.*, p. 16 (1775).
[4] Jefferson, *Writings*, iv, 360, 479; v, 121; i, 168.

Jefferson's strength did not lie in his logic and political philosophy. Adams, on the other hand, was the ablest political philosopher of his day; and the study of the development of his mind repays attention. It has been alleged that Adams changed his principles. 'The bold champion of the Revolution' became 'equally fearless in his advocacy of strong government and of aristocratic principles'.[1] But there was no inconsistency in John Adams's thought; there was merely logical development. 'The fundamental article of my political creed', he wrote in 1815, 'is, that despotism, or unlimited sovereignty, or absolute power, is the same in a majority of a popular assembly, an aristocratical council, an oligarchical junto, and a single emperor.'[2] And what was fundamental to Adams in 1815 was also fundamental in 1775.

Always a constitutional lawyer, Adams had come to perceive the necessity of independence reluctantly enough. In his opposition to the sovereign authority of parliament, he would have been 'very happy', as he remarked in his Autobiography, 'if the constitution could carry us safely through all our difficulties without having recourse to higher powers, not written'. He appealed exhaustively to precedent. But he was quite prepared to resort to higher powers, not written, should the necessity arise.[3] He was clear that the authority which parliament claimed was contrary both to constitutional and natural law, and that the law of nature was the foundation of rights in general, of the British constitution in particular, and indeed of all just government. Government, he declared, was a 'plain, simple, intelligible thing, founded in nature and reason, and quite comprehensible by common sense'.[4] But the common sense view of the matter did not lead Adams to the conclusion that because by natural law men had equal rights, because government rested on the consent of the governed, that therefore a majority should have the power to trample on a minority. On the contrary, as he remarked to Jefferson in 1798, 'as to trusting to a popular assembly for the preservation of our liberties it was the merest chimera imaginable, they never had any rule of decision but their own will'.[5]

There was the crux of the matter. How was it possible to main-

---

[1] Merriam, *op. cit.*, p. 123.
[2] *Works*, x, 174; quoted by Merriam, *op. cit.*, p. 141.
[3] *Works*, ii, 331, 374.
[4] *Ibid.*, ii, 155, 157, 159; iii, 463, 454.
[5] Jefferson, *Writings*, i, 277.

tain a controlling rule of law? That was the question which Adams
had in mind in 1815, in 1798, and in 1775. The basis of government must admittedly be broad; but its powers must be confined.
A good government, said Adams, in the words of Harrington,
must be an empire of laws.[1] Ecclesiastical controversies, he alleges
in his Autobiography, had quite early helped to show him 'in all
their dismal colours, the deceptions to which the people in their
passions are liable'. He had, he affirms, small respect for that
'popular talk' and 'those democratical principles which have done
so much mischief in this country'. And a circumstantial and
amusing story relates his alarm at the 'spirit' and 'principles' which
the revolution had engendered.[2] Adam's faith in the steady and
rational character of the American people grew weaker rather
than stronger; and these observations may not reflect contemporary states of mind at all. But his reflections on government in
1775 and 1776 reveal a mind already made up on the fundamental
principles of liberty and constitutional organization. 'A legislative,
an executive, and a judicial power,' he wrote, 'comprehend the
whole of what is meant and understood by government. It is by
balancing each of these powers against the other two, that the
efforts in human nature towards tyranny can alone be checked and
restrained, and any degree of freedom preserved in the constitution.' Adams had been attacking absolutism, but to no purpose if
that absolutism was to be replaced by another nearer home. 'A
people,' he wrote, 'cannot be long free, nor ever happy, whose
government is in one assembly.'[3]

These principles Adams ever retained and developed. 'It is a
fixed principle with me,' he wrote in 1790, 'that all good government is and must be republican.' The people must have 'collec-
tively, or by representation, an essential share in the sovereignty'.
But the 'multitude' must also 'have a check'.[4] 'Power,' he declared,
'is always abused when unlimited and unbalanced.' For 'since all
men are so inclined to act according to their own wills and interests in making, expounding, and executing laws, to the prejudice
of the people's liberty and security, the sovereign authority, the
legislative, executive, and judicial power, can never be safely

[1] *Works,* iv, 194 (1776).
[2] Autobiography, under dates 1768, 1772, 1775; *Works,* ii, 214, 310, 420.
[3] Adams to Lee, 15 Nov. 1775; 'Thoughts on Government', (1776); *Works,* iv,
186, 194–5. See also Wright, *op. cit.,* p. 121.
[4] *Works,* vi, 415, 418.

lodged in one assembly, though chosen annually by the people; because the majority and their leaders, the *principes populi*, will as certainly oppress the minority . . . as hereditary kings or standing senates'.[1]

To Adams, then, sovereignty must be limited and divided, checked and balanced. The only true sovereign was the law and the constitution. Adams, in short, attacked not the absolutism of a given body at a given time, but of any body at any time. The experience of the revolution and its aftermath confirmed his belief in the principles with which he set out. The law of nature, the rule of right and reason, whose ultimate authority he continued to exalt, meant for him that in human institutions and constitutions must be enshrined a rule of law to preserve the natural rights of men against the tyranny either of majorities or minorities. A republic must be an empire of laws, not of men.

Such was the republic which the authors of the Federal Constitution tried to build. They were concerned not to make America safe for democracy, but to make democracy safe for America. From Lord Chief Justice Coke to the Supreme Court of the United States is a long way, but a clear one. The controlling rule of law which the seventeenth century set above king or parliament, which the Puritans exalted in matters both civil and ecclesiastical, which the philosophers saw as the governing principle of the universe, which the colonists invoked against the absolutism of parliament, this 'was now made the essential principle of federalism'.[2]

---

[1] *Ibid.*, vi, 73, 114.
[2] A. C. McLaughlin, *The Foundations of American Constitutionalism*, p. 155.

5

The Fall of the Spanish American Empire*

At the time of the Napoleonic invasions of the Spanish peninsula in 1807–8, the Spanish empire in America stretched in unbroken line from California to Cape Horn. From Stockholm to Cape Town is less distant, and within the area ruled by Spain all western Europe from Madrid to Moscow might lie and be lost.

A hundred years earlier, at the beginning of the eighteenth century, Spain had been a major battlefield of Europe. That experience was now to be repeated, and this time foreign invasion spelt imperial destruction. The French Revolution in its Napoleonic aspect was the occasion, if not the cause, of the emancipation of Spanish America.[1] But in the years between the war of the Spanish Succession and the wars of Napoleon, Spain herself had risen with remarkable resilience from the decrepitude into which she had fallen in the seventeenth century. Her economic decline had been first arrested and then reversed, and under Charles iii and during the early years of Charles iv she enjoyed what seems in retrospect to have been an Indian summer of prosperity.

What was true of Spain was true also of her empire. Of the empire during the long years of Spain's weakness and decay we know all too little. But of its material and intellectual advance during the so-called century of enlightenment there is abundant evidence. And Spain, like Britain, undertook in the eighteenth century the task of imperial reorganization and reform. At home and in the empire the administrative system was overhauled. New vice-royalties and captaincies-general were created. The establishment, in the very year of the North American Declaration of

* [*History*, n.s. xxxvii (1952), pp. 213–27.]
[1] *Cf.* Sir Charles Webster, *Britain and the Independence of Latin America, 1812–1830* (2 vols., London, 1938), i, 8.

Independence, of the viceroyalty of the Río de la Plata,[1] covering the whole, indeed more than the whole, of what is now Argentina, marked a period in the history of Spanish America. And the attempt to systematize and centralize colonial government by the division of the colonies into intendancies – 'to unify the government of the great empires which God has intrusted to me', as Charles III expressed it in the great Ordinance of Intendants for New Spain[2] – was scarcely less important.

The reforms in the imperial economic system were equally radical. The Spanish system of colonial and commercial monopoly differed not in kind from the colonial policy of other powers, but in the extraordinary rigour with which it was applied. There were special reasons for the severity and minuteness of these economic regulations, and special reasons for the quite disastrous consequences that followed. But though the policy of colonial monopoly was never abandoned, it was, in the eighteenth century, liberalized. Slowly and cautiously the natural trade routes of the Indies were opened up. Where once Cádiz and Seville had enjoyed a monopoly within a monopoly, and the fleets and galleons had divided between them the commerce and treasure of Mexico and Peru, step by step the ports of America and the ports of Spain were opened, the age-old restrictions on inter-colonial commerce were lightened, and the tariffs and duties hampering trade revised. The so-called Decree of Free Trade[3] of 1778, by which all the more important ports of Spain and of Central and South America were allowed to trade, if not freely at least directly, with one another, was as much a landmark in the economic history of the later empire as was the establishment of the viceroyalty of the Río de la Plata in its political history.

The reasons for these striking innovations were, in the broadest sense of the word, strategic. Efficiency in administration, the rehabilitation of colonial trade, were not so much ends in themselves as means to an end; and the end was imperial defence, the protection of the empire against foreign aggression, particularly English aggression, the elimination of foreign economic competition, and the restoration of Spanish maritime and military

---

[1] Made permanent in 1777.

[2] Printed in L. E. Fisher, *The Intendant System in Spanish America* (Berkeley, 1929), p. 97.

[3] Printed in *Documentos para la Historia Argentina* (Facultad de Filosofía y Letras, Buenos Aires, 1913–), vi, 3.

power in Europe. And as in British colonial policy after 1763, so in Spanish, the financial problem was paramount.[1] Defence demanded revenue, 'it being necessary', as Charles III instructed his visitor-general to New Spain, 'on account of the large sums needed in attending to the obligations of my royal crown, to exhaust all means which may appear conducive to increasing as much as possible the income from the revenues.'[2] This was a dominant consideration both in administrative and in economic reform. And what Britain in part proposed to effect by tightening up the acts of trade, Spain in part proposed to effect by their relaxation.

The results, or the apparent results, were remarkable. The volume of imperial trade notably increased.[3] At Buenos Aires, now the capital of the viceroyalty of the Río de la Plata and no longer a dependency of Lima, the economic life of the colony was transformed. Its customs receipts, its exports, its shipping, its population, all alike rapidly increased.[4] At Havana, Cuba, where six vessels had sufficed for the trade of Spain in 1760, two hundred were insufficient in 1778, and more than a thousand, Spanish and foreign, entered in 1801.[5] New Spain, or Mexico, repeats the same story – a larger volume of shipping, swelling revenues, greater exports.[6] In Peru, when the legislation of 1778 first came into effect, 'speculations were multiplied to so extraordinary a degree' in the first fervour of novelty that the merchants resorted to the now familiar device of destroying their goods in order to maintain

---

[1] *Cf.* C. H. Haring, *The Spanish Empire in America* (New York, 1947), pp. 145–6. This is the most important single volume on the history of the Spanish empire since the publication of R. B. Merriman, *The Rise of the Spanish Empire in the Old World and the New* (4 vols., New York, 1918–34).

[2] The instructions are in H. I. Priestley, *José de Gálvez, Visitor-General of New Spain, 1765–1771* (Berkeley, 1916), p. 404.

[3] For an index, but no more than an index, see the table of imports and exports in C. Calvo, *Anales Históricos de la Revolución de la América Latina*, i (Paris, 1864), cxxvii.

[4] See the figures and references assembled in my *British Consular Reports on the Trade and Politics of Latin America, 1824–1826* (Royal Historical Society, *Camden Third Series*, lxiii, London, 1940), pp. 18, 28–31.

[5] Haring, *op. cit.*, p. 342; Alexander von Humboldt, *Personal Narrative of Travels to the Equinoctial Regions of the New Continent* ... (trans. H. M. Williams, 7 vols., London, 1818–29), vii, 228–30.

[6] The shipping figures are given in M. Lerdo de Tejada, *Comercio Esterior de México desde la Conquista hasta Hoy* (Mexico, 1853), Docs. 12 and 13, and the revenue figures in Alexander von Humboldt, *Essai Politique sur le Royaume de la Nouvelle-Espagne* (5 vols., Paris, 1811), v, 4–5.

the price level.[1] And even remote Chile experienced a new and vigorous impulse of economic change.[2]

Whatever truth, therefore, there may be in the legend of the stagnation and decay of Spain and of the Spanish American empire in the seventeenth century, it does not hold for the eighteenth. Within Spain's transatlantic dominions the signs of an expanding economy and of a growing prosperity were everywhere, or almost everywhere, writ large. 'It is just . . . to observe,' wrote a competent British observer, that Peru, during the late eighteenth century 'was not only in a flourishing state both in respect to her mines and to her commerce, but also as referable to the capitals possessed by individuals, to the comparative extent of her manufactures, and to her navigation. Between the years 1790 and 1800 there existed in Lima a *commercial* capital of above 15 millions of dollars; whereas in the present year [1826] it is under one million.'[3] Humboldt, in Venezuela, noted that 'everything seemed to announce the increase of population and industry'.[4] In New Spain the public revenues increased more than sixfold in the eighteenth century, and so also did the produce of the mines.[5] And though more than half of the world output of the precious metals still flowed from Spanish America, and though there is a lively superstition that the Spanish American colonies were made of gold and silver and nothing else, agriculture as well as mining, as the great Gálvez tells us,[6] were the basis of their prosperity. The value of the gold and silver of the Mexican mines, says Humboldt, was less 'by almost a fourth' than that of the agricultural produce.[7] Of Venezuela and Cuba he observes that agriculture 'founded more considerable fortunes' than had been accumulated by the working

---

[1] *British Consular Reports*, p. 112; *Mercurio Peruano de Historia, Literatura, y Noticias Públicas* (12 vols., Lima, 1791–5), i, 209, etc.

[2] See Diego Barros Arana, *Historia Jeneral de Chile* (16 vols., Santiago, 1884–1902), vii, 427–8. For an excellent survey of the developments described above see B. W. Diffie, *Latin-American Civilization, Colonial Period* (Harrisburg, Pa., 1945), pp. 417–40.

[3] *British Consular Reports*, p. 114. [This statement now seems to me exaggerated. I should add also that the material and economic progress of the colonies was not uniform and there were examples of decay as well as of advance. For conflicts of economic interests within them see R. A. Humphreys and John Lynch, *The Origins of the Latin American Revolutions, 1808–1826* (New York, 1966), pp. 19–22.]

[4] *Personal Narrative*, iv, 210.

[5] Humboldt, *Essai Politique*, v, 4–5; iv, 99. On the Mexican mines see the useful, little book of C. G. Motten, *Mexican Silver and the Enlightenment* (Philadelphia, 1950).

[6] *Hispanic American Historical Review*, iv (1921), 274.

[7] *Essai Politique*, iii, 286.

of the mines in Peru,[1] and in southern South America, where the mines were few, but where Buenos Aires and even Montevideo were rapidly rising in importance, the pastoral and agricultural industries, then as now, were the economic staples.

It is reasonable to conclude, with Professor Haring,[2] that as the eighteenth century closed the peoples of Spanish America were probably more prosperous than at any time in their history. True, in a colonial and developing area, there was no considerable growth of manufactures. Nor was there in the English colonies. But domestic manufacturing was in fact more widespread than is commonly supposed. True, also, the whole population of Spanish America was certainly not greater than that of the British Isles in 1811. But its increase in the eighteenth century was remarkable. In 1800 Mexico City was the leading city of the western hemisphere, larger than any city of Great Britain and Ireland except London and Dublin. Its rival, Lima, compared with Bristol and was itself outstripped by Havana. Even long-neglected Buenos Aires was as large as New York or Philadelphia in 1790.[3] And the growth and embellishment of the cities (not merely the capital cities) illustrates the same expansionist trend. Here, at least, in public buildings and public display, were the marks of opulence; and it is no accident that here also, at the end of the century, there was an efflorescence of intellectual activity, in the universities and academies, in the growth of a periodical press, in literary societies and in clubs. In Santa Fé, Peru and Mexico, observed an English merchant in 1804, there was not only a greater degree of knowledge and a greater degree of progress in civilization than was commonly supposed in Europe, but, he added, though perhaps with prejudice, 'much more than exists in Old Spain'.[4]

The disruption of this society by a violent cataclysm which would, within a few years, destroy much of its wealth, would seem, at first sight, an improbable event. The Conde de Aranda, one of the more far-sighted of Spanish statesmen, indeed foresaw it. 'We must imagine', he wrote in 1782, 'that sooner or later in [Spanish] America there will occur revolutions like those of the

---

[1] *Ibid.,* ii, 25.
[2] *Op. cit.,* p. 344.
[3] On the population figures see Diffie, *op. cit.,* pp. 449–59.
[4] The quotation is from William Jacob, 'Plan for Occupying Spanish America', 26 Oct. 1804, P[ublic] R[ecord] O[ffice], Chatham Papers, 30/8/345. *Cf.* Humboldt, *Personal Narrative,* ii, 240; iii, 474.

English colonies.'[1] And Canning's retrospective judgement, on the effect of the American Revolution, that 'the operation of that example' was 'sooner or later inevitable',[2] is well known. The influences of eighteenth-century rationalism and of the French Revolution were equally powerful dissolvents. The continent, despite the censorship of the Inquisition, was not closed to ideas. Forbidden literature is always the most enticing of literature. A cultivated minority was certainly acquainted with the writings of the *philosophes*, of Rousseau, of Locke, even of Adam Smith. These were to be echoed, along with the Declarations of Independence and of the Rights of Man, in the pronouncements and charters of revolutionary leaders and revolutionary governments. Yet despite the activities of an adventurer like Francisco de Miranda, who knew the 'brace of Adamses' and had seen the French Revolution at first hand, despite occasional conspiracies and even outright rebellion, there was little specifically revolutionary activity in Spanish America before Spain herself fell a prey to Napoleon. The revolution, when it came, rose like a sudden tide from still, or comparatively still, waters.

Yet Spain's colonies were lost before the revolution began. The Bourbon reforms came too late, they did not go far enough, they were given insufficient time, to save the empire. And politically at least they contained no concession to the newer movement of ideas. 'Instead of considering its colonies as a place of refuge for the idle, the profligate, and the disaffected, where they might learn to amend their lives, and, if possible, forget their errors', wrote the *Edinburgh Review* in 1806[3], 'the Spanish Crown has watched over its foreign settlements with the solicitude of a duenna, and regulated their government as if they were to be inhabited by Carthusians'. The quotation, perhaps, is mainly interesting for the light it throws on the value placed on colonies in early nineteenth-century Britain. But it contains a solid grain of truth. The empire, from first to last, was built on paternalist and absolutist lines. It could not, in point of fact, be quite so centralized as theory might imply. The royal will was always limited by circumstance. But the price of paternalism was procrastination and inefficiency, a tradi-

[1] Manuel Conrotte, *La Intervención de España en la Independencia de los Estados Unidos* . . . (Madrid, 1920), p. 166.
[2] Webster, *op. cit.*, i, 6; ii, 193.
[3] *Edinburgh Review*, viii (July 1806), 383.

tion of legalism and a disrespect for law, a class system which almost, but not quite, became a caste system, and a mounting jealousy between Spaniards born in Spain and Spaniards born in America, between, that is, the governors and the governed. 'The most miserable European,' wrote Humboldt, 'without education, and without intellectual cultivation, thinks himself superior to the whites born in the new continent.'[1] The creoles, excluded generally from the higher administrative posts, found almost their sole representation in municipal institutions. 'Even in the most despotic states,' says Robertson in his famous *History*, 'this feeble spark of liberty is not extinguished.'[2] But even here it was the local, not the representative, character of the *cabildos*, or town councils, too often closed corporations, petty oligarchies, which caused them to play so prominent a part in the events of 1808 to 1810.

There was no relaxation of this paternalistic system in the eighteenth century. On the contrary, enlightened despotism sought to rationalize and simplify the machinery of imperial administration both in Spain and in America in the interests of order, uniformity, centralization, efficiency. And though, for a time, a new life was breathed into the imperial system, the political aspirations of the creoles were forgotten, or ignored. In so far as the newly appointed intendants, invariably Spaniards, superseded minor, but creole, officials, and trespassed, moreover, on the functions of the *cabildos,* the Spanish American creoles were, in fact, still further removed from the work of government. 'We were left,' Bolívar was to say, 'in a state of permanent childhood.'[3]

And, paradoxically enough, the measures designed to secure a still closer integration between Spain and her colonies had precisely the opposite effect. In Spanish America, as in Spain, local and regional loyalties were always strong. Customs, conditions, varied enormously. Cities and squares, law and administration, might be drawn to a pattern, but the life of the colonies flowed in its own individual channels; and at a time when the Bourbon economic reforms gave to the several regions of Spanish America a new economic autonomy, the creation of new viceroyalties and

---

[1] *Essai Politique*, ii, 2.

[2] William Robertson, *The History of America* (5th edn., 3 vols., Edinburgh, 1788), iii, 262. *Cf.* Humboldt, *Personal Narrative*, iv, 102. Perhaps the best discussion of the *cabildo* is to be found in Haring, *op. cit.*, pp. 158–78.

[3] D. F. O'Leary, *Bolívar y la Emancipación de Sur-América, Memorias del General O'Leary* (2 vols., Madrid, n.d.), i, 379.

captaincies-general promoted and consolidated a growing sense of regional nationalism. Colonial self-consciousness was directly stimulated. It can be no accident that the revolution, when it came, gained its first successes in those areas whose economic and political status had thus been raised. The origins of the new Spanish American nations must properly be sought in the developing life of the eighteenth century.

Apart from a small minority, an intellectual *élite*, it is possible that the rising creole middle class of lawyers, merchants, landowners and soldiers might have reconciled themselves for some time longer to their political inferiority, however much they resented their social inferiority, to the Spaniards. The loyalists, or royalists, were always far more numerous during the Spanish American revolutions than they were during the revolution for North American independence. But whatever the prosperity of Spanish America, whatever the rehabilitation of Spain, in the second half of the eighteenth century, the economic foundations of the empire had been irretrievably undermined. The recovery of Spain had failed to keep pace with the expanding economy of her colonies, and the imperial economic reforms of Charles III were no more than palliatives of a condition imperfectly understood. The trade of the empire was still a closed monopoly of Spain, but the monopoly was imposed by a country which still could not successfully apply it, a country outstripped in financial and technical resources, in facilities and skills, by its greatest colonial rival, Britain. The empire, Professor Whitaker has observed, 'fell not so much because of decay within as because of pressure from without';[1] and from this point of view its fall was no more than a corollary of the commercial expansion of Europe and particularly of England.

What really stimulated the economic expansion of Spanish America in the eighteenth century, perhaps, were not so much the imperial economic reforms as the European search for Latin American markets and the European demand for Latin American products. And for the continued growth of European interest in Spanish America there were, apart from considerations of strategy

---

[1] A. P. Whitaker, 'The Commerce of Louisiana and the Floridas at the end of the Eighteenth Century', *Hispanic American Historical Review*, viii (1928), 203. See also on the above paragraph Allan Christelow, 'Great Britain and the Trades from Cádiz and Lisbon to Spanish America and Brazil, 1759–1783', *ibid.*, xxvii (1947), 9, 18–21, and Ricardo Levene's introduction to *Documentos para la Historia Argentina*, pp. v, xxiv.

and politics, three main reasons. First, Spanish America provided dollars, the gold and silver coin and specie which was the lubricant of international trade. The bullion supply was as interesting to the continental as it was to the British and North American merchant. Secondly, Spanish America supplied a number of raw materials, such as drugs and dyewoods, hides and skins, increasingly important for industrial and commercial purposes.[1] Thirdly, it afforded a market for manufactured goods, particularly textiles and hardware. The market, perhaps, was not so infinitely extensible as was sometimes imagined, but its potentialities were great; some English and some continental merchants knew it far better than might be supposed, and it was undoubtedly profitable.

There were, also, two ways of tapping the resources and trade of Spanish America. The first was to do so indirectly by way of Cádiz and, still more indirectly, by way of Lisbon and Rio de Janeiro. The second was the direct or contraband trade. Both had long been practised. At the end of the seventeenth century everybody knew that the fleets and galleons at Cádiz were stocked with foreign, principally French and English, not Spanish goods, that the Spanish merchants were little more than agents or shippers, and that the returns which flowed to Spain immediately flowed out again. 'We owe to Divine Providence,' Philip v complained, 'the special blessing of vast dominions in America, the centre of abundant precious metals; [yet] the Crown has always seen that . . . this is the kingdom which retains the least.'[2] Or, in Pufendorff's phrase, which Mr Christelow has recently quoted, 'Spain kept the cow and the rest of Europe drank the milk.'[3]

Spain, in short, could not supply her colonies herself. But she maintained the pretence of so doing. What was more, she insisted that colonial products should flow only to Spain. Since the tonnage of the galleons fell by three-quarters in the seventeenth century, it is obvious that the volume of imperial trade had seriously contracted. Not only this, high duties and restrictive freights combined with the monopolistic interests of the merchant houses in Seville and Cádiz to raise the price level in America to

[1] On the problem of raw materials see Allan Christelow, 'Contraband Trade between Jamaica and the Spanish Main, and the Free Port Act of 1766', *Hispanic American Historical Review*, xxii (1942), 310–11.

[2] E. J. Hamilton, *War and Prices in Spain, 1651–1800* (Cambridge, Mass., 1947), p. 46.

[3] 'Great Britain and the Trades from Cádiz and Lisbon . . .', p. 3.

fantastic heights. An increase of two to three hundred per cent above the prices in Spain was not uncommon.[1] And if Spain could not herself supply her colonies with enough or cheap enough goods, neither could Europe obtain from Spain all that she wanted of colonial products. The result was an enormous contraband trade. This was the second method employed by the French, the English and the Dutch, the direct or contraband trade; and the more debilitated Spain became, the greater grew the contraband; the more the contraband, the greater Spain's debility, and the weaker her empire.

Mr Christelow has shown how the British merchants, at least, in the eighteenth century were losing their interest in the old limited commercial system based on Cádiz, how they welcomed the reforms of Charles III, and how they looked forward, indeed, to the ending of all restraints.[2] The full story of the growth of the direct or contraband trade has yet to be told. Already serious in the seventeenth century, the contraband trade grew more so in the eighteenth century. And its hold was certainly strengthened by the operations of the South Sea Company under the *Asiento* of 1713. The legal trade of the company in the annual ships and in the supply of negroes cloaked a still greater general but illicit trade carried on through the company's factors and agents in Jamaica, Panamá, Vera Cruz, Caracas, Santiago de Cuba, Buenos Aires, Santiago de Chile, and even Lima and Potosí. Between 1730 and 1739, when its property was confiscated, the company realized at least five million pounds by this illicit activity.[3] Even so, it had to face the competition of private traders as well as the hostility of Spain; and it was into the hands of the private traders that the trade fell when the company's operations ceased. 'This commerce in time of peace, and this with the prizes that are made in time of war,' wrote the author of the *European Settlements in America*, 'pour into Jamaica an astonishing quantity of treasure; great fortunes are made in a manner instantly';[4] and what Jamaica was to the

---

[1] See the references and figures in *British Consular Reports*, pp. 29, 30, 111, 352.

[2] 'Great Britain and the Trades from Cádiz and Lisbon . . .', pp. 2–29.

[3] G. H. Nelson, 'Contraband Trade under the Asiento, 1730–1739', *American Historical Review*, li (1945), 63–4. The literature on the contraband is too extensive to be cited here. The more important references, however, will be found in Nelson's article.

[4] *An Account of the European Settlements in America* (2 vols., 3rd edn., London, 1760), ii, 78. For the figures of the trade of Jamaica in the first half of the eighteenth century see Richard Pares, *War and Trade in the West Indies, 1739–1763* (Oxford, 1936), pp. 474–5.

Spanish Main, Colonia do Sacramento, just opposite to Buenos Aires, was, when in Portuguese hands, to the River Plate.

The effect on Spain can partly be measured in the continued decline in the tonnage of the fleets and galleons and in the irregularity of their sailings. When the galleons sailed for the last time in 1737 they were unable to dispose of their goods because the markets were already overstocked. Royal decree after royal decree complained of the presence of foreigners and foreign goods in the Indies. Foreigners must be expelled. Officials who connived at contraband trade should be punished with death. Even their immortal souls would be imperilled, for in 1776 the church was recommended to teach that contraband was a mortal sin.[1] Finally, of course, the great series of economic and commercial reforms which began in 1740 with the permission given to register ships to sail round Cape Horn, and culminated in the legislation of Charles III, reflected the acute anxieties of the crown.

These reforms could alleviate, but they failed to remedy the situation. It is true that they did much to rehabilitate Spanish commerce. Though the old monopolists protested, new and more enterprising Spaniards and Spanish Americans entered trade. Shipping and revenue increased. But the contraband continued. To tap the trade of the Gulf of Mexico and the Spanish Main, the British, in 1766, established free ports in Dominica and Jamaica, extending the system, after 1787, to other strategic points in the West Indies.[2] And there is no doubt that, despite temporary vicissitudes, the free port trade, encouraged in time of peace and specially licensed in time of war, was, as the Board of Trade found it, when reviewing the Free Port Acts themselves, highly 'beneficial'.[3] The Spaniards might properly complain. But it was no part of British policy to enforce the Laws of the Indies. And whatever may have been the prospects that the imperial reforms of Charles III could have arrested foreign economic pressure upon the walls of the empire and that Spain herself could have been brought successfully to compete in the swelling volume of international trade, the doom of Spanish hopes was sealed by two events. The

[1] *Documentos para la Historia Argentina*, v, 380.

[2] See, in particular, Christelow, 'Contraband Trade between Jamaica and the Spanish Main . . .', pp. 309–43, and D. B. Goebel, 'British Trade to the Spanish Colonies, 1796–1823', *American Historical Review*, xliii (1938), 289–94.

[3] Minutes of the Committee of Trade, 15 March 1805, PRO, B[oard of] T[rade Records], 5/15, p. 76.

first was the death of Charles himself in 1788 and the accession of
the incompetent Charles IV. The second was the entry of Spain
into the French revolutionary wars.

The war of 1779 to 1783, when Spain had actively promoted
the independence of England's colonies, had been costly enough.
For the first time in Spanish history the crown was forced to issue
paper money, soon to be inflated.[1] The brief war with France, from
1793 to 1795, was a further blow. But when, in 1796, Spain again
went to war with England, and, with a brief interval of only two
and a half years, remained at war for twelve years more, the result
was disaster. This was the crisis of the empire. Spain and her
colonies were severed. The Spanish economy was seriously
deranged. The Spanish navy was almost destroyed. And the
colonies were thrown upon their own and foreign resources.

There had been occasions, in earlier years, when Spain had been
compelled to tolerate the trade of friends or neutrals in Spanish
America. In 1782, for example, Louisiana had been allowed to
trade with France. Cuba, in 1793, was permitted to trade with the
United States. In the years after 1789, moreover, the slave trade
had been thrown open and foreigners allowed to engage in it.[2]
But when, on 18 November 1797, the crown opened the ports of
Spanish America to neutral shipping, the measure was one of
desperation. The order was indeed revoked in 1799 because it had
'redounded entirely', as the decree of revocation complained, to
the injury of the state and of the interests of its subjects.[3] But what
the law forbade, local regulation continued to tolerate and the
crown itself to license; and though the old system was restored at
the peace in 1802, with the renewal of the war once again the ports
were opened.[4]

The result, or partial result, was the rapid growth of North
American shipping and North American trade, from Cuba to
Buenos Aires and Buenos Aires to Chile. And more than one
American, perhaps, like the young Richard Cleveland of Massa-

---

[1] Hamilton, *op. cit.*, p. 152.

[2] Whitaker, *op. cit.*, p. 192; R. F. Nichols, 'Trade Relations and the Establishment
of the United States Consulates in Spanish America, 1779–1809', *Hispanic American
Historical Review*, xiii (1933), 293; J. F. King, 'Evolution of the Free Slave Trade
Principle in Spanish Colonial Administration', *ibid.*, xxii (1942), 49–56.

[3] *Documentos para la Historia Argentina*, vii, 134, 157.

[4] A. P. Whitaker, *The United States and the Independence of Latin America, 1800–1830*
(Baltimore, 1941), pp. 8–9.

chusetts, carried in his cargo a copy of the Federal Constitution and of the Declaration of Independence, conveniently translated into Spanish.[1] But it was not only American trade, legitimate and illegitimate, that grew. So also did British trade. The contraband flourished at the free ports in the West Indies. It flourished at Trinidad, which alone was said to supply the Spanish colonies with goods to the value of one million pounds a year.[2] It flourished at Vera Cruz, as Viceroy Marquina bitterly complained. It flourished at Buenos Aires. And, even on the Pacific coast, where the South Sea whalers were actively engaged in it, it extended and strengthened its hold.[3]

There was still to be fought out in Spanish America the battle between monopoly and free enterprise, between the beneficiaries of an old order and the partisans of a new. But the issue was already resolved. It was impossible to re-enact the Laws of the Indies. The economic emancipation of Spanish America was determined before its political emancipation began.

And so far as political emancipation was concerned, the years from 1796 to 1808 were equally decisive. As Britain had formerly wavered between plundering the Spanish American colonies and trading with them, so now she hesitated between their conquest and their emancipation. In 1797 the governor of Trinidad was specifically instructed to encourage revolution on the mainland. The invasion of Buenos Aires was prepared, and cancelled, in the same year. And there were other plans, in the mind of the British government as well as in that of Francisco de Miranda, so long plotting in England and America the emancipation of Venezuela. But fundamentally Britain was more interested in trade than territory. Her designs were commercial and strategic rather than imperial, and when, in 1806, Sir Home Popham captured Buenos Aires, it was at his own responsibility. *The Times*, indeed, rejoiced.

---

[1] H. Bernstein, *Origins of Inter-American Interest, 1700–1812* (Philadelphia, 1945), p. 80. On American trade see also Goebel, *op. cit.*, pp. 295–7, and Whitaker, *The United States and the Independence of Latin America*, pp. 5–16, 23–6.

[2] Minutes of the Committee of Trade, 11 June 1808, PRO, B.T. 5/18, p. 167; *Memorandum on Trinidad*, Colonial Office Records, 318/2, f. 275; Goebel, *op. cit.*, pp. 291–4.

[3] *Cf. British Consular Reports*, pp. 256–7, 31, 127; Goebel, *op. cit.*, pp. 304–9; and see the complaints of Viceroy Marquina of New Spain (1803) in *Instrucciones que los Vireyes de Nueva España dejaron a sus Sucesores* (Mexico, 1867), p. 205, and of Viceroy Abascal y Sousa of Peru in his *Relación* printed in Manuel de Odriozola, *Documentos Históricos del Perú* (10 vols., Lima, 1863–79), ii, 23.

It knew not, it said, how to express itself in terms adequate to the national advantage obtained.[1] But the government vacillated. It did too little and that little too late. Buenos Aires was recaptured and Montevideo lost. The whole affair, said *The Times*, was 'a dirty, sordid enterprise, conceived and executed in a spirit of avarice and plunder', and the chief source of the calamity was the unauthorised beginning of it.[2]

But for Spanish America its end was all important. The viceroy of the Río de la Plata had fled. It was the creoles who defeated the British, deposed the incompetent viceroy and appointed a new one. Spanish America had seen the deposition and imprisonment of the legal representative of the king. It had seen a creole militia defeat a European army. It had seen a colonial port crowded with British ships and flooded with British goods. It was not a revolution that took place at Buenos Aires as a result of the British invasions. But it was a political and economic transformation that contained the seeds of revolution.

Suddenly, however, the situation changed. Napoleon invaded Spain. The crown fell into captivity. A usurper sat upon the throne. From an enemy Britain became, overnight, the ally of Spain, and the army which Wellesley was preparing in Ireland for the liberation of Spanish America sailed, not to emancipate Spanish America from Spain, but to liberate Spain from France.

The news of the fall of the monarchy, and of the invasion of the mother country, stirred the loyalty and moved the indignation of the colonies; superficially, the resistance movement in Spain was almost exactly imitated in Spanish America. As juntas sprang up in Spain in the name of Ferdinand vii, so in Spanish America juntas and *cabildos* assumed the powers of viceroys, presidents and captains-general, the agents, now, of an authority which had ceased to exist. Extraordinary circumstances called for extraordinary measures. The colonists took thought for their own protection and their own future. Power reverted to the people, though by 'the people' nothing more can be meant than a small but active creole minority: the revolutions in Spanish America were the work of the few, not of the many.

But that a movement which began as an assertion of independence from France should have ended as an assertion of indepen-

[1] *The Times*, 13 Sept. 1806.
[2] *Ibid.*, 14, 15 Sept. 1807.

dence from Spain was due quite as much to Spain herself as to the creole minority in her colonies whose thwarted aspirations in government and trade were thus fulfilled. For though the monarchy had collapsed, though the Peninsula was overrun, the Spaniards still clung to the principles of imperial monopoly and colonial subordination. Crown, regency, cortes, showed themselves equally blind, equally determined. The colonies, declared the Junta Central, in 1809, were an integral part of the Spanish monarchy, and the deduction soon followed that they owed obedience to the extraordinary authorities erected in Spain.[1] That was not the Spanish American view. Nor had it been the Habsburg view. 'Estos y esos reinos', 'these and those kingdoms', was the famous phrase used to define the royal possessions in Spain and the Indies. The Indies had never belonged to Spain. They were the property of the crown of Castile, united to the kingdoms of Spain merely by a dynastic tie. The Bourbons forgot, or ignored this Habsburg view; and so did the Spaniards. But the creoles remembered it. Just as the English colonies, in the eighteenth century, refused to accept subordination to the sovereignty of parliament, so the Spanish Americans refused to accept subordination to the people of the Peninsula. And in both cases what reason failed to arrange, force was left to decide.

[1] *Cf.* Haring, *op. cit.*, p. 117.

6

The Historiography of the Spanish
American Revolutions*

The literature relating to the fall of the Spanish American empire
and to the establishment, in the first quarter of the nineteenth
century, of the independent states of Spanish America is already
vast and is rapidly increasing. No other period, with the possible
exception of that of the conquest, has so closely and continuously
engaged the attention of historians in Spanish America itself. The
pioneers of the last century, Bartolomé Mitre in Argentina, Diego
Barros Arana in Chile, José María Restrepo in Colombia, Lucas
Alamán in Mexico – to mention only a few outstanding names,
none of which, incidentally, has attracted the notice of G. P.
Gooch in his well-known *History and Historians in the Nineteenth
Century* – have been followed by a host of investigators (though
unevenly distributed as between the Spanish American states
themselves), who have devoted themselves to the political, biographical, military, institutional and diplomatic aspects of the
revolutionary period, though much less to its social and economic
aspects.[1] And if the subject lends itself both to *pietas* and polemics,
such names as those of Ricardo Levene and of Emilio Ravignani

* [X Congresso Internazionale di Scienze Storiche, *Relazioni* (6 vols., Firenze,
1955), i, 207–33. This article was reprinted in the *Hispanic American Historical Review*,
xxxvi (1956), 81–93. It was attacked by I. R. Lavretskii in his survey of the *Review* in
Voprosi istorii (Dec. 1959), pp. 94–107, reprinted in translation both in the *Review*
itself (xl, 1960, 340–60) and in H. F. Cline, ed., *Latin American History, Essays on its
Study and Teaching, 1898–1965* (2 vols., Austin and London, 1967), i, 144–56. Since
Professor Lavretskii attributes to me not only statements which I have never made
but opinions which I have never held, I take this opportunity of saying so. For a
further discussion of the historiography of the Spanish American revolutions see
R. A. Humphreys and John Lynch, 'The Emancipation of Latin America', XII
Congrès International des Sciences Historiques, *Rapports* (4 vols., Vienna, 1965),
iii, 39–56.]

[1] For an indication of the extent and variety of current writing see the *Handbook
of Latin American Studies* (Harvard University Press, 1936–51; University of Florida
Press, 1951–).

92

in Argentina, of Ricardo Donoso in Chile, and of Eduardo Acevedo and Vicente Lecuna in Uruguay and Venezuela – names chosen almost at random from the ranks of older scholars and easily to be supplemented by those of younger men in Argentina, Uruguay, Chile, Peru, Colombia, Venezuela and Mexico in particular – testify to the past and present vigour of historical scholarship and to the high quality of much of the work produced.

Outside Spanish America the case is different. When the late F. A. Kirkpatrick wrote his chapter on 'The Establishment of Independence in Spanish America' in volume 10 of the *Cambridge Modern History*, published in 1907, he was able to refer to the works of Mariano Torrente (1792–1856) and of José Coroleu (1839–95) in Spain and of H. H. Bancroft (1832–1918) in the United States, but, among Europeans and North American scholars, to little else. Nearly half a century has passed. In the United States of America these years have seen the rapid development and professionalization of Spanish American historical studies – a development whose importance it would be difficult to over-estimate and whose influence is far-reaching – and there, so far as the revolutionary period is concerned, the seeds early sown by Bernard Moses,[1] F. L. Paxson,[2] and W. S. Robertson[3] have borne a rich harvest in the fields of biography, diplomatic history and international relations, and in studies of the antecedents of the independence movement in Spanish America. But there has been no parallel development in Europe. The rise of the Spanish empire and the problems of its political and economic organization have always engaged the attention of European scholars. Its fall, and the subsequent history of the independent Spanish American states, have done so much less. In Spain, it is true, there has been a notable resurgence of interest in the later years of the empire – a field in which much work remains to be done, particularly in assessing the effects in Spanish America of the Bourbon political and economic reforms and of the continued pressure of European commercial expansion – and where the late Pedro Leturia ploughed a rather lonely furrow such scholars as Jaime Delgado and Manuel Giménez Fernández are making valuable contributions to the history of the independence period

[1] *South America on the Eve of Emancipation* (New York, 1908).
[2] *The Independence of the South-American Republics* (Philadelphia, 1903).
[3] *Francisco de Miranda and the Revolutionizing of Spanish America* (Washington, 1909).

itself. But this welcome development is comparatively new. Sweden, in recent years, has been represented by the work of Sven Ola Swärd,[1] and Britain principally by Sir Charles Webster's publication of selected documents from the Foreign Office archives.[2] For the rest the European contribution to the historiography of the independence period is slender in volume, despite the political, diplomatic and economic importance of the revolutions for independence to the European powers. And though there may be signs of better things to come, their promise has yet to be fulfilled.

It is, of course, not easy for the European scholar to visit Spanish America, and rich, and not yet fully exploited, as is the material in European repositories,[3] the principal archives for the study of the independence period, apart from those of the mother-country, Spain herself, are in Spanish American lands. Fortunately the publication of source materials makes steady progress. Associated with such names as those of Carlos Calvo (Argentina), Manuel de Odriozola (Peru) and J. E. Hernández Dávalos (Mexico) in the nineteenth century, it made great strides in the present century with the gradual establishment of Spanish American historiography on a firmer professional basis, and the work of the last generation has added greatly to that of its predecessors.

Only a brief survey of recent developments is possible. In Chile the *Archivo de don Bernardo O'Higgins*, which the Archivo Nacional began to publish in 1946 under the distinguished editorship of Ricardo Donoso, Jaime Eyzaguirre, Guillermo Feliú Cruz, Eugenio Pereira Salas, and Luis Valencia Avaria, reached its twelfth volume in 1953, and so rich are its contents that it might more properly be called the *Archivo de la época de don Bernardo O'Higgins*. Under the direction of the Comisión Nacional Archivo

---

[1] *Latinamerika i svensk politik under 1810 -och 1820 -talen* (Uppsala, 1949).

[2] *Britain and the Independence of Latin America, 1812–1830. Select Documents from the Foreign Office Archives* (2 vols., London, 1938).

[3] *Cf.* as examples of this material in three quite different fields Pedro Leturia's *La emancipación hispanoamericana en los informes episcopales a Pio VII* (Buenos Aires, 1935); my *British Consular Reports on the Trade and Politics of Latin America, 1824–1826* (London, 1940); and J. F. Guillén's *Independencia de América. Indice de los papeles de expediciones de Indias* (3 vols., Madrid, Archivo General de Marina don Alvaro de Bazán, 1953). See also C. Bermúdez Plata, *Catálogo de documentos de la sección novena del Archivo General de Indias*, vol. i (Sevilla, 1949); and, of course, the older catalogues of Pedro Torres Lanzas, *Independencia de América. Fuentes para su estudio. Catálogo de los documentos conservados en el Archivo General de Indias* (6 vols., Madrid, 1912), and segunda serie (2 vols., Sevilla, 1924–5).

Artigas, the monumental *Archivo Artigas* (Montevideo, 1950–)
is being added to the *Archivo del General Juan A. Lavalleja* (6 vols.,
Montevideo, 1935–49), published by the Archivo General de la
Nación, in Uruguay;[1] and the *Archivo del doctor Gregorio Funes*
(Buenos Aires, Biblioteca Nacional, 1944–), in Argentina, to
the older editions, published by the Museo Mitre, of the *Docu-
mentos del Archivo de Belgrano* (7 vols., 1913–17), the *Documentos del
Archivo de San Martín* (12 vols., 1910–11), and the *Documentos del
Archivo de Pueyrredón* (4 vols., 1912). In Venezuela the *Archivo del
General Miranda* was at last completed in twenty-four volumes in
1950, and in Colombia the first, and so far the only, volume of a
new edition of the *Archivo Santander* appeared in 1940. Meanwhile
Dr Otero Muñoz has performed[2] for the old edition (24 vols.,
1913–32) a similar service to that performed by Sir Lewis Namier
for Sir John Fortescue's *Correspondence of King George III*, and Dr
Roberto Cortázar has begun publication of the *Cartas y mensajes de
Santander* (Bogotá, 1952–). Finally, so far as this type of material
is concerned, the late Dr Vicente Lecuna produced in 1948 an
eleventh, supplementary volume to his splendid edition of the
Cartas del Libertador (10 vols., Caracas, 1929–30),[3] which is the
most impressive contribution to Bolivarian source material since
the publication of the *Documentos* of Blanco and Azpurúa (14 vols.,
1875–7) and of O'Leary's so-called *Memorias* (32 vols., 1879–88);
and of the celebrated narrative portion of these last there is a new
and definitive edition (3 vols., Caracas, 1952) to which Monseñor
Nicolás Navarro has contributed a valuable introduction. The
appearance in 1940 of the alleged 'nuevos documentos definitivos',
which the late Sr Colombres Mármol[4] purported to have discovered on the relations between San Martín and Bolívar, sufficiently emphasizes the need for the more exacting standards now
generally applied to the editing of documents relating to the lives
of the revolutionary leaders.

Equally welcome, because of the rarity of the originals, is the

---

[1] *Cf.* also *Correspondencia del General José Artigas al cabildo de Montevideo, 1814–1816*
. . . (Montevideo, 1940; 2nd ed., 1946).

[2] 'Archivo Santander. Erratas sustanciales en los veinticuatro tomos', *Boletín de
Historia y Antigüedades* (Bogotá), xxx, Núms. 339–40 (1943), 1–222.

[3] See also Vicente Lecuna and Esther Barret de Nazaris, *Cartas de Santander* (3 vols.,
Caracas, 1942), and Laureano García Ortiz, *Bolívar y Santander. Correspondencia,
1819–1820* (Bogotá, 1940).

[4] E. L. Colombres Mármol, *San Martín y Bolívar en la entrevista de Guayaquil* (Buenos
Aires, 1940).

continued reproduction of contemporary journals. The *Gaceta de gobierno de Lima independiente,* which the Universidad Nacional de La Plata began to publish in 1950, and the *Colección de antiguos periódicos chilenos* of the Biblioteca Nacional of Chile (Santiago de Chile, 1951–   ) are late examples.[1] Legislative and congressional records, since the appearance of Emilio Ravignani's monumental *Asambleas constituyentes argentinas,* published by the Instituto de Investigaciones Históricas of Buenos Aires (7 vols., 1937–40),[2] are represented by such examples as the *Documentos del Congreso de Tucumán* (La Plata, 1947), in the invaluable series of the Archivo Histórico de la Provincia de Buenos Aires,[3] and by the continued publication of Colombian congressional proceedings, completed to the close of the year 1825 with the volume edited by Roberto Cortázar and Luis Augusto Cuervo, *Congreso de 1825. Senado. Actas,* in the Biblioteca de Historia Nacional (Bogotá, 1952). In the diplomatic field W. R. Manning's *Diplomatic Correspondence of the United States concerning the Independence of the Latin American Nations* (3 vols., New York, 1925) and Sir Charles Webster's volumes, already cited, remain the outstanding compilations. But the *Correspondencia de Lord Strangford y de la estación naval británica en el Río de la Plata con el gobierno de Buenos Aires, 1810–1822,* published by the Archivo General de la Nación in Argentina in 1941, formed a valuable supplement,[4] fresh material is appearing in the *Archivo de don Bernardo O'Higgins,* and much has been made available on the relations between the infant Latin American states themselves. It must suffice to refer here to such examples as Rafael Heliodoro Valle's collection on *La anexión de Centroamérica a México,* of which

[1] See also *Gaceta de Caracas* (4 vols., Paris, 1939) and *Correo del Orinoco* (Paris, 1939), published by the Academia Nacional de la Historia de Venezuela; *El Eco de los Andes* (Universidad Nacional de Cuyo, Mendoza, 1943); *La Estrella del Sur* (Instituto Histórico y Geográfico del Uruguay, 1942); *Gazeta de Montevideo* (Instituto de Investigaciones Históricas of Montevideo, 1948–   ); and *El Argos de Buenos Aires,* completed by the Academia Nacional de la Historia of Argentina in 1942. The Academia Nacional de la Historia of Argentina, like its predecessor, the Junta de Historia y Numismática Americana, and like the Museo Mitre, has done much to make early Argentine periodicals available.

[2] Vols. i–iii relate to the independence period, and so also in part does vol. vi, part ii.

[3] *Cf. Acuerdos de la honorable junta de representantes de la provincia de Buenos Aires (1820–1821)* (2 vols., La Plata, 1932–3), and *Libro de sesiones reservados de la honorable junta de la provincia de Buenos Aires (1820–1823)* . . . (La Plata, 1936).

[4] *Cf.* also the Archivo's *Misiones diplomáticas* (Buenos Aires, 1937), and Emilio Ravignani's *Comisión de Bernardino Rivadavia ante España y otras potencias de Europa (1814–1820)* (2 vols., Buenos Aires, 1933–6).

the sixth and final volume in the Archivo Histórico Diplomático Mexicano appeared in 1949, and to the documents gathered together and reprinted by J. E. Pivel Devoto and Rodolfo Muñoz, *La diplomacia de la patria vieja, 1811–1820* (Montevideo, 1943), in the Archivo Histórico Diplomático del Uruguay. Finally, of course, the documentation of the years immediately preceding the independence period and of the last days of Spanish rule has been enlarged, as, for example, in Spanish America by the publications of the Comité de Orígenes de la Emancipación, which is a sub-committee, in Venezuela, of the Comisión de Historia of the Instituto Pan-americano de Geografía e Historia, and in Spain by those of the Escuela de Estudios Hispano-Americanos at Seville.[1]

All in all, the work of the last fifteen or twenty years makes an impressive addition to the older corpus of printed materials.[2] A regrettable silence fell for a time upon the Instituto de Investigaciones Históricas at Buenos Aires, whose *Documentos para la historia argentina* (22 vols., 1913–36) and earlier documentary publications had made so distinguished a contribution to the economic, institutional and diplomatic history of Argentina in the late eighteenth and early nineteenth centuries. But new volumes continued to be added to the great *Colección de historiadores y de documentos relativos a la independencia de Chile* (Santiago de Chile, 1900–) and a formidable body of documentary material made its appearance in historical and archival periodicals. Activity was very much greater in some countries than in others and, on the whole, it followed familiar lines, reflecting a sustained interest in all that pertains to the great actors in the revolutionary drama and a greater emphasis on the sources for institutional, military, and diplomatic history than on those for economic or social history. The *Catálogo de la sección republicana* of the Archivo Histórico of the Ministerio de Hacienda y Comercio in Peru (2 vols., Lima, 1945–6) revealed something, however, of the wealth that economic historians may exploit. And it is, indeed, more tools of this kind

---

[1] *Cf.* Pedro Grases, *La conspiración de Gual y España y el ideario de la independencia* (Caracas, 1949); Miguel Batllori, *El abate Viscardo. Historia y mito de la intervención de los jesuítas en la independencia de hispanoamérica* (Caracas, 1953); V. Rodríguez Casado y G. Lohmann Villena, eds., *Memoria de gobierno del Virrey Joaquín de la Pezuela* (Sevilla, 1947), and V. Rodríguez Casado y J. A. Calderón Quijano, eds., *Memoria de gobierno del Virrey Abascal* (2 vols., Sevilla, 1944).

[2] *Cf.* the sources listed in B. Sánchez Alonso, *Fuentes de la historia española e hispano-americana* (3rd ed., 3 vols., Madrid, 1952).

that are perhaps most urgently needed.[1] Catalogues, and then more catalogues, and after that the documents;[2] systematic surveys of the material available in Spanish American archives; more attention to municipal and local records[3] as well as to the records of central and regional administration, and more to the records of social and economic life:[4] these are the needs of the present. And it is still too often true that documents are published either with inadequate indexes or with no indexes at all.

With the intellectual, institutional, and economic history of the eighteenth century, this paper is not concerned. But it is obvious at a glance that one of the most impressive contributions which modern historiography is making to the better understanding of the Spanish American revolutions lies in the fuller exploration of the late colonial period. The age of reform in Spanish America preceded the age of revolution. The empire, under the later Bourbons, enjoyed an Indian summer of prosperity. The 'leyenda negra' of 'un excès de misère, l'ignorance, l'abrutissement de tous par un despotisme royal et la "sombre théocratie" ', against which Marius André so vigorously protested,[5] has, of course, long since been discarded. There is even a tendency to invest the final years of Spanish rule with a golden glow and not only to minimize colonial grievances, but even to deny that they existed. Slowly but surely, however, our knowledge of the later history of the empire is being deepened and widened. The changes in its administrative structure, together with their political and economic repercussions within the Spanish dominions, are gradually being brought under review. The debate on the influence of the American and the French revolutions has been widened, on the one hand, by a closer inspection of the ideas of the 'age of enlightenment' and their reception in Spanish America, and, on the other, by the emphasis now placed not only in Spain, but in Spanish America as well, on the persistence of the traditional doctrines of Spanish

---

[1] *Cf.* Guillén, and Bermúdez Plata, *op. cit.* (see above, page 94, note 3).

[2] *Cf.* J. L. Trenti Rocamora, *Catálogo de documentos del Museo Histórico Nacional.* Tomo I (Buenos Aires, 1952), and *Selección de documentos del Museo Histórico Nacional.* Tomo I. *Guerras de la independencia* (Buenos Aires, 1952).

[3] A number of *cabildo* records, of course, are already in print. See the list given by Agustín Millares Carlo in *Contribuciones a la historia municipal de América* (Mexico, Instituto Panamericano de Geografía e Historia, 1951).

[4] *Cf. La libertad de comercio en la Nueva España en la segunda década del siglo xix* (Mexico, Archivo Histórico de Hacienda, 1943).

[5] *La fin de l'empire espagnol d'Amérique* (Paris, 1922), p. 32.

scholasticism, what Manuel Giménez Fernández calls 'la doctrina suareziana de la soberanía popular.'[1] And while the social tensions within the colonies are being more fully revealed, more attention has been paid to economic history, to the effects, for example, of the innovations introduced into the old commercial system, to the impact on Spanish America of the commercial expansion of Europe, and to the economic intercourse between Spanish America and the outside world.[2]

The picture which is emerging can as yet only be sketched in its broad outlines and at every turn new fields of enquiry are being opened up.[3] A whole series of regional and specialized economic, social, administrative and financial studies is yet to be demanded, and we need to know much more than we do, to take one example alone, of the situation created by the entry of Spain into the Napoleonic wars and the partial breakdown of the imperial economic system. But while, on the one hand, the revolutions for independence are being placed yet more firmly in the general setting of the commercial, the intellectual, and the political revolutions of the eighteenth and early nineteenth centuries, on the other they are being more closely related to the developing life within the Spanish dominions of differing Spanish American societies, to the rise of *criollismo*, and to the slow unfolding of a 'conciencia de sí'.[4] The Spanish American revolutions were precipitated by the Napoleonic invasions of the Iberian peninsula and the consequent crisis of the Spanish monarchy; and it may be true, as Jaime Eyzaguirre has remarked, in lapidary phrase, that 'las colonias hispanas, a diferencia de las inglesas del continente, no consiguen su emancipación por la mayor edad, sino por la orfandad'.[5] But the Spanish American revolutions are no longer to

[1] *Las doctrinas populistas en la independencia de Hispano-América* (Sevilla, 1947).

[2] Like the political and intellectual antecedents of the revolutions, their economic antecedents have long engaged the attention of scholars. It suffices to refer here to the contributions of A. P. Whitaker, Allan Christelow, Dorothy B. Goebel, E. J. Hamilton, R. S. Smith, Harry Bernstein and others writing in the United States, and to those of Ricardo Levene, Emilio Ravignani, José Torre Revello and Ricardo Caillet-Bois in Argentina, of Eugenio Pereira Salas in Chile, Eduardo Arcila Farías in Venezuela, Luis Chávez Orozco in Mexico, Olga Pantaleão in Brazil, and Guillermo Céspedes del Castillo in Spain.

[3] *Cf.* María del Carmen Velázquez, *El estado de guerra en Nueva España, 1760–1808* (Mexico, 1950).

[4] *Cf.* A. P. Whitaker and Jorge Basadre in *Ensayos sobre la historia del nuevo mundo* (Mexico, 1951), pp. 81, 367.

[5] *Fisonomía histórica de Chile* (Mexico, 1948), p. 98.

be seen as separating what was to come after from what had gone before. Here, as elsewhere in Spanish American historiography, a broader conception of the historical process is superseding the nationalistic and provincial outlook which tended to dominate so much of the earlier writing on the revolutionary period.

While the background of the revolutionary period is thus being more fully explored, renewed attention has been directed to the beginnings of the revolutionary movements in Spanish America in the critical years between 1808 and 1810. Here the part played by the cabildos or town councils in the incipient movement for self-government, the minority character of so-called popular revolutions, the nature of the political doctrines then gaining currency, the great diversity of conditions in the several parts of the Spanish American empire, and the activities of the 'comparatively few enlightened, keen-witted leaders, who in many areas', as Professor Haring has observed, 'represented the ambitions of the educated creole class to supplant the peninsular Spaniards in government and trade',[1] are the major themes, and the debate which continues to rage in Argentina over the origins of the revolution of May 1810 (despite the earlier and very substantial contributions of Clemente Fregeiro, Diego Molinari and Ricardo Levene) is a lively illustration.[2]

Much of this, of course, is a re-examination of familiar ground. And the historiography of the revolutionary period in general follows, for the most part, well-established lines. As in the past, the concentration of interest upon the personalities of the period, the tendency to see the liberation of Spanish America through the lives of its liberators, are notable characteristics. Few modern biographies have attained to the stature of Bartolomé Mitre's classic studies of San Martín and Belgrano (to the latter of which Mario Belgrano's *Historia de Belgrano*[3] is an indispensable supplement), or are to be regarded, like W. S. Robertson's *Life of Miranda* (2 vols., Chapel Hill, 1929), as historiographical milestones. And not many have resulted, as the late Eduardo Acevedo's biography of the Uruguayan national hero, José Artigas,[4] resulted,

[1] *The Spanish Empire in America* (New York, 1947), p. 346.
[2] *E.g.*, Roberto F. Marfany, '¿Dónde está el pueblo?', *Humanidades*, xxxi (1948), 253–313; Enrique Ruiz-Guiñazú, *Epifanía de la libertad* (Buenos Aires, 1952); C. A. Pueyrredón, *1810. La revolución de mayo* (Buenos Aires, 1953).
[3] Rev. ed., Buenos Aires, 1944.
[4] 3 vols., Montevideo, 1909–10. Reprinted, 1950.

in a drastic revision of conventional views. But among recent works Ricardo Piccirilli's *Rivadavia y su tiempo* (2 vols., Buenos Aires, 1943) was a notable contribution to the understanding of the Argentine statesman who attempted, as Sarmiento suggested, to bring Europe to America; W. S. Robertson, in his *Iturbide of Mexico* (Durham, N. C., 1952), has written what must long be regarded as the definitive biography of the liberator who made himself an emperor; among the numerous biographies of Bolívar, Gerhard Masur's *Simón Bolívar* (Albuquerque, 1949) is outstanding; and traversing ground covered not only by Mitre but by J. P. Otero and so many others, J. M. Yrarrazaval Larraín's *San Martín y sus enigmas* (2 vols., Santiago de Chile, 1949), though its conclusions are controversial, provides a valuable critique of source materials already in print.[1] Meanwhile, though the greater figures of the revolutionary period command a major share of attention, and though their conduct, their services to the cause of independence, and their political purposes continue to provoke animated debate, not always divorced, in Spanish America, from partisan devotion or ideological conviction,[2] lesser figures – so great is the attraction of what Sir Lewis Namier has described as 'the ritual form' of historiography – are also finding their biographers. The portrait gallery is steadily being enlarged. And the addition of such works as H. A. Bierck's biography of the Colombian foreign minister, Pedro Gual (Caracas, 1947), of Julio César Chaves' life of Castelli, 'el adalid de Mayo' (Buenos Aires, 1944), of Mariano de Vedia y Mitre's life of Monteagudo (3 vols., Buenos Aires, 1950), or of Enrique Martínez Paz's study of Deán Funes (Córdoba, 1950) – and there are many others – can only be welcomed.

Biographical studies of this kind may contribute, on the one hand, to a more systematic examination of the political ideas of the revolutionary period, and, on the other to a clearer understanding of local forces and regional influences. Both are needed. It is only slowly that local and regional history is being integrated with the

[1] See also Luis Castillo Ledón, *Hidalgo, La vida del héroe* (2 vols., Mexico, 1948–9); and, as a contribution to the military side of the career of Bolívar, Vicente Lecuna, *Crónica razonada de las guerras de Bolívar* (3 vols., New York, 1950) – an outstanding example of the attention lavished upon the military operations of the great revolutionary leaders.

[2] The evidence upon which to determine what took place at the celebrated interview between Bolívar and San Martín at Guayaquil in 1822 is, for example, scanty indeed. But the commentary upon it threatens to assume encyclopedic proportions.

several national histories of the emerging Spanish American states. And despite the work of Moses, Belaunde, José Ingenieros, Ricardo Donoso, Giménez Fernández and many others, the field of political thought – and experimentation – has only partially been explored. Belaunde's pregnant observation that 'we should consider not only the Spanish tradition and the philosophy of the enlightenment but American federalism, French jacobinism, British realism, and constitutional monarchism' cannot too closely be kept in mind.[1] And here it may also be observed that though the role of the pulpit and of the clergy in the revolutions for independence has long engaged, and still engages, the interest of historians, it is only in comparatively recent years that attention has been called to the role of the press.[2]

The political and military history of the revolutions, so much the preoccupation of nineteenth-century historians, has, of course, long been buttressed by constitutional and diplomatic history. The great contribution made by United States scholars in this last field has already been mentioned. It is sufficient to refer here to the pioneer researches of F. L. Paxson, W. R. Manning, J. B. Lockey and J. F. Rippy, continued in the late 'thirties and early 'forties by C. C. Griffin, W. S. Robertson, A. P. Whitaker and S. F. Bemis. This tradition of diplomatic studies, somewhat weakened of late years in the United States, has been maintained in Spain by Jaime Delgado[3] and in Cuba by J. L. Franco,[4] both of whom have concerned themselves with the Spanish side of the story.[5] And where so much has been done to elucidate United States interests, to

[1] Víctor Andrés Belaunde, *Bolívar and the Political Thought of the Spanish American Revolution* (Baltimore, 1938), p. 1. French jacobinism, the Spanish tradition and the philosophy of the enlightenment have received a good deal more attention than the other influences of which Belaunde speaks. On constitutional monarchism see J. A. de la Puente Candamo, *San Martín y el Perú. Planteamiento doctrinario* (Lima, 1948). See also A. Rojas, 'La batalla de Bentham en Colombia', *Revista de Historia de América*, Núm. 29 (1950), pp. 37–66.

[2] *Cf.* R. Vargas Ugarte, *El episcopado en los tiempos de la emancipación sudamericana* (2nd ed., Buenos Aires, 1945); R. Jaramillo Arango, *El clero en la independencia* (Antioquia, 1946); J. M. Miquel i Vergés, *La independencia mexicana y la prensa insurgente* (Mexico, 1941).

[3] *España y México en el siglo* xix (3 vols., Madrid, 1950–53). *Cf.* also his *La independencia de América en la prensa española* (Madrid, 1949) and Melchor Fernández Almagro, *La emancipación de América y su reflejo en la conciencia española* (Madrid, 1944).

[4] *Política continental americana de España en Cuba, 1812–1830* (Havana, 1947).

[5] See also R. O. Fraboschi, *La comisión regia española al Río de la Plata, 1820–1821* (Buenos Aires, 1945) and Mario Belgrano, *Rivadavia y sus gestiones diplomáticas con España* (3rd ed., Buenos Aires, 1945).

clarify French and Vatican policy, and to disentangle the diplomatic negotiations of the new Spanish American states themselves,[1] a revival of interest in the policies of the mother country is a development not only due but overdue. Meanwhile, despite the intensive study devoted in England both to Castlereagh and Canning, despite the brilliant essay which Sir Charles Webster has prefaced to his collection of documents on Britain and the independence of Latin America, and despite also a recent synthesis by William W. Kaufmann,[2] British policy in relation to the independence of Spanish America still awaits its fuller exploration. Sir Charles Webster, it is true, has laid down the main lines with clarity and precision, and Canning's role, often grossly exaggerated, can now be seen in better perspective. But the diplomacy of the years before 1812 has not yet been studied with the attention it deserves.[3] Our knowledge of British economic interests in the Spanish American area and of British economic penetration therein, at a time when new links were being forged and new interests created between Spanish America and Europe, is as yet only fragmentary, and unsystematic.[4] And we shall need a series of studies comparable, on the one hand, to A. K. Manchester's *British Pre-eminence in Brazil* (Chapel Hill, 1933) or similar in type, on the other, to Laura Bornholdt's *Baltimore and Early Panamericanism* (Northampton, 1949) before Britain's role in the liberation of Latin America can properly be assessed.

At this point the student of politics and diplomacy must call the economic historian to his aid. And the economic history of Spanish America in the age of its emancipation remains to be written. It is not only the phenomena associated with the opening of the con-

---

[1] *E.g.,* to consider the last twenty-five years alone, by R. Montaner Bello in Chile, F. J. Urrutia in Colombia, and Mario Belgrano, Ricardo Caillet-Bois and Enrique Ruiz-Guiñazú in Argentina.

[2] *British Policy and the Independence of Latin America, 1804–1828* (New Haven, 1951).

[3] For an example of recent 'revisionist' study of one aspect of British diplomacy see J. Street, 'Lord Strangford and Río de la Plata, 1808–1815', *Hispanic American Review*, xxxiii (1953), 477–510.

[4] I have tried to illustrate some of these interests and connections in my *Liberation in South America, 1806–1827. The Career of James Paroissien* (London, 1952). See also H. S. Ferns, 'Beginnings of British Investment in Argentina', *Economic History Review*, 2nd series, iv (1952), 341–352; J. Fred Rippy, 'Latin America and the British Investment "Boom" of the 1820s', *Journal of Modern History*, xix (1947), 122–9, as well as earlier articles by D. B. Goebel, J. B. Williams, C. W. Centner, Domingo Amunátegui Solar, Eugenio Pereira Salas and others; and, more recently, J. Street.

tinent to the trade of the world – the rise, and effects, of foreign commercial penetration, the beginnings of foreign capital investment, the opening of a new European frontier – that require more detailed investigation. So also do the disruptive effects of war and revolution – the flight of Spanish capital and capitalists, the abandonment of the mines, the destruction of livestock, the dislocation of the labour supply. It is unnecessary to labour the point. The problem has been admirably stated by Professor C. C. Griffin.[1] It is, however, easier to state than to solve. And, in tackling it, only a beginning has yet been made, in scattered articles on finance and trade, in incidental discussions in works concerned with local or regional history, and in an occasional full-length study such as Miron Burgin's brilliant examination of *The Economic Aspects of Argentine Federalism, 1820–1852* (Cambridge, Mass., 1946).[2] Nor has the cultural and social history of the revolutionary period fared much better. It is only in part that the effects of the wars of independence on different social groups – the Indian peoples, the coloured castes, the mestizo populations – have yet been studied.[3] Here the historian must join hands with the sociologist and the demographer. And there is no shortage of questions to be asked and of work to be done. 'Acá,' observes Professor Griffin, of the wars of independence, 'eran casi guerras sociales de raza; allá tenían una dirección nacionalista bien desarrollada; acullá parecen más bien guerras personalistas de caudillos rivales.'[4] It is, indeed, the variety and the complexity of the scene that arrest the attention of the modern historian, and his shafts must yet be sunk into layers so far barely touched.

Will the focus of interest shift, in the next twenty-five years, from the political, the constitutional and the diplomatic aspects of the revolutions to their economic and social aspects? It would be hazardous to guess. But fresh winds are blowing. The field of vision is widening. And the revolutions are now to be seen in the

[1] 'Economic and Social Aspects of the Era of Spanish-American Independence', *Hispanic American Historical Review*, xxix (1949), 170–87. And note the references there given to the economic literature on the revolutionary period.

[2] *Cf.* also David Bushnell, *The Santander Regime in Gran Colombia* (Newark, Delaware, 1954).

[3] *Cf. e.g.*, George Kubler, *The Indian Caste of Peru, 1795–1940* (Washington, 1952); J. R. King, 'A Royalist View of the Colored Castes in the Venezuelan War of Independence', *Hispanic American Historical Review*, xxxiii (1953), 526–37; and see the references in Griffin, *op. cit.*

[4] *Ensayos sobre la historia del nuevo mundo*, p. 113.

light not only of what preceded them but of what came after. Meanwhile, the gains of the past are being consolidated and so far as individual Spanish American countries are concerned, the general history of the revolutionary period is being re-interpreted and re-written.[1] But we still await the synoptic view, a general synthesis which shall be full and adequate. Perhaps the time is not yet ripe. But may we not hope for an interim report?

[1] *Cf.* the great *Historia de la nación argentina,* which Ricardo Levene has edited, and the work of Jorge Basadre in Peru, Luis Chávez Orozco in Mexico, Francisco Encina in Chile and Joaquín Tamayo in Colombia.

7

British Merchants and South American Independence*

The economic history of Latin America in its age of emancipation is still unwritten. There is an immense literature relating to political, constitutional, diplomatic, and military history.[1] It is possible to follow, if not hour by hour, almost, at least, day by day, the movements of Bolívar and, on occasion, of San Martín, the two greatest of the 'liberators'. But the disruptive effects of war and revolution, on the one hand, and the stimulating, but also in part disruptive, effects of the rise of foreign trade, the arrival of the foreign merchant, and the beginnings of foreign capital investment, on the other, still await their historian.[2] Much of the trade was British trade. A majority of the merchants were British merchants. And the foreign capital investment was almost wholly British. What sort of people were these merchants, adventurers, and commission agents who laid the foundations of British economic enterprise in South America in the first quarter of the nineteenth century? What kinds of risk did they run and what kinds of reward did they gain? How far did British capital help to fill the gap left by the flight of Spanish capital? And what was the contribution of this overseas commercial penetration to the political and economic development of the new Spanish American states?

* [The Raleigh Lecture on History, 1965, published in the *Proceedings of the British Academy*, li (London, 1966), 151–74.]

[1] See my paper on 'The Historiography of the Spanish American Revolutions', above, pp. 92–105.

[2] *Cf.* the stimulating essay of C. C. Griffin, 'Economic and Social Aspects of the Era of Spanish-American Independence', *ibid.*, xxix (1949), 170–87, together with his 'Aspectos económico-sociales de la época de la emancipación hispanoamericana: una bibliografía selecta de la historiografía reciente, 1949–1959', Academia Nacional de la Historia, *El Movimiento Emancipador de Hispanoamérica* (4 vols., Caracas, 1961), i, 349–60, and his three lectures, *Los Temas Sociales y Económicos en la Epoca de la Independencia* (Caracas, 1962).

Not all these questions can yet be answered, and I cannot hope to do more than illustrate the kinds of answer that may be given to some of them. But one further question must be examined first. What was the legal status of British trade in South America? British merchants in London and Bristol, Liverpool and Jamaica, had long hoped for free and open access to those Spanish American markets and sources of supply, of gold and silver, drugs and dyewoods, hides and skins, which some of them knew fairly well, either through the trades of Lisbon and Cádiz or through the operation of the free port system in the West Indies[1] – though there were other ways, too, of trading with Spanish America. In Spain, during the long reign of Charles III, the regulations governing the conduct of imperial trade had been revised and liberalized. Foreigners, late in the eighteenth century, had been admitted to a share in the slave trade.[2] Still later, during the long struggle between the sea-power of England and the land-power of France, and while Spain was still an ally of France, the crown had been compelled to tolerate for limited periods neutral shipping in Spanish American ports.[3] But, with these exceptions, the trade of the empire still remained the close preserve of Spain, and British anxieties to end the monopoly were matched by Spanish anxieties to maintain it.

The Napoleonic invasions of the Iberian peninsula, the overthrow of the Spanish royal house, the rising of the Spanish people, and the transformation of Britain from an enemy to an ally of Spain in July 1808, made no difference to this situation. Canning, at the Foreign Office, in 1808 and 1809, repeatedly tried to persuade the Spanish government that 'an intercourse with

[1] Allan Christelow, 'Great Britain and the Trades from Cadiz and Lisbon to Spanish America and Brazil, 1759–1783', *Hispanic American Historical Review*, xxvii (1947), 2–29, and 'Contraband Trade between Jamaica and the Spanish Main, and the Free Port Act of 1766', *ibid.*, xxii (1942), 309–43; Frances Armytage, *The Free Port System in the British West Indies. A study in commercial policy, 1766–1822* (London, 1953); D. B. Goebel, 'British Trade to the Spanish Colonies, 1796–1823', *American Historical Review*, xliii (1938), 289–94.

[2] J. F. King, 'Evolution of the Free Slave Trade Principle in Spanish Colonial Administration', *Hispanic American Historical Review*, xxii (1942), 34–56.

[3] *Cf.* Sergio Villalobos R., 'El Comercio Extranjero a fines de la Dominación Española', *Journal of Inter-American Studies*, iv (1962), 517–44; R. F. Nichols, 'Trade Relations and the Establishment of the United States Consulates in Spanish America, 1779–1809', *Hispanic American Historical Review*, xiii (1933), 289–313; and A. P. Whitaker, *The United States and the Independence of Latin America, 1800–1830* (Baltimore, 1941), pp. 4–9, 14–16.

South America is indispensably necessary for the obtaining, by this country, the means of continuing its aid to the Spanish cause'[1] – the bullion supply was always a major concern of the British government – and he protested also that 'it would not be unreasonable to expect' that the same relaxation of the restrictions on colonial trade which had been made in favour of neutrals should be extended to an ally.[2] Richard Wellesley, in 1810 and 1811, was equally emphatic.[3] But these representations were made in vain. It is true that on 17 May 1810 a decree was signed and thereafter printed purporting to open the ports of the Indies at least in part to the trade of all friendly nations. But this decree, according to Henry Wellesley at Cádiz, was the impudent fabrication of a Spanish American under-secretary in the ministry of finance; and it was, in any event, quickly disavowed.[4] As for Richard Wellesley's own proposal of a commercial treaty legalizing British trade with the Indies during the continuance of the war,[5] this was rejected outright.[6] Spanish suspicions of British intentions were too ingrained, the government was dominated by Cádiz and the prejudices of the Cádiz merchants were too strong, to give such a proposal any chance of success. After all, it was only in 1797 that that 'rough foul-mouthed devil', Sir Thomas Picton (to use the Duke of Wellington's words),[7] had been encouraged at Trinidad to promote revolution on the mainland; only in 1806 that Sir Home Popham (on his own responsibility)

[1] Canning to John Hookham Frere, no. 3, 5 Oct. 1808, P[ublic] R[ecord] O[ffice], F[oreign] O[ffice Records] 72/60. *Cf.* Canning to Frere, no. 30, 16 Nov. 1808, F.O. 72/60; to Admiral Apodaca, 17 Nov. 1808, F.O. 72/67; to Marquess Wellesley, no. 4, 27 June 1809; nos. 36 and 38, 24 Aug., 16 Sept. 1809, F.O. 72/75.

[2] Canning to Marquess Wellesley, no. 26, 17 Aug. 1809, F.O. 72/75.

[3] *Cf.* Marquess Wellesley to Henry Wellesley, no. 21, 13 July 1810, F.O. 72/93.

[4] Henry Wellesley to Marquess Wellesley, no. 56, 11 July 1810, F.O. 72/96. See also J. M. Zamora y Coronado, *Biblioteca de Legislación Ultramarina* (6 vols., Madrid, 1844–6), ii, 264–5.

[5] He thought, alternatively, of measures to liberalize the conditions of trade by the Cádiz route and to allow of the export of specie directly from Spanish America to Britain. Marquess Wellesley to Henry Wellesley, no. 24, 24 July; no. 26, 11 Aug.; no. 27, 4 Aug. 1810, F.O. 72/93.

[6] H. Wellesley to Marquess Wellesley, no. 77, 22 Aug. 1810, F.O. 72/96: no. 81, 25 Aug.; Bardaxí to H. Wellesley, 24 Aug. 1810, F.O. 72/97; C. R. Crawley, 'French and English Influences in the Cortes of Cadiz, 1810–1814', *Cambridge Historical Journal*, vi (1939), 182–3; H. Wellesley to Viscount Wellington, 16 Aug. 1810, *Supplementary Despatches, Correspondence, and Memoranda of Field Marshal Arthur Duke of Wellington, K.G.* (15 vols., London, 1858–72), vi, 574.

[7] Philip Henry, Fifth Earl Stanhope, *Notes of Conversations with the Duke of Wellington, 1831–1851* (Oxford, 1938), p. 68.

had attacked, captured, and briefly held Buenos Aires; only in 1807 that Sir Samuel Auchmuty had stormed Montevideo. Agents from Venezuela, where the Spanish authorities had been deposed, were actually in England, brought by a British naval corvette. As for British trade with Spanish America in general, Spain had been trying to put a stop to it for more than a century.

The question was raised again in 1811: first, when Britain offered to mediate between Spain and her rebellious colonies,[1] and the cortes, which had now been summoned, agreed that she should have the right to trade with Spanish America while mediation was in progress; and, later, when the cortes passed a resolution authorizing the conclusion of a subsidy treaty under which Britain would be granted a share in the Indies trade in return for a loan.[2] But the conditions of mediation which the cortes laid down were wholly unacceptable to Britain,[3] and the proposed subsidy treaty was equally unsatisfactory.[4] Both were rejected. Twelve years later, in one of his most celebrated state papers, the Polignac Memorandum of October 1823, Canning stated 'that permission to trade with the Spanish colonies had been conceded to Great Britain in the year 1810, when the mediation of Great Britain between Spain and her colonies was asked by Spain and granted by Great Britain' and 'that it had been ever since distinctly understood that the trade was open to British subjects, and that the ancient coast laws of Spain were, so far as regarded them at least, tacitly repealed'.[5] But the basis for these assertions is slender indeed. When, in 1812, Castlereagh succeeded Wellesley at the Foreign Office, what Canning called the 'coast

[1] Marquess Wellesley to H. Wellesley, no. 18, 4 May 1811, F.O. 72/108.

[2] H. Wellesley to Marquess Wellesley, no. 130, 20 Dec.; no. 141, 31 Dec. 1811, F.O. 72/115.

[3] H. Wellesley to Marquess Wellesley, no. 69, 30 June 1811, F.O. 72/112; Bardaxí to H. Wellesley, 29 June 1811, *ibid.*; John Rydjord, 'British Mediation between Spain and her Colonies, 1811–1813', *Hispanic American Historical Review*, xxi (1941), 33–4. This article makes use of Spanish but not of British archives.

[4] Bardaxí to H. Wellesley, 29 Dec., Wellesley to Bardaxí, 30 Dec. 1811, F.O. 72/115.

[5] Printed in C. K. Webster, *Britain and the Independence of Latin America, 1812–1830. Select Documents from the Foreign Office Archives* (2 vols., London, 1938), ii, 117. See also *Parliamentary Debates*, N.S., x, 753, for Canning's further statement, in March 1824, that no treaty existed, merely an understanding. *Cf.* Goebel, *op. cit.,* pp. 288–9. H. W. V. Temperley and Lillian M. Penson, *Foundations of British Foreign Policy from Pitt (1792) to Salisbury (1902)* (Cambridge, 1938), pp. 523–6, attempt to explain away Canning's words, but not, I think, with great success. Webster asserts that 'a sort of permission to trade was given by the Cadiz Government' (*op. cit.,* i, 10).

laws of Spain' were, theoretically at least, as much in force as they had always been.

In practice a very different situation prevailed. What Spain refused to concede, Spanish Americans took for themselves. Everywhere in South America, except in the old viceroyalty of Peru and the neighbouring presidencies of Quito and Charcas, the years between 1808 and 1812 saw the beginnings of the transition from the closed to the open door. In the great Portuguese colony of Brazil, to which the prince regent and the royal family of Portugal had fled, the Carta Régia of January 1808, issued soon after the arrival of the prince, put an end to the old system of colonial monopoly. Sir Home Popham's assault on Buenos Aires, eighteen months earlier, foreshadowed a similar conclusion in the Río de la Plata. Popham and his fellow conquerors of Buenos Aires, it is true, believed not so much in free trade as in freer trade, and, for Britain in particular, preferential trade.[1] But Buenos Aires in 1806 and Montevideo in 1807 had tasted, under British rule, a commercial freedom which they had never known before, and it was not for long that the great river would again be closed to foreign trade. However illegally, British merchants continued to reside at Buenos Aires in 1808 and 1809 and British merchant ships to unload their cargoes. Finally, on 6 November 1809, a recently-appointed viceroy, faced with an empty treasury, reluctantly agreed that the port must be opened to the trade of allies and neutrals.[2] Stringent restrictions were imposed, and, under pressure from the old Spanish merchants, the viceroy soon sought to retreat from the concessions he had made.[3] On 25 May 1810, however, he was deposed. From that moment Buenos Aires was independent in fact if not in name and its port remained open to the ships of all friendly nations.

[1] Brigadier-General W. C. Beresford to Castlereagh, Fort of Buenos Ayres, 11 July 1806, PRO, War Office Records, 1/161; H. S. Ferns, *Britain and Argentina in the Nineteenth Century* (Oxford, 1960), pp. 49–51.

[2] Acta de la Junta Consultiva de 6 de Nov., sobre la permisión provisoria de comercio con los extranjeros . . . , *Documentos para la Historia Argentina*, vii (Buenos Aires, 1916), p. 379; R. A. Humphreys, *Liberation in South America, 1806–1827. The Career of James Paroissien* (London, 1952), pp. 38–40; Goebel, *op. cit.*, pp. 308–12; John Street, 'La influencia británica en la independencia de las provincias del Río de la Plata, con especial referencia al período comprendido entre 1806 y 1816', *Revista Histórica* (Montevideo), xxi (1954), nos. 61–3, pp. 379–91.

[3] Alexander Mackinnon to Secretary of State for Foreign Affairs, Buenos Aires, 4 Feb., 1 June 1810, F.O. 72/107. Mackinnon first arrived in the Río de la Plata in June 1809.

The struggle which took place at Buenos Aires from 1808 to 1810 between those who wanted the port opened and those who wished to keep it closed, between agricultural and consumer interests on the one hand and the interests of the Spanish monopolistic merchant houses on the other, was paralleled in other parts of South America.[1] Just as the monopolists of Buenos Aires subscribed to a loan in 1809 to induce the viceroy to maintain the old exclusionist system, so, nine years later, the monopolists of Lima took precisely the same action.[2] But the issue was everywhere the same. As juntas and cabildos took the place of viceroys and governors, one after another the ports of South America were opened to the foreign trader – in Venezuela in May 1810, at Cartagena de las Indias on 1 January 1811, in Chile in February 1811.[3] Thereafter the fortunes of trade followed the fortunes of war and the vicissitudes of royalist or patriot blockades and victories. At the last, even in Peru, for so long the stronghold of Spanish power in South America, the viceroy was compelled to connive at foreign trade,[4] and there also, with the patriot occupation of Lima in 1821, the ports were opened.

While this transformation took place in South America, in England the legend of El Dorado wove again its ancient spell. 'There can be no field of enterprise,' said Brougham in 1817, 'so magnificent in promise, so well calculated to raise sanguine hopes, so congenial to the most generous sympathies, so consistent with the best and the highest interests of England, as the

[1] See, for Buenos Aires, the celebrated *Representación, en nombre de los labradores y hacendados de las campañas del Río de la Plata,* of Mariano Moreno (1809), printed in D. L. Molinari, *Le representación de los hacendados de Mariano Moreno* (Buenos Aires, 1914), for the prolonged conflict of economic interests in Venezuela, E. Arcila Farías, *Economía colonial de Venezuela* (Mexico, 1946), pp. 318–20, 368–70, and for Chile, Hernán Ramírez Necochea, *Antecedentes Económicos de la Independencia de Chile* (Santiago de Chile, 1959), pp. 81–105.

[2] See my *British Consular Reports on the Trade and Politics of Latin America, 1824–1826* (Camden 3rd series, lxiii, London, Royal Historical Society, 1940), p. 29, n. 1, p. 127, n. 2.

[3] The captain-general of Venezuela had allowed British trade from Curaçao in 1807 and this privilege, though hampered by heavy duties, was further extended in 1808. Proclamation of Captain-General of Venezuela, 1 Sept. 1808, PRO Ad[miralty Records] 1/258; Alexander Cochrane to W. W. Pole, 21 Oct. 1808, Ad. 1/329. The junta of Caracas in 1810 offered preferential rates to British trade. Goebel, *op. cit.,* p. 299. For the decree of the supreme junta of Cartagena, dated 10 Dec. 1810, opening the port of Cartagena as from 1 Jan. 1811, see Vice-Admiral B. S. Rowley to J. W. Croker, 5 Feb. 1811, Ad. 1/262, and, for Chile, *British Consular Reports,* p. 91.

[4] *British Consular Reports,* p. 127, n. 2.

vast continent of South America. He must indeed be more than temperate, he must be a cold reasoner, who can glance at those regions, and not grow warm.'[1] At the news, rather more than ten years earlier, of Popham's conquest of Buenos Aires, so great had been the popular enthusiasm, enhanced, no doubt, by the sight of the wagon-loads of silver which Popham sent home, that within a few weeks perhaps a hundred ships were fitting out for the Río de la Plata; and when Montevideo fell into British hands in February 1807, 6,000 British subjects are said to have entered the town, of whom 2,000 were 'merchants, traders, adventurers'. Immense sums in money and goods were realized in a short space of time,[2] and the gloom into which the mercantile community was cast by the loss of these conquests – a loss followed so soon by the fall of Lisbon and by the application of the American Non-Importation and Embargo Acts – was proportionately great. It was only relieved by the opening of the ports of Brazil, when, in the words of an English visitor, 'so great and so unexpected was the influx of English manufactures into Rio de Janiero . . . that the rent of the houses to put them into became enormously dear. The bay was covered with ships, and the custom-house soon overflowed with goods.'[3] John Luccock, a partner in the firm of Luptons of Leeds, arriving in June 1808, found that the stock of fine cloth was 'sufficient for several years';[4] and the descriptions given by McCulloch and others of the services of cut-glass, the skates, the stays, the warming-pans, and the coffins which found their way to Rio de Janeiro, and later to Buenos Aires, between 1808 and 1810, are too well known to be repeated.[5] It is not surprising that the select committee on the state of commercial credit in 1811 attributed a principal part of the commercial distress which prevailed in Britain in 1810 to the 'great and extensive

[1] 13 March 1817. *Parliamentary Debates*, xxxv, 1026.

[2] J. P. and W. P. Robertson, *Letters on Paraguay* (3 vols., 2nd ed., London, 1839), i, 94, 101–2; Humphreys, *Liberation in South America,* pp. 4–9; J. B. Williams, 'The Establishment of British Commerce with Argentina', *Hispanic American Historical Review,* xiv (1935), 47.

[3] John Mawe, *Travels in the Interior of Brazil* (London, 1812), p. 324. Mawe was a mineralogist.

[4] Herbert Heaton, 'A Merchant Adventurer in Brazil, 1808–1818', *Journal of Economic History,* vi (1946), 9.

[5] Mawe, *op. cit.,* pp. 324–6; Thomas Tooke, *A History of Prices, and of the State of Circulation from 1793 to 1837* (2 vols., London, 1838), i, 276–7; W. R. Manning, ed., *Diplomatic Correspondence of the United States concerning the Independence of the Latin-American Nations* (3 vols., New York, 1925), i, 454.

speculations, which commenced upon the opening of the South American markets in the Brazils and elsewhere, to the adventures of British merchants'.[1]

From now on, British trade with the east coast of South America was firmly established and British merchants were looking to the opening of the west coast also.[2] It was not, of course, free trade. Tariffs were often high. Rates varied with bewildering rapidity. And merchants were subjected to arbitrary regulations and arbitrary exactions. Only in Brazil were their rights safeguarded by treaty – the Anglo-Portuguese commercial treaty of 1810. But Brazil was also the seat of the British South American naval station, established in May 1808, and the commanders of His Majesty's ships at Rio de Janeiro, in the Río de la Plata, and, later, in Pacific waters, acted as unofficial consuls and diplomats, protected British trade, safeguarded the rights of British merchants, and, incidentally, transported on their behalf immense quantities of specie to England.[3] These, then, were the conditions under which the British communities in Rio de Janeiro and Buenos Aires were founded. That at Buenos Aires already numbered more than 50 persons in 1809 and more than 120 in 1810, and by that year the property which British merchants had at stake there, as one of them reported, was 'seldom less than £750,000 sterling', and sometimes more than a million.[4]

One member of this small community in 1810 was a young Scotsman, John Parish Robertson by name. Robertson had first visited the Río de la Plata in 1807, brought there by his father, a former assistant secretary to the Bank of Scotland,[5] in the hope

---

[1] *Parliamentary Debates*, xix, 250; Tooke, *op. cit.*, i, 306. *Cf.* A. D. Gayer, W. W. Rostow, and Anna J. Schwartz, *The Growth and Fluctuation of the British Economy, 1790–1850* (2 vols., Oxford, 1953), i, 92–3.

[2] There is evidence of eleven ships fitting out for trade with Chile and Peru as early as 1807–8, the earlier vessels sailing with the avowed purpose of contraband, the latter in the hope that since Britain and Spain had become allies, trade would be free. Hullett Bros. *et al.* to Canning, 3 April 1809, F.O. 72/90. Their fate was not happy.

[3] G. S. Graham and R. A. Humphreys, eds., *The Navy and South America, 1807–1823. Correspondence of the Commanders-in-Chief on the South American Station* (London, Navy Records Society, 1962), *passim*.

[4] Alexander Mackinnon to Canning, 2 Nov. 1809, F.O. 72/90, 12 Aug. 1810, F.O. 72/107; *British Consular Reports*, p. 26, n. 2, p. 32, n. 1.

[5] William Robertson, Sr, was appointed assistant secretary, after being a senior clerk in the Secretary's Office, on 24 March 1796. Bank of Scotland, Minutes of Courts of Directors, vol. 8. According to *Chambers's Edinburgh Journal*, N.S., no. 1, 6 Jan. 1844, he resigned this post (it is not clear precisely when) on account of ill-health and entered 'a mercantile house in Glasgow'.

of turning to good commercial advantage the recent conquest of Buenos Aires. He returned to South America, this time by himself, after the emigration of the Portuguese court to Brazil in 1808, landed at Rio de Janeiro in October of that year, and moved to Buenos Aires a few months later. Here he was employed as a clerk until in December 1811 he made his way to Asunción, the capital of the former intendancy of Paraguay, more than 1,000 miles away, to dispose of a large consignment of goods which was to follow him up-river. The intendancy, when Robertson arrived, had only recently established its virtual independence both of Spain and of Buenos Aires and was soon to fall under the iron rule of Dr José Gaspar Rodríguez de Francia, who in 1813 became one of the republic's two 'consuls' and in 1814 its dictator. To the rest of the world it was as unknown as Tibet. Robertson was the first British subject to attempt to trade with the country, and one of the very few foreigners (apart from some of the old Jesuit missionaries) to have entered it at all. He was not yet twenty.

The Paraguayan venture lasted more than three years. At first regarded with suspicion and his every transaction watched, Robertson quickly won his way and was soon privileged to buy and sell freely. If later dealings, when $200 worth of salt in Buenos Aires sold for $4,000 in Asunción,[1] are any guide, his profits must have been large indeed. They were sufficient, at any rate, to tempt his younger brother, William, to come out from Scotland to join him in 1814. He then proposed to pay a visit to England himself, was entrusted by Francia with specimens of Paraguayan tea, sugar, tobacco, and cloth, and was told to present these to the House of Commons and to announce the dictator's wish to sign a treaty of friendship and commerce with England.[2] He went no further than Buenos Aires, however. On his way back to Asunción he was robbed of part of his property and nearly of his life, and, when he did arrive, it was to find that he had incurred Francia's violent hostility. He was instantly expelled, withdrew to the little town of Corrientes in the province of the same name, and was there joined by his brother a few weeks later with what had been saved from their Paraguayan venture. And he was probably fortunate. Within a few years

[1] *Letters on Paraguay*, iii, 255.
[2] *Ibid.*, ii, 281-4.

Paraguay had become a country barely possible either to enter or to leave, and it so remained till Francia's death in 1840.

The Robertsons, meanwhile, saw and grasped a new opportunity. The territory of Corrientes, together with that of Entre Ríos, lying between the Paraná and Uruguay rivers, had been the great cattle country of the viceroyalty of the Río de la Plata. Devastated during the civil wars which followed the dissolution of the viceroyalty, it was slowly returning to tranquillity. Europe needed hides. Corrientes could supply them, if the landowners could be induced to put their properties in order and if the hides could be collected. Dried hides could be bought in Corrientes for 1½d. a pound, sold at Buenos Aires for 5½d., and resold at Liverpool for 9d. or 10d. A horse cost 3d. Its hide sold for 3s. in Buenos Aires and for 7s. or 8s. in England.[1] The Robertsons turned themselves into the 'hide-merchants' and 'carriers' of the province,[2] organizing the hide trade as it had never been organized before. A partnership with a fellow Scot at Buenos Aires, Thomas Fair (later a large landowner), assured them the means of giving credit to the *estancieros* to induce them to return to their estates and collect together their herds of cattle. They established two headquarter-stations about 150 miles apart and a dozen or so outposts. They organized a system of wagon trains to collect hides and skins. They engaged an Irish-born gaucho, whose name struck terror into the hearts of other gauchos, to maintain order. And they paid good wages and prices.

By the end of 1816 not only was prosperity returning to Corrientes,[3] it had returned to the Robertsons, and the time had come for larger operations. John Parish Robertson, who had arrived in South America allegedly with only a guinea in his pocket in 1808,[4] sailed for England in a specially chartered vessel early in 1817, with the primary purpose of visiting his grandfather at Bath.[5] For this there was good reason. Robertson's grandfather was John Parish, the founder of the great merchant

[1] J. P. and W. P. Robertson, *Letters on South America* (3 vols., London, 1843), i, 262–3.

[2] *Ibid.,* i, 181.

[3] *Ibid.,* iii, 70–1. On the Robertsons' activities in Corrientes see also John Street, *Artigas and the Emancipation of Uruguay* (Cambridge, 1959), pp. 274–7, and Ferns, *op. cit.,* pp. 61, 81–2.

[4] *Chambers's Edinburgh Journal,* 6 Jan. 1844.

[5] *Letters on South America,* iii, 3; 'My Grandfather. A Tale of Bath', *Fraser's Magazine for Town and Country,* xiii (Jan. to June 1836), 569.

banking house of John Parish & Co. of Hamburg and the father of David Parish, who had established his own merchant house at Antwerp and had managed on behalf of Charles IV of Spain, G. J. Ouvrard of Paris, the Hopes of Amsterdam and the Barings the extraordinary operation of shipping Mexican silver on Spanish account to Napoleon in 1805 and 1806.[1] John Parish was himself a Scot, born at Leith. He had retired from the Hamburg firm at the end of 1796 with a fortune estimated at 2,000,000 marks and in 1807 established himself at Bath, where, in the next sixteen years, he gave 579 dinners and 76 balls and suppers and disposed of 14,750 bottles of wine. Hitherto he had ignored his grandsons. But he now recognized John as 'a chip of the old block', and John, having been provided with letters of introduction 'for all parts of the country',[2] finally set up a house of his own at Liverpool, while his brother and their partner remained at Buenos Aires. John and William Parish Robertson of Buenos Aires and Liverpool were no longer provincial traders. They were the correspondents of the Barings, the Gladstones, and the Parishes, importing German linens from Hamburg, shipping Spanish dollars for Bombay and Calcutta, freighting jerked beef for Havana.[3]

In Corrientes the Robertsons had lived a hard and dangerous life. They had incurred, also, the hostility of local traders, and it was with relief that they settled down into more conventional grooves, William, at Buenos Aires, classifying himself for the first time, in December 1817, 'as an English merchant in a foreign

---

[1] On John Parish see Richard Ehrenberg, *Das Haus Parish in Hamburg* (2nd ed. Jena, 1925), and A. Raffalovich, 'John Parish, banquier et negociant à Hambourg', *Journal des Économistes*, 6th series, vii (1905), 199–208; on David Parish, P. G. Walters and R. Walters Jr., 'The American Career of David Parish', *Journal of Economic History*, iv (1944), 149–66, John Rydjord, 'Napoleon and Mexican Silver', *Southwestern Social Science Quarterly*, xix (1938), 171–82, R. W. Hidy, *The House of Baring in American Trade and Finance* (Cambridge, Mass., 1949), pp. 35–7, and Vincent Nolte, *Fifty Years in Both Hemispheres, or Reminiscences of the Life of a Former Merchant* (New York, 1854). John Parish died in 1829 and is buried in Bath Abbey. David became a partner in the banking house of Fries & Co. of Vienna, was ruined when it was ruined in 1825, and threw himself into the Danube in 1826.

[2] *Letters on South America*, iii, 10. *Cf.* John Parish Robertson to Baring Bros., London, 21 July 1817, Baring Papers, H.C. 4.1.3.1A, detailing the nature of the import and export trade of Buenos Aires. I am much indebted to the partners of Baring Brothers and Company for their courtesy in allowing me access to their records.

[3] *Letters on South America*, iii, 101, 145, 151–8.

country'.[1] Even at Buenos Aires, of course, life and property were not invariably secure. The growing community of British merchants had its troubles, and it appealed from time to time for the help of the British naval commanders in South American waters.[2] But the city grew and flourished on foreign trade. It was never reconquered. In contrast to what happened in most of the other Spanish ports of South America, the British community never suffered disruption. And William Parish Robertson, in later life, could look back to these early years almost as to a golden age.[3]

On the Caribbean shores of South America a very different situation prevailed. Here the captaincy-general of Venezuela in 1810, like Buenos Aires in the same year, had welcomed the foreign trader, and its example had been followed in the neighbouring viceroyalty of New Granada by the port of Cartagena. But not all the cities of Venezuela recognized the new republican régime set up in the capital, Caracas; the rebel ports were soon put under blockade from Puerto Rico; neither the first nor the second Venezuelan republic long survived; and it was not till 1823 that all danger from the Spaniards vanished. Cartagena, which declared its independence in 1811 but then joined the United Provinces of New Granada, was, for a time, more fortunate. As one of the great fortified towns of the Indies, it enjoyed a special fame, and the opening of its port inevitably attracted the British merchant, more particularly the British merchant in Jamaica, so long a centre of the contraband trade with the Spanish main. And of the Jamaican merchants trading to the main Maxwell and Wellwood Hyslop of Kingston are outstanding examples.

The Hyslops came from Kirkcudbrightshire.[4] Wellwood, born in 1780, appears at the age of 22 as deputy commissary-general to His Majesty's forces in Jamaica.[5] Maxwell, three years younger, is known to all biographers of Bolívar as Bolívar's friend and

---

[1] *Ibid.,* ii, 70–1, iii, 100.
[2] *Cf. The Navy and South America,* Docs. 149, 150.
[3] *Letters on South America,* ii, 67–72, iii, 102, 114–15.
[4] They were the third and fifth sons of William Hyslop of Lochend (afterwards Lotus). Maxwell Hyslop Papers, in the possession of R. A. M. Maxwell-Hyslop, Esq., to whom I am much indebted for the privilege of examining them.
[5] Frank Cundall, ed., *Lady Nugent's Journal* (London, 1907), p. xxxiii, and entry under 29 April 1802.

benefactor when the future liberator was a penniless refugee in Jamaica in 1815.[1] The brothers traded as general merchants and their business was in part under-written by their cousins, W. and A. Maxwell & Co. of Liverpool. The Liverpool firm, in 1811, was exporting butter, soap, earthenware, hams, and cheese on joint-account; the Jamaica firm sent home rum and logwood, coffee and cocoa, pimento and indigo, ginger and cotton.

Exactly when the Hyslops' South American connexions began is not clear. What is certain is that they had long kept a close eye on the changes which were occurring on the mainland. What were the prospects, they wrote to the Maxwells in November 1812, for Cartagena cotton and cochineal, and what was the value of gold and silver, milled and in bars?

It is very probable that we shall have to do a good deal in these articles, in consequence of our having been appointed agents for the Government of Carthagena. The cause of independence has taken a very favourable change of late, and as it is now almost reduced to a certainty that it will succeed, we shall have great trade with the River Magdalena. We have got powerful friends in that quarter, and we shall hope to benefit ourselves as well as you by it. We are now shipping a considerable quantity of goods there for the Government . . . indeed we have it in contemplation to establish a house at Carthagena solely for the conduction of commission business. . . . .[2]

Accordingly, while Maxwell Hyslop remained at Kingston, Wellwood, in 1813, removed to Cartagena. Bolívar's celebrated march from New Granada to Caracas in this same year gave substance to their hopes for 'the cause of independence' and the future of British commerce. Wellwood, painting a glowing picture for the Board of Trade of the market in New Granada for British hardware, textiles, and machinery and of the supply, in return, of 'raw materials of the first necessity to our manufacturers, and bullion for the surplus', looked forward to a 'monopoly of the trade of these countries' for Great Britain.[3] The Liverpool Maxwells gave increased credit. 'We are working

[1] Bolívar to Hyslop, 19 May, 19 June, 30 Oct., 8 Nov., 4, 17, 26 Dec. 1815, Simón Bolívar, *Obras Completas* (ed. Vicente Lecuna and Esther Barret de Nazaris, 2 vols., La Habana, 1947), i, 131, 139, 182, 183, 186, and see Bolívar to Hyslop, 20 April 1830: 'the services which you have rendered to Colombia and to me personally I shall never forget . . .' (*ibid.*, ii, 874).

[2] Hyslops to Maxwells, Kingston, 28 Nov. 1812, Maxwell Hyslop Papers.

[3] W. Hyslop to Lord Bathurst, Cartagena, 20 Dec. 1813, F.O. 72/167.

double tides,' wrote Maxwell Hyslop in October;[1] and for a time all went well. Venezuela, it is true, again succumbed to the royalists, and Bolívar, who had already fled to Cartagena once, was forced to do so for a second time. But Maxwell, as late as April 1815, feared United States competition more than Spanish reconquest, anticipated the time when Britain would acknowledge the 'Confederate Government of New Granada', and hoped that when that time came Wellwood would be appointed 'British agent' at Cartagena.[2]

These sanguine hopes received a sharp check when the news reached Kingston a few days later that a Spanish expeditionary force under the command of General Pablo Morillo had reached Venezuela. 'How far this will affect the independence of New Granada,' wrote Maxwell, 'we are not competent to state at present, but if the expedition be extensive, it surely will be ag^t the cause, and if that cause fail, goodbye to British commerce on the main, which loss may be fairly attributed to our Ministers for not giving countenance to so noble an effort to throw open the bosom of a most fertile country.'[3] And the news of Morillo's expedition was followed in May by Bolívar's own arrival in Kingston, driven from New Granada as a result of civil and military dissensions, and by that of two commissioners from Cartagena seeking British military and naval aid and offering to place the town and fortress 'in deposit' in British hands until proper terms could be reached with Spain.[4] 'We hope the British Parliament will be obliged to take up this important subject,' wrote Maxwell. 'If England refuse to give assistance, she may depend that the U. States, or some other power will, and in that case the preference to Britain will be lost. Were Carth^a garrisoned by British troops, what a field would be open to our country!'[5]

But the doom of Cartagena was already sealed. In August Morillo moved from Venezuela to New Granada to begin the siege of the city. Maxwell, believing it to be impregnable – after all it had resisted Vernon in the eighteenth century – sent

[1] M. Hyslop to W. Maxwell, Kingston, 24 Oct. 1813, Maxwell Hyslop Papers.
[2] Hyslops to Maxwells, Kingston, 10 April 1815, *ibid*.
[3] Hyslops to Maxwells, Kingston, 28 April 1815, Maxwell Hyslop Papers.
[4] Rear-Admiral J. E. Douglas to Croker, 16 June 1815, enclosing Juan de Dios Amador to Douglas, 26 May 1815, Ad. 1/266. See also Salvador de Madariaga, *Bolívar* (London, 1952), pp. 260, 674.
[5] Hyslops to Maxwells, Kingston, 17 June 1815, Maxwell Hyslop Papers.

flour for the relief of its defenders, and Wellwood, eluding Morillo's blockade, suddenly appeared at Kingston. He came with two more commissioners and armed with the authority of the governor and provincial legislature of Cartagena to surrender the city and province in full sovereignty to Britain,[1] or, as Maxwell magniloquently but inaccurately put it, 'to lay the whole empire of New Granada at the feet of the Prince Regent thro his Grace the Duke of Manchester', the then governor of Jamaica.[2] But the duke declined to receive the commissioners. Wellwood, having written in much indignation to Lord Castlereagh,[3] returned to Cartagena and he was still there when the city fell on 6 December. Failing to make his escape, he was thrown into prison, and in prison he remained for four months until he was liberated at last through the intervention of Rear-Admiral Douglas, the commander-in-chief on the Jamaica station.[4]

Though Wellwood fell into the hands of the Spaniards, his property did not: he had shipped it off under the care of one of his clerks.[5] And Maxwell, despite his anxiety about Wellwood, was planning even now, in anticipation of the success of a fresh expedition which Bolívar was leading to Venezuela, to establish a house at La Guaira, Puerto Cabello, or Maracaibo. Indeed, the head-clerk of the Cartagena house himself accompanied the expedition.[6] By June 1816, with Wellwood safely back at Kingston, the brothers were describing themselves as the commercial agents of General Bolívar as well as of New Granada,[7] and when, with the revival of republican fortunes in Venezuela, a so-called Congress was installed at Cariaco in May 1817 and a new, though

[1] Manchester to Bathurst, 4 Nov. 1815, PRO C[olonial] O[ffice Records], 137/141; Douglas to Admiralty, 27 Oct. 1815, enclosing Juan de Dios Amador to Douglas, 14 Oct. 1815, Ad. 1/266; *The Star* (London), 27, 30 Jan., 1 Feb. 1816; *Documentos para la Historia de la Provincia de Cartagena de Indias* (ed. M. E. Corráles, 2 vols., Bogotá, 1883), ii, 156, 238, 284–5; Madariaga, *op. cit.,* pp. 261–2.

[2] Hyslops to Maxwells, Kingston, 18 Nov. 1815, Maxwell Hyslop Papers.

[3] W. Hyslop to Castlereagh, 7 Nov. 1815, F.O. 72/178.

[4] Douglas to Viceroy of New Granada, 10 April 1816; Viceroy to Douglas, May 1816, Fundación John Boulton, Caracas, Sección Venezolana del Archivo de la Gran Colombia, C, xx, 95–8. See also Memorial of Maxwell Hyslop to Castlereagh, 12 April 1816, F.O. 72/189; Goulburn to Hamilton, 12 March, 10 April 1816, C.O. 138/46; *The Star,* 7 March 1816.

[5] Hyslops to Maxwells, 30 Dec. 1815, Maxwell Hyslop Papers.

[6] P. Bartlett to Maxwell Hyslop, 23 March 1816; Hyslops to Maxwells, 2 April 1816, Maxwell Hyslop Papers.

[7] Hyslop & Co. to Brougham, 5 June 1816; Hyslops to Maxwells, 25 July 1816, Maxwell Hyslop Papers.

transient, executive power established, Wellwood was appointed minister plenipotentiary to Great Britain, charged with the negotiation of a commercial treaty. As it happened, Maxwell had already left for England, and the nomination was therefore altered in his favour,[1] though, naturally, to no purpose.

For some time longer the Hyslops continued to flourish. They acted as agents in Jamaica of the government of Colombia, when that state was founded, and contracted to supply it with arms; they formed a branch house at Maracaibo in 1821 and re-established the house at Cartagena;[2] and when the government toyed with the idea of constructing a canal or railway across the isthmus of Panama, the Hyslops were thought of as the contractors.[3] But their relations with the Maxwells had already begun to cool in 1818; there were disagreements over credit which grew more acute in 1820 and 1821; and the old terms of intimate friendship were never renewed. Finally, the firm was brought to the verge of ruin when B. A. Goldschmidt & Co., the Colombian loan contractors, suspended payment in January 1826. The Hyslops were caught short with dishonoured bills and their affairs had to be put into the hands of trustees.[4]

As Venezuela and New Granada were reconquered by Spain, so, on the west coast of South America, Chile was reconquered from Peru. Its ports, opened in 1811, were again closed in 1814. Not many adventurers made their way to Chile in these early years. Some British ships were seized by the Spaniards. Others, mostly South Sea whalers, were captured, during the war of 1812, by the United States frigate, *Essex*, till she in turn was captured by Captain Hillyar in Valparaiso Bay in March 1814.[5] But with San Martín's crossing of the Andes in January 1817 and the royalist defeat, on 12 February, at the battle of Chacabuco,

[1] Maxwell Hyslop to Castlereagh, 13 Aug. 1817; Hyslop to the Executive Power of the United Provinces of Venezuela, 22 Aug. 1817; Hyslop to Bolívar, 13 Feb. 1818, Fundación John Boulton, Sección Venezolana del Archivo de la Gran Colombia, C, xxiii, 1–5, and W, vi 8–14. See also F.O. 72/202.

[2] M. Hyslop to Castlereagh, 16 Jan. 1822, F.O. 72/263.

[3] *British Consular Reports,* p. 242; David Bushnell, *The Santander Regime in Gran Colombia* (Newark, Del., 1954), pp. 139–40.

[4] Hyslops to Maxwells, 29 April 1826, Maxwell Hyslop Papers. Maxwell Hyslop died at Falmouth, Jamaica, on 12 March 1837. R. R. Madden, *A Twelvemonth's Residence in the West Indies* . . . (2 vols., London, 1835), i, 229, refers to him as 'one of the most respectable men in the island'. Wellwood, who became a member of the House of Assembly, survived till 1845.

[5] *The Navy and South America,* pp. 99, 105, 109–10, 113, 132–3, 141–2.

E

Chile's experience more nearly resembled that of Buenos Aires and Rio de Janeiro than that of Venezuela and Cartagena. The markets, as one English visitor reported, were 'quite glutted with every description of goods and wares'.[1] Valparaiso, whose population multiplied five times in as many years, soon resembled, in the opinion of another, a 'coast town' of Britain,[2] and its reputation as the most important port on the Pacific was already established by the middle twenties.[3]

But Chile was provincial, Peru metropolitan, Chile was an agricultural, Peru a mineral-producing region; and it was to Peru, and to San Martín's preparations for its sea-borne invasion, that the British merchants now looked. Antony Gibbs & Sons, for example, the bulk of whose business was done with Spain, were already preparing in 1819 to establish a branch house in Lima, and their representative actually arrived there while the city was still in royalist hands.[4] Similarly, the Robertsons, in 1820, decided that the time had come for a further extension of their activities. William Parish Robertson, who had paid a brief visit to England in that year, returned to Buenos Aires with a handsome cargo of Manchester dry goods. John Parish Robertson, winding up his domestic affairs at Liverpool, followed him in a much larger vessel, chartered to sail round the Horn, his purpose now to lay 'the foundation of prosperous and extensive establishments in Santiago' and, so soon as possible, Lima.[5] Travelling overland from Buenos Aires, he reached Santiago in April 1821. 'The utmost anxiety,' he wrote to his grandfather, 'prevails to hear from San Martín who is besieging Lima; no doubt is entertained of its ultimate fall; but the poverty of the Treasury here and the large stocks of goods in the hands of the merchants, make the Government impatient and the English uneasy about the delay.' If Lima fell before his ship arrived, he added, he would certainly

[1] Samuel Haigh, *Sketches of Buenos Ayres, Chile, and Peru* (London, 1831), p. 253.

[2] B. Vicuña Mackenna, *The First Britons in Valparaiso, 1817–27* (Valparaiso, 1884), pp. 35–6; Maria Graham, *Journal of a Residence in Chile, during the year 1822* (London, 1824), p. 131.

[3] *British Consular Reports,* p. 94, n. 1. See also, for the growth of trade, Claudio Véliz, *Historia de la Marina Mercante de Chile* (Santiago, 1961), pp. 24–41.

[4] J. A. Gibbs, *The History of Antony and Dorothea Gibbs and of their Contemporary Relatives, including the history of the origin and early years of the House of Antony Gibbs and Sons* (London, 1922), pp. 354, 393, 395. Antony Gibbs & Sons had long had friends and correspondents in Lima.

[5] *Letters on South America,* iii, 214, 231–2.

go on there with her cargo.[1] It was not, however, till July that San Martín entered Lima, and not till April 1822 that Robertson left Chile for Peru,[2] to remain there for fifteen months.

There are a few glimpses only to be had of the Robertsons' operations at this time: of William, at Buenos Aires, investing in the public funds and in the stock of the new Bank of Buenos Aires, and persuading his grandfather to do likewise;[3] of John, at Lima, contracting to supply provisions to Callao,[4] and helping, with 'great talent', to fit out a military expedition against the royalist troops in the interior of the country.[5] In August 1823, however, at his own request, he was appointed commercial agent in England for the government of Peru,[6] part of his duties, in that capacity, being to superintend the affairs of the Peruvian loan recently floated in London. And in January 1824, William, on behalf of John Parish Robertson & Co., and in association with a Buenos Aires merchant, Félix Castro, and three other merchant houses, contracted with the government of Buenos Aires Province to negotiate a loan of £1,000,000 in Europe at a price of not less than 70 per cent, the government to receive £700,000 at its absolute disposal, and the contractors a premium of 1 per cent. Substantial sums from the general revenues of the province were to be allocated to the payment of interest and principal. In return for an advance of $250,000 the contractors were to enjoy all profits over the agreed minimum price. John Parish Robertson and Félix Castro were authorized to raise the loan in Europe, and they were directed to employ the House of Baring if possible.[7] 'If you undertake the management of the business,' wrote William to the Barings, 'I look for unqualified success.'[8]

The Barings, to their subsequent regret, agreed. A British

[1] J. P. Robertson to John Parish, Santiago, 17 April 1821, Paroissien Papers, Essex Record Office; *Liberation in South America*, p. 92.
[2] J. P. Robertson to James Paroissien, Valparaiso, 18 April 1822, Paroissien Papers.
[3] W. P. Robertson to John Parish, 11 June, 25 July 1823, F.O. 6/1; *British Consular Reports*, p. 23, n. 4.
[4] W. P. Robertson to John Parish, 11 June 1823, F.O. 6/1. William adds that eight ships were on their way to John's consignment with goods to the value of $600,000.
[5] The Santa Cruz expedition. General William Miller to James Paroissien, 29 Nov. 1823, Paroissien Papers.
[6] *Liberation in South America*, pp. 128–9.
[7] Loan Contract, 16 Jan. 1824, Public Archives of Canada, Baring Papers, A. Letters Received, 3. j, Agents and Correspondents, Buenos Ayres, 1824–7; Robertsons to Barings, 8 Jan., 8 Mar. 1824, *ibid*.
[8] W. P. Robertson to S. C. Holland, 26 Apr. 1824, *ibid*.

consul-general, Woodbine Parish (no relation of the Parish Robertsons), had lately been sent to Buenos Aires – just as other consular officials, much to the satisfaction of the London, Liverpool, and Manchester merchants, had also been sent to Montevideo, Chile, and Peru. The provincial government of Buenos Aires had earned a high reputation, which Woodbine Parish, it should be noted, held to be fully justified, during the past three years; and the proposal seemed attractive. Fortunately, the agreement which the Barings signed with Robertson and Castro in July has survived. The loan was to be issued at 85 per cent. Barings were to be given £200,000 worth of stock at the original contract price of 70, and the profits on the remaining £800,000 would go to Robertson and Castro. The government of Buenos Aires Province, that is to say, would receive a nominal £700,000; Barings would make £30,000, together with a commission of 1 per cent on the sale of stock and on the annual amount of the sinking fund and dividends; and Robertson and Castro would receive £120,000.[1] It is a substantial sum, and, not surprisingly, a Barings' representative, at a later date, thought that Robertson and Castro had indeed 'realized pretty pickings'.[2]

So much for the Buenos Aires loan. The Peruvian loan, with which Robertson was also concerned, had been floated in October 1822 by Thomas Kinder and had had an unhappy history.[3] But in the general atmosphere of euphoria which pervaded the London capital market in 1824 and 1825 Robertson succeeded in rescuing it and even indeed in launching a second loan. Meanwhile, he and his brother had already signed a further contract with the provincial government of Buenos Aires for the settlement of 200 families on a tract of land which the government was to provide in the southern part of the province.[4] And at the time of the great joint-stock company boom and of that mania for speculation in Spanish American mines which McCulloch thought so 'remarkable' and 'disgraceful' an 'era in our commercial history',[5] it is not

[1] J. P. Robertson and Félix Castro to Barings, 25 June 1824; Agreement between Baring Bros., John Parish Robertson and Félix Castro, 26 July 1824, Baring Papers (Canada), A.3.j.

[2] Ferns, op. cit., p. 311.

[3] I have described this in detail in my Liberation in South America, pp. 122 ff.

[4] The contract, dated 11 March 1824, is printed in James Dodds, Records of the Scottish Settlers in the River Plate and their Churches (Buenos Aires, 1897), pp. 21–3.

[5] J. R. McCulloch, A Dictionary, Practical, Theoretical, and Historical, of Commerce and Commercial Navigation (2 vols., Philadelphia, 1840), ii, 187–8.

surprising to find John Parish Robertson becoming in January 1825 a director of the Pasco Peruvian Mining Company and promoting in June the Famatina Mining Company, with a commission to himself of 5 per cent on the capital raised.[1]

But these golden days were quickly ended. Peru suspended interest payments on its loans in October 1825, and Robertson, who was heavily involved in Peruvian bills, found himself hard pressed to meet drafts from his Lima house of Cochran and Robertson.[2] The Famatina Mining Company turned out to lay claim to the same mines as another company formed six months earlier; the miners it sent out were shipwrecked in the Río de la Plata and then temporarily detained at Montevideo as the result of the outbreak of war between Buenos Aires and Brazil;[3] and nothing whatever resulted from the company's plans. The Pasco Peruvian Mining Company was equally unfortunate. It paid dearly for its mines in the first place, and then, after sending out miners, engineers, and machinery, had to sell the equipment it had bought in order to meet its expenses.[4] These disasters were followed by the suspension of payments on the Buenos Aires loan in July 1827, and by the financial collapse of Thomas Kinder, with whom Robertson had been closely linked in his Peruvian operations.[5] Finally, the colonization scheme failed. The first emigrants sailed from Leith in May 1825. They came from the 'west and south of Scotland, and were chosen with a view at once to their agricultural skill and their religious and moral character'. But they were settled, not on land provided by the government, but on land which the Robertsons had themselves decided to buy at Monte Grande, no great distance from Buenos Aires, and though by 1828 the colony consisted of over 500 persons and was doing fairly well, it had cost the Robertsons some £60,000 and their funds were exhausted.[6]

By this time both the Lima house and the Buenos Aires house

[1] Henry English, *A General Guide to the Companies formed for Working Foreign Mines* . . . (London, 1825). See also his *A Complete View of the Joint Stock Companies, formed during the years 1824 and 1825* (London, 1827).

[2] J. P. Robertson to Alexander Baring, 2 Nov. 1825; to S. C. Holland, 9 Nov. 1825, Baring Papers (Canada), A.3.j. See also C. M. Ricketts to Canning, 10 June 1827, enclosure, F.O. 61/11.

[3] W. P. Robertson to Woodbine Parish, Jan. 1825, F.O. 118/2.

[4] C. M. Ricketts to Canning, 16 Sept. 1826, F.O. 61/8; 14 May 1827, F.O. 61/11.

[5] J. P. Robertson to Barings, 14 Dec. 1827, Baring Papers (London), H.C. 4.1.3.11.

[6] Dodds, *op. cit.*, pp. 3, 6–62. See also Ferns, *op. cit.*, pp. 138–40.

had been forced into liquidation.[1] John Parish Robertson, who had gone out to Buenos Aires to supervise the Monte Grande colony and to straighten out his affairs as best he could, returned to England in 1829 a comparatively ruined man. At the age of 37 he entered himself as a pensioner at Corpus Christi College, Cambridge, matriculated in the Lent Term of 1830, and headed Class 3 of the Junior Sophs in 1831.[2] Leaving Cambridge without taking a degree, he settled down to a journalistic and literary life, producing in collaboration with his brother his *Letters on Paraguay* and his *Letters on South America*. He died at Calais in 1843.[3]

In February 1824, her colonies lost, Spain at last permitted foreigners to trade with them.[4] By this time, according to contemporary estimates, between eighty and a hundred British commercial houses were established in Spanish American cities.[5] In Peru, where the struggle between royalists and patriots still continued, there were some sixteen British establishments or agencies in Arequipa alone in September 1824;[6] and Peru had been flooded with British goods.[7] Britain and British India supplied a major part of the wants of Chile;[8] and at Buenos Aires, where the British community now numbered 3,000, half the public debt and the best part of the most valuable property were allegedly in British hands.[9] Already in 1822 four Latin American loans had been floated in London, including, alas, a loan to the almost wholly fictitious Kingdom of Poyais in Central America. Five more were floated in 1824, when petition after petition, from London, Liverpool, Manchester, Birmingham, Leeds, was presented to parliament for British recognition of the new Spanish American states, and five

[1] J. P. Robertson to Barings, 6 June 1827, Baring Papers (Canada), A.3.j; 14 Dec. 1827, Baring Papers (London), H.C. 4.1.3.11.

[2] Corpus Christi College Cambridge Muniments, Cautions Book, 1781–1860; Register, 1822–44; Buttery Book, 1826–35; Examinations Book, 1821–. I am indebted for these references to Professor C. R. Cheney.

[3] William Parish Robertson left South America in 1834, became head clerk of Antony Gibbs & Sons, London, in 1839, consul for Peru in London in 1845 and consul-general for Ecuador in 1847. He visited Mexico on behalf of the Mexican bondholders in 1849 and is said to have died at Valparaiso in 1861.

[4] Decree of 4 Feb. 1824. *British and Foreign State Papers* (London, 1825–), xi, 864.

[5] Sundry British Merchants to Canning, 21 July 1823, F.O. 72/283; Sir James Mackintosh, 15 June 1824, *Parliamentary Debates*, N.S. xi, 1381.

[6] Memorandum on Arequipa, by Thomas Rowcroft, 18 Sept. 1824, F.O. 61/3.

[7] *Cf. British Consular Reports,* pp. 93, n. 2, 117, 124, 129–30.

[8] *Ibid.,* pp. 92–8.   [9] *Ibid.,* pp. 26, n. 2, 23, n. 4.

again in 1825, at a time when the process of recognition, through the negotiation of commercial treaties in effect dictated by Canning, had been begun. Of the joint-stock companies formed in these years, moreover, it was the Latin American enterprises, more particularly the Latin American mining companies, some twenty-six in all, which were, as the American minister in London observed, 'the great objects of attention with monied men'.[1]

What were the results? The 'Mexican and South American mining subscriptions, with only one or two exceptions,' wrote Tooke, 'proved to be a total loss of the capital paid.'[2] But the capital paid, by the end of 1826, was only a seventh of the authorized capital. Of the two companies with which John Parish Robertson was associated, the Famatina Mining Company and the Pasco Peruvian Mining Company, one had a paid up capital of £50,000, the other of £150,000. C. M. Ricketts, the British consul-general in Peru in 1826, thought that with prudence, skill, capital, and industry the mines of Peru and Bolivia could not fail to be restored to operation.[3] But prudence was not the distinguishing quality of the boards of directors in London, nor, perhaps, where they existed, of the managers in South America, and sums of the order of £150,000 turned out to be sufficient only to meet the original capital outlay and the costs of transportation to the mines and of preliminary works in difficult and disturbed conditions. Since the financial panic which swept the money market at the end of 1825 generally precluded the companies from making further calls upon their shareholders, in Peruvian and Bolivian mines, at any rate, there was no large investment of British capital to replace Spanish capital.

The loans, to quote Tooke again, also entailed a severe loss upon the subscribers, and heavy liabilities, it may be added, upon the borrowers. Their nominal value was over £21,000,000. But the amounts realized were very much less and the sums credited to the Latin American states very much smaller still.[4] For a debt of

---

[1] J. F. Rippy, *British Investments in Latin America, 1822–1949* (Minneapolis, 1959), pp. 17–25; L. H. Jenks, *The Migration of British Capital to 1875* (London, 1938), pp. 46–9; Manning, *Diplomatic Correspondence*, iii, 1529.

[2] *History of Prices*, ii, 159.

[3] *British Consular Reports*, p. 118. See also C. M. Ricketts to Canning, 16 Sept. 1826, F.O. 61/8.

[4] Under £17,000,000 and perhaps £12,000,000 respectively. Rippy, *op. cit.,* pp. 20–2.

£1,000,000, for example, the province of Buenos Aires received less than £600,000.[1] Most of this was spent, not on the objects originally intended, but on the prosecution of a war with Brazil. The loans, indeed, were employed for the most part in meeting previous obligations to British merchants and others and in current military and naval expenditures. Only small proportions were turned to productive purposes, and every government had ceased to pay interest charges by the end of 1827.

Whoever profited from the loans – the Robertsons, for example, and other financial agents – it was not the original investors; and it may be questioned also whether the Latin American states themselves gained immediately more than they lost eventually, in credit and reputation. The assistance which they had earlier derived, in arms, provisions, and supplies, from British and American merchants was solid enough. The European merchants, said John Miller, in the memoirs of his brother, General William Miller, were apt to assume 'rather more credit than they were entitled to, from the circumstances of their happening to be the consignees of a few old ships, and of second-hand slops and stores'.[2] Perhaps they did, though I do not know what the evidence is for saying so. But, 'second-hand slops and stores' or not, without the resources which were made available through British and foreign trade in general victory would have been far harder to achieve. In this sense the opening of the ports of the continent to the trade of the world was an event of decisive importance. But the benefits which it brought were not unmixed. The competition of foreign goods bore hardly, for example, on the small domestic producers of coarse cotton fabrics or wines. A silver-producing region, such as Peru, found itself drained of bullion in exchange for consumer goods and weapons of war. Bullion to the value of nearly $27,000,000 was shipped from Lima in British men-of-war alone between 1819 and 1825,[3] though some of this was refugee capital; and it was estimated that the 'commercial capital' of the country in 1826 was only a fifteenth of what it had been in 1800.[4] Agricultural areas, on the other hand, such as the Río de la Plata and Chile,

---

[1] Woodbine Parish, *Buenos Ayres and the Provinces of the Río de la Plata* (2nd ed., London, 1852), p. 373; H. E. Peters, *The Foreign Debt of the Argentine Republic* (Baltimore, 1934), pp. 13–14, 16.

[2] John Miller, *Memoirs of General Miller, in the service of the Republic of Peru* (2 vols., London, 1828), ii, 221.

[3] See the table in *British Consular Reports*, p. 195.   [4] *Ibid.*, p. 114.

responded immediately to the new currents of foreign trade, the increased demand, and the larger markets for their products. Buenos Aires above all, as the gateway between Europe and the plains, showed the signs of social and economic change.

The British government, in its negotiations both with Spain and with Spanish America after the close of the Napoleonic wars, sought no exclusive trading privileges for itself, however warmly these might have been welcomed by some of the British merchants. Nor, when independence had been won, did it propose to act as a debt-collecting agency on behalf of distressed British subjects. The complaints which it received were both loud and long. But, as the British consul-general in Peru observed of the claims made against the Peruvian government, the merchants had adventured 'in a game of lottery'. They had chosen to 'embark in speculations at a period of eminent risk'; sometimes they had 'assisted the royalists and at other times the patriots: and in all instances they were alone influenced by their own temporary advantage'.[1] John Miller said much the same thing. As 'men of business', he observed, 'these gentlemen were right to make the most of the market and their commodities; but then their claims to ardent patriotism, unmixed with views of profit, must be disallowed. It is true that many of them displayed that liberality of feeling which is generally found to exist in the commercial world; but in this case their sympathies and their interests went hand in hand. When these became unhappily at variance, poor Sympathy often went to the wall. . . . Thus, speaking of the merchants as a body, and within the sphere of their counting-houses, their pretensions to disinterested liberalism fall to the ground.' Nevertheless, added Miller, 'speaking of them individually, a very great many may be instanced as having given unequivocal proofs of their zeal and adherence to the cause of independence'.[2] It is a reasonable verdict.

---

[1] C. M. Ricketts to Canning, 10 June 1827, F.O. 61/11.
[2] *Op. cit.*, ii, 221–2.

B*

8

Anglo-American Rivalries and Spanish American Emancipation*

From the beginning of the revolutionary movement in Spanish America, wrote Sir Charles Webster, nearly thirty years ago, the influence of Great Britain was established 'by two main agencies – her trade and her fleet'.[1]

Only rarely, in the eighteenth century, had a British vessel-of-war appeared in Spanish American waters except with hostile intent. The list of British naval officers – Anson, Vernon, Knowles Pocock, Nelson, Harvey – who commanded expeditions against one or another Spanish American port on the mainland or in the islands is long and distinguished; and the tale of these expeditions was completed only in the nineteenth century with the invasions of the Río de la Plata in 1806 and 1807.[2] But in the winter of 1807–8, while Napoleon's armies were overrunning Portugal, ships of the Royal Navy escorted the Portuguese royal family and the Portuguese fleet from Lisbon to Rio de Janeiro; and there, in May 1808, the British South American naval station was established. The primary purpose of the squadron so based was to patrol the South Atlantic and to defend Brazilian shores from French attack.[3] But when Spain, too, fell under the Napoleonic

* [Presidential Address to the Royal Historical Society, December 1965. *Transactions of the Royal Historical Society*, 5th Series, xvi (1966), 131–56.]

[1] Sir Charles K. Webster, *Britain and the Independence of Latin America, 1812–1830. Select Documents from the Foreign Office Archives* (2 vols., London, 1938), i, 11.

[2] Britain, the future Baron Stuart de Rothesay told the Foreign Office in 1809, was only 'known in South America by the exercise of our power to the disadvantage of the inhabitants, by a long succession of injurious and predatory acts, by unsuccessful expeditions against the vulnerable parts of their coast'. Communication from Mr C. Stuart on the Spanish Colonies in South America, 15 Sept. 1809, P[ublic] R[ecord] O[ffice], F[oreign] O[ffice Records] 72/90.

[3] W. W. Pole to Sir William Sidney Smith, 25 Jan. 1808, G. S. Graham and R. A. Humphreys, *The Navy and South America, 1807–1823. Correspondence of the Commanders-in-Chief on the South American Station* (London, Navy Records Society, 1962), Doc. 2.

harrow and, in one of the great diplomatic revolutions of modern times, was converted, in July 1808, from an enemy to an ally of England, the squadron's activities were extended. As the Leeward Islands and Jamaica squadrons already guarded the sea-lanes of the Caribbean, so now, from the South American station, ships were regularly stationed in the Río de la Plata; after the outbreak of the Anglo-American war of 1812 they were sent round the Horn, principally at first for the protection of the southern whale fishery, not from French but from American aggression;[1] and thereafter the South American squadron was a two-ocean squadron, operating both in the Atlantic and in the Pacific.

The squadron was disbanded in 1815 (after the ratification of the Treaty of Ghent),[2] only a couple of detached ships remaining in the Río de la Plata and the Pacific. But it was soon, and wisely, re-established.[3] It was reinforced in 1817, partly 'to keep up a proper impression in our favour', as the first lord of the Admiralty put it,[4] and when, at the end of 1819, Commodore Sir Thomas Hardy – Nelson's Hardy – took over its command from Commodore William Bowles, it was a more formidable force than the Mediterranean fleet at the same period.[5] Its ships, in the words of Captain Basil Hall, who served under Hardy, were 'distributed at those points where the presence of a British naval authority was most essentially required, namely, Rio de Janeiro in Brazil; Buenos Ayres in the River Plate; Valparaiso in Chili; Lima in Peru; and San Blas on the coast of Mexico',[6] and not only did its officers provide a stream of information for the Admiralty and the Foreign Office, but – to quote Hall again – 'the whole of the consulate affairs fell to their charge, every dispute which arose between

[1] Manley Dixon to J. W. Croker 30 April, 11, 21 June, 1813, *ibid.*, Docs. 62, 68, 69.

[2] Croker to Dixon, 27 Dec. 1814, Dixon to Croker, 28 April 1815, *ibid.*, Docs. 100, 105.

[3] *Ibid.*, p. 158.

[4] Melville to Bathurst, 11 Aug. 1817, National Library of Scotland, Melville MSS. 3835. I am indebted for this reference to Dr C. J. Bartlett.

[5] Hardy to Croker, 27 Oct. 1819, Graham and Humphreys, *op. cit.*, Doc. 168; C. J. Bartlett, *Great Britain and Sea Power, 1815-1853* (Oxford, 1963), pp. 64-5. The squadron had been considerably reduced by the end of September 1822, but was again reinforced in 1823, and at the end of 1824 consisted of two ships of the line, six frigates and three sloops.

[6] Basil Hall, *Extracts from a Journal, written on the Coasts of Chili, Peru, and Mexico, in the years 1820, 1821, 1822* (2 vols., 3rd ed., Edinburgh, 1824), i, 42. The squadron only operated 'south of the line' in the Atlantic.

British subjects and the local governments was necessarily carried on through them'.[1] They had been ordered to take no part in political disputes, nor were they to assist Spaniard against Spaniard; but Britons, as Admiral de Courcy had told his officers, they were to defend against the world.[2] These war-time instructions still held in peace, when the naval officers were mainly concerned with the protection of British trade and British property. Both in war and peace, however, they acted on occasion as diplomats as well as consuls, serving as intermediaries not only between British subjects and the old or newly-constituted authorities in Spanish America but also between patriots and loyalists.

Just as few British naval vessels, before 1808, had approached the mainland of Spanish America except with hostile intent, so also few British merchantmen, transports or whalers anchored off its coasts or touched at one of its ports, at any time between the suspension in 1738 of the English *asiento* for the supply of slaves to Spanish America and the invasions of the Río de la Plata in 1806–7, unless in distress or for the purposes of contraband trade.[3] The contraband trade, through the free ports in the West Indies and through Lisbon, Rio de Janeiro and the Río de la Plata, had been an important branch of British commerce in the eighteenth century;[4] it was still important in the early nineteenth century. William Jacob, who, as an economist and a merchant with great experience of the Spanish and Spanish American trades, had long argued in favour of a 'free intercourse with Spanish America', pointed out in 1806 that even in the middle of an Anglo-Spanish war British goods were bought with avidity in Spanish America. The 'free ports in the West Indies, the neutrals, and some British

[1] *Ibid.*, i, 43.
[2] De Courcy to Croker, 29 Sept. 1810, Graham and Humphreys, *op. cit.*, Doc. 34.
[3] But slavers were permitted to enter specified ports in the West Indies and on the Main after 1789, and this privilege was extended to Cartagena and the Río de la Plata in 1791 and to certain Pacific ports later. See J. F. King, 'Evolution of the Free Slave Trade Principle in Spanish Colonial Administration', *Hispanic American Historical Review*, xxii (1942), 50 ff.
[4] *Cf.* Allan Christelow, 'Great Britain and the Trades from Cadiz and Lisbon to Spanish America and Brazil, 1759–1783', *ibid.*, xxvii (1947), 2–29, and D. B. Goebel, 'British Trade to the Spanish Colonies, 1796–1823', *American Historical Review*, xliii (1938), 288–320, and, for the free port system, extended after 1787 from Jamaica and Dominica to other strategic points in the West Indies, Frances Armytage, *The Free Port System in the British West Indies. A study in commercial policy, 1766–1822* (London, 1953).

ships', he observed, were 'channels of conveyance', so far as they operated, 'highly beneficial'.[1] But most of the trade, as he also observed, was contraband. Contraband meant risk, high prices and limited sales; and what British merchants and manufacturers had increasingly demanded were safer channels, quicker returns and larger sales. They wanted, in short, complete freedom of access to Spanish American markets and sources of supply; and in 1806–7, with Sir Home Popham's filibustering expedition against Buenos Aires and the subsequent capture of Montevideo, they seemed about to attain it, at least in the Río de la Plata.

But Buenos Aires was reconquered and Montevideo lost. It needed the Napoleonic invasions of Portugal and Spain to open the continent to the trade of the world. In 1808 the Portuguese crown in exile threw open the ports of Brazil, and between 1808 and 1822 impecunious colonial governors or new revolutionary authorities threw open the ports of Spanish America. British merchants, brokers and adventurers were quick to take advantage. British firms and agencies were established in the ports and in the capitals. British manufactures flooded the markets. And by the time Spain herself, in 1824, had acknowledged that the age of monopoly was past, there were few parts of Spanish America with which London, Liverpool and Glasgow merchants had not established some connexion.[2]

These pioneers of British economic enterprise in Spanish America were, like the naval officers, important channels of influence and information.[3] But they were not the only channels. British soldiers, for example, served in the revolutionary armies and British sailors in the revolutionary navies, providing generals and admirals as well as many officers of lesser rank. The Treasury, deeply interested in the bullion supply, had its own financial representatives in Mexico and sometimes elsewhere. It had bought

[1] Memorial on the Advantages to be obtained by Great Britain from a Free Intercourse with Spanish America, 14 Feb. 1806 [?], F.O. 72/90. See also his Plan for Occupying Spanish America . . . , 26 Oct. 1804, PRO, Chatham Papers, 30/8/345. Jacob was M.P. for Rye 1808–12, and was made an FRS in 1807.

[2] See, on this paragraph, Goebel, *op. cit.,* and, above, 'British Merchants and South American Independence', pp. 106–29.

[3] Thus, Alexander Mackinnon, who arrived at Montevideo on 1 June 1809 as supercargo and part owner of the *Richard* of London, and became president of the committee of British merchants in Buenos Aires early in 1810, corresponded regularly with the Foreign Office till June 1811. Robert Staples (see below, p. 134) and the Parish Robertson brothers are further examples.

dollars at Vera Cruz under licence from the Spanish crown even when Spain and Britain were at war,[1] and, peace made, it was so misguided in 1809 as to send out Lord Cochrane's disreputable uncle, Andrew Cochrane Johnstone, as its purchasing agent.[2] It was still regretting this mistake, and trying to recoup its losses, long after Johnstone had been dismissed and replaced by two Irishmen, Thomas and Matthew Murphy, and later still by Charles Parke and James Dick of Jamaica.[3] Finally, at the embassy in Rio de Janeiro, where Lord Strangford exercised an almost viceregal influence from 1808 to 1815, the Foreign Office maintained one very important diplomatic post. It had a listening post, also, at Havana, where Henry T. Kilbee served as a highly informative member of the mixed commission for the regulation of the slave trade set up under the Anglo-Spanish Convention of 1817. And it tried, in 1811, to establish a consul, one Robert Ponsonby Staples, of the Belfast firm of Montgomery, Staples and Co., 'on the banks of the Río de la Plata'. But the regency in Spain declined to grant an exequatur to Staples and the government of Buenos Aires refused to recognize him.[4] Not, indeed, till many years later, at the end of 1823, were the first British consuls and commissioners of enquiry sent to Spanish America.

But the United States also had a navy. It too had a merchant fleet. American merchants, like British merchants, provided arms and supplies to Spanish American insurgents. American soldiers and sailors, like British soldiers and sailors, though in far fewer

[1] Spencer Perceval to Canning, 6 Mar. 1809; William Huskisson to George Hammond, 19 July 1809, F.O. 72/90. *Cf.* Armytage, *op. cit.*, pp. 110–11, 118–19.

[2] G. Harrison to Hon. A. C. Johnstone, 17 March 1809, Secret, F.O. 72/90.

[3] The amount of silver obtained by direct purchase was never large. W. F. Cody, 'British Interest in the Independence of Mexico, 1808–1827', an unpublished doctoral thesis of the University of London (1954), p. 70, gives a figure of under $11 million for the years 1810 to 1820.

[4] The appointment of Staples was dated 16 March 1811. Having been refused recognition, he returned to England in June 1812 and was given £1,200 to compensate him for losses and expenses. He again went to Buenos Aires in 1813 to prosecute certain mercantile speculations of his own and also to procure bullion for the Treasury, and this time stayed there. On his own responsibility he acceded in 1816 to the request of the British merchants in the city to represent them in an official manner and even assumed the title of consul, which he continued to employ until an official rebuke reached him in 1819. See Memorandum respecting Mr Staples and the Consulship of Buenos Aires, F.O. 6/1; Staples to Planta, 6 Dec. 1825, F.O. 6/10; and, for further details of his career, my *British Consular Reports on the Trade and Politics of Latin America, 1824–1826* (Royal Historical Society, Camden Third Series, lxiii, London, 1940), p. 331, note 2, hereinafter cited as *B.C.R.*

numbers, fought in the revolutionary armies and navies.[1] And American consuls and commissioners of enquiry were sent to Spanish America at a far earlier date than were British.

The navy, it is true, on the eve of the war of 1812, was little more than 'a scratch force of fighting ships'.[2] And though, after the war, it provided a limited protection to American commerce in Spanish American waters, no permanent naval patrol was established in the South Pacific until 1821 or in the South Atlantic till 1826.[3] But whatever the neglect of the navy as an effective fighting force both before and after the war of 1812, there could be no doubts about the strength of the merchant marine. And just as the merchant marine had steadily expanded during the Napoleonic wars,[4] so also, by contraband trade on the one hand and through concessions granted to neutral traders by local regulation or imperial decree on the other, had American trade with Spanish America. Without this trade Cuba might have starved.[5] But not in the Caribbean only, where the volume of trade was largest, did Britons watch with jealous eyes what William Jacob called 'the rapid growth of the navigation of our former fellow subjects but now commercial rivals';[6] American ships sailed southwards to the Río de la Plata; they rounded the Horn; they sailed to the north-west coast and to Canton, and they touched at Pacific ports on their way.[7] Jefferson's famous embargo and the war of

[1] *Cf.* W. F. Neumann, 'United States Aid to the Chilean Wars of Independence', *Hispanic American Historical Review*, xxvii (1947), 204–19, and C. L. Chandler, *Inter-American Acquaintances* (Sewanee, Tennessee, 1915).

[2] G. S. Graham, *Empire of the North Atlantic. The maritime struggle for North America* (Toronto, 1950), p. 242.

[3] A. P. Whitaker, *The United States and the Independence of Latin America, 1800–1830* (Baltimore, 1941), pp. 279, 298–9.

[4] 558,000 tons in 1802, 981,000 tons at the end of 1812. Bradford Perkins, *Prologue to War: England and the United States, 1805–1812* (Berkeley and Los Angeles, 1961), p. 29.

[5] *Cf.* R. F. Nichols, 'Trade Relations and the Establishment of the United States Consulates in Spanish America, 1779–1809', *Hispanic American Historical Review*, xiii (1933), 289–313; Goebel, *op. cit.*, pp. 295–9.

[6] See above, p. 133, n. 1.

[7] R. F. Nichols, *Advance Agents of American Destiny* (Philadelphia, 1956), pp. 223–5, gives statistics of the Spanish West Indian trade with the United States. *Cf.* also C. L. Chandler, 'United States Merchant Ships in the Rio de la Plata (1801–8) as shown by Early Newspapers', *Hispanic American Historical Review*, ii (1919), 26–54; Eugenio Pereira Salas, *Buques norte-americanos en Chile a fines de la era colonial (1788–1810)* (Prensas de la Universidad de Chile, 1936); Whitaker, *op. cit.*, pp. 11–16; and Harry Bernstein, *Origins of Inter-American Interest, 1700–1812* (Philadelphia, 1945), pp. 33–42.

1812 alike restricted this rising commerce. But its recovery from the effects first of the one and then of the other, despite diversionary interests elsewhere, is some index of the vigour of American enterprise and initiative.

To protect its commerce and assist its traders the United States had long sought to establish consuls or consular agents in Cuba and elsewhere in the Caribbean;[1] and with the beginnings of the revolutionary movements in South America in 1810 'agents for commerce and seamen' were at once appointed not only in Venezuela and the Río de la Plata but in Mexico also. These were Robert Lowry of Baltimore, Joel Poinsett of Charleston, South Carolina, and William Shaler, an adventurous sailor from Bridgeport, Connecticut. Shaler got no further than Cuba, where he remained for more than a twelve-month.[2] Lowry, who served intermittently in Venezuela for many years, early came to fear that Britain intended to seize the province of Guayana,[3] and, naturally resenting the preferential rates which were at this time accorded to British shipping,[4] was reported in 1812 to be 'something more than industrious in circulating reports unfavourable to the British'.[5] Of Poinsett it has been said that 'his mind had been conditioned by an unquenchable loyalty to his native land and an unquestioned antipathy for things English'.[6] His stay in Buenos Aires was brief. 'He has lived much in France,' wrote a British merchant, 'and has assumed most of their insinuating, frivolous manners and customs. . . . After infusing his political poison here, he named a vice-consul, also gifted with propaganda faculties, and he is gone to Chile himself.'[7] There he remained, with the title of consul-general, for nearly two years, was 'busy as a fiend', Captain Peter Heywood reported, in 'contaminating the whole population on that side of the continent' (by which Heywood

[1] At Cuba, for example, as early as 1797 and at La Guaira in 1800.

[2] His career is described in Nichols, *Advance Agents,* pp. 50–156.

[3] W. R. Manning, ed., *Diplomatic Correspondence of the United States concerning the Independence of the Latin-American Nations* (3 vols., New York, 1925), ii, 1153.

[4] Manning, *op. cit.,* ii, 1151, 1156; Luis López Méndez to Castlereagh, 12 Oct. 1812, F.O. 72/157, that duties had been reduced in favour of Great Britain as a result of an agreement between the supreme junta and the governor of Curaçao.

[5] Gregor MacGregor to Spencer Perceval, Caracas, 18 Jan. 1812, F.O. 72/171.

[6] H. F. Peterson, *Argentina and the United States, 1810–1960* (New York, 1964), p. 17. There is more than one biography of Poinsett. See J. F. Rippy, *Joel R. Poinsett, Versatile American* (Durham, N.C., 1935).

[7] Alexander Mackinnon to Strangford, 31 March 1812, F.O. 72/156. *Cf.* Staples to Castlereagh, 30 July 1812, F.O. 72/157.

meant spreading reports hostile to Britain),[1] conducted himself with much indiscretion, and finally left the country having done more, as events turned out, to damage American than British prestige.

Such were the beginnings of the American consular service in South America. Comparatively few North American merchants settled in Spanish American cities.[2] But after 1810 the State Department was fairly regularly represented by consuls or consular agents, though they were not always most suitably chosen. A commission of enquiry was dispatched to the Río de la Plata in 1817, but the commissioners' reports were contradictory and the incidental horticultural and botanical results of the expedition were more important than the political.[3] Finally, the United States, like Britain, had early accredited a diplomatic representative to the Portuguese court in Brazil, and in 1823 it appointed diplomatic representatives in Spanish America also.

Not all these early American consuls, envoys and diplomats were so strongly inimical to Britain as was Poinsett. When Richard Anderson, the first American minister to Colombia, met Charles McNeal, the acting American consul at Cartagena, he noted that McNeal was the first American he had ever seen who was 'British in his feelings'.[4] But McNeal was the exception. Most American agents shared in some degree a distrust, dislike and jealousy of Britain, natural enough, perhaps, in the circumstances of the times. After all, the sons of the men who fought in the war of independence fought in the war of 1812. And these feelings were not all on one side. 'I don't like Americans;' says Tom Cringle in *Tom Cringle's Log*; 'I never did, and never shall like them; I have seldom met with an American gentleman, in the large and complete sense of the term. I have no wish to eat with

[1] Heywood to Melville, 4 Dec. 1812, F.O. 72/152, and, for a somewhat different version, Edward Tagart, *A Memoir of the late Captain Peter Heywood, R.N.* . . . (London, 1832), pp. 245–61. See also the comments of Captain Bowles in Graham and Humphreys, *op. cit.*, pp. 113, 117.

[2] See, however, for two examples, Benjamin Keen, *David Curtis DeForest and the Revolution of Buenos Aires* (New Haven, 1947), and Eugenio Pereira Salas, *Henry Hill, Comerciante, Vice-Consul y Misionero* (Santiago de Chile, 1940).

[3] *Cf.* Watt Stewart, 'The South American Commission 1817–1818', *Hispanic American Historical Review*, ix (1929), 31–59, and W. D. Rasmussen, 'Diplomats and Plant Collectors: the South American Commission, 1817–1818', *Agricultural History*, xxix (1955), 22–31.

[4] 20 April 1825. Alfred Tischendorf and E. Taylor Parks, eds., *The Diary and Journal of Richard Clough Anderson, Jr., 1814–1826* (Durham, N.C., 1964), p. 202.

them, drink with them, deal with, or consort with them in any way; but,' he adds, 'let me tell the whole truth, *nor fight* with them, were it not for the laurels to be acquired, by overcoming an enemy so brave, determined, and alert, and every way so worthy of one's steel, as they have always proved.'[1] That, at least, was a generous qualification, and it would have been well, perhaps, if all Englishmen – and Scotsmen – had shown something of its spirit.

At the Foreign Office neither Castlereagh nor Canning allowed animosities such as these to affect the language of diplomacy, and Richard Rush, who succeeded John Quincy Adams as American minister in London in 1817, so successfully concealed his dislike of England that he has even been mistaken for an Anglophil. Whatever other problems, moreover, might threaten to divide Britain and the United States, or to embarrass their relations, once the war of 1812 was ended, there was at least common ground between them in their attitudes to Spanish America. Their official policies were alike cautious, though the reasons for this caution certainly differed. In both countries a growing body of liberal and commercial opinion vigorously favoured the rebels.[2] Both governments found it difficult to restrain the private activities of their peoples in support of the insurgent cause – the recruiting of mercenaries in England, for example, or privateering based on such ports as Baltimore in the United States. But both made genuine efforts to uphold the correct principles of neutrality: American neutrality legislation, indeed, preceded British. Each maintained the right to trade freely with any part of the Spanish American area, and, except for the duplication or near-duplication in Brazil of the special privileges which Britain had enjoyed in Portugal, neither sought exclusive commercial advantages. Finally, neither was prepared to contemplate with indifference the intervention in Spanish America of the European powers, whether on

[1] Michael Scott, *Tom Cringle's Log* (William Blackwood, Edinburgh and London, n.d.), p. 170. *Tom Cringle's Log* was first published in *Blackwood's Magazine* in 1829–33. Scott had lived for many years in Jamaica and the principal scenes of the book are laid there and in the Caribbean generally in 1815 and 1816.

[2] Alongside the speeches of Brougham, Mackintosh and Lansdowne in England and of Clay in the United States the remarks of Sir Oswald Mosley on 9 Feb. 1818 deserve to be remembered: 'He hoped in God that such a separation [of the Spanish colonies from Spain] would take place. It was the interest of mankind that it should: it was particularly the interest of this fine and commercial country, that other countries should be free, and in a condition to reciprocate commercial advantages upon liberal and enlightened principles.' *Parliamentary Debates*, xxxvii, 249.

Spain's behalf or on their own.[1] To this extent, therefore, both upheld not only the principle of the open door but, ultimately, that of self-determination.

But though Britain and the United States thus shared a certain community of purpose, the conflict of interests between them was only thinly veiled. Republics – sometimes confounded with democracies – were admired in America and distrusted in Europe. Castlereagh would have been glad to see Bourbon princes – could the princes have been found – at the head of the new Spanish American states. Canning regarded the preservation of the principle of monarchy in Brazil as a cardinal point in his grand design to link Latin America to Europe – or to England. But to these ideas the United States was resolutely opposed. Neither Castlereagh nor Canning was prepared to contemplate, in Canning's famous words, 'a division of the world into European and American, Republican and Monarchical'.[2] But, in the western hemisphere, it was an American system and an American policy which the United States wished to see predominate. 'There can not be a doubt,' said Clay in 1818, 'that Spanish America, once independent, whatever may be the form of the governments established in its several parts, these governments will be animated by an American feeling, and guided by an American policy. They will obey the laws of the system of the New World, of which they will compose a part, in contradistinction to that of Europe.'[3] Jefferson had expressed the same idea many years earlier; Adams and Monroe were to express it later.[4]

This clash of ideas was not, of course, the only barrier to Anglo-American amity. The two countries held opposing doctrines of maritime and neutral rights, and each wished to win the new states to its own conception.[5] Each, moreover, suspected the territorial

---

[1] For Castlereagh's warning against the use of force see the Foreign Office 'Confidential Memorandum' of Aug. 1817, Webster, *op. cit.,* ii, 352–8, and his *The Foreign Policy of Castlereagh, 1815–1822* (London, 1934), pp. 413–21.

[2] Canning to Hookham Frere, 8 Jan. 1825, G. Festing, *John Hookham Frere and his Friends* (London, 1899), p. 267.

[3] Calvin Colton, ed., *The Works of Henry Clay* . . . (10 vols., New York and London, 1901), vi, 145; C. C. Griffin, *The United States and the Disruption of the Spanish Empire, 1810–1822* (New York, 1937), p. 136.

[4] See, more particularly, A. P. Whitaker, *The Western Hemisphere Idea: its rise and decline* (Ithaca, N.Y., 1954), pp. 28–31, 35–9.

[5] J. F. Rippy, *Rivalry of the United States and Great Britain over Latin America (1808–1830)* (Baltimore, 1929), pp. 109–11, 228–9, 234–5, 238.

ambitions of the other. 'North America,' observed *The Times* in 1820, 'aims at aggrandizement; South America fights for liberty.'[1] And British fears lest the United States, having acquired Florida, should next acquire Cuba, and might even, indeed, in Sir Robert Wilson's words, 'extend her views of aggrandizement to Mexico' and 'push her frontier from the Atlantic to the Pacific Ocean',[2] were matched across the Atlantic by the counter-fears that Britain would take Cuba for herself. The lengths to which suspicion could go were strikingly illustrated by the alarums, on the one hand, of the American representative in Bogotá in 1823 that Britain, by getting possession of Maracaibo and the south bank of the Orinoco, would reduce Colombia to the status of a colony, and by those, on the other, of the American minister in Buenos Aires, three years later, that she intended to establish a protectorate over Uruguay.[3]

Finally, to political rivalry and the struggle for pre-eminence and prestige, there were added also commercial jealousy and the struggle for markets. Brougham had argued in 1808 that the prosperity of the United States benefited Britain: – 'the less she traded with other nations, the less she will trade with ourselves.'[4] But it was a more responsive chord that he struck when, eight years later, he warned the House of Commons of the 'indefatigable activity and vast commercial resources' of the United States and argued that her rising manufactures should be stifled 'in the cradle'.[5] British merchants and their spokesmen constantly expressed their fears lest the United States, by cementing friendly relations with the new Spanish American states, should reap decisive commercial advantages, monopolize the carrying trade, and undersell British goods.[6] And though the commercial classes in general welcomed the announcement in 1822 of American

[1] 8 Jan. 1820.
[2] 3 June 1819. *Parliamentary Debates*, xl, 871–2.
[3] C. S. Todd to J. Q. Adams, Bogotá, 29 March, 17 April 1823, Manning, *op. cit.*, ii, 1248, 1250; John M. Forbes to Clay, 21 June, 3 Aug. 1826, *ibid.*, i, 654, 656. *Cf.* the still more absurd fears of J. G. A. Williamson in Venezuela in 1829, *ibid.*, ii, 1343–4.
[4] Perkins, *Prologue to War*, p. 20.
[5] 9 April 1816. *Parliamentary Debates*, xxxiii, 1099, 1119.
[6] *Cf.* Tierney, 18 May, Wilson, 3 June, Davies, 10 June 1819, *Parliamentary Debates*, xl, 482–3, 859, 1087; Lushington, 11 July 1820, *ibid.*, n.s., ii, 381; Memorial of Merchants, Ship-Owners, Manufacturers and Traders of London, 23 April 1822, *Times*, 30 April 1822; *ibid.*, 3 July 1822.

recognition of Spanish American independence,[1] approbation was mingled with dismay. From now on pressure for British recognition steadily grew.

What substance was there to these rivalries and fears? The 'ideological' differences, if such they may be called, between Britain and the United States, and the struggle for political leadership and prestige, were real enough. They are apparent at every turn. American agents and British agents, but American agents more particularly, were prone to insinuate in Spanish American ears that 'Codlin's the friend, not Short'; and few are likely to dissent from the view of Professor Bemis that 'the Monroe Doctrine and the Polignac Memorandum' became 'rival placards over Latin America competing for the diplomatic allegiance of the new states. . . .'[2]

The suspicions which each country entertained of the other's territorial ambitions were, by contrast, often baseless. So far as British policy was concerned, they were, indeed, wholly baseless. The invasions of the Río de la Plata in 1806–7 were Britain's last attempt at conquest in Spanish America, and even these, as Castlereagh rightly judged, were an aberration.[3] Britain's interests were commercial and political, not imperial. She looked, not to territory, but to trade. She had no wish to annex Maracaibo, or Panama, or the Orinoco, no desire to occupy Cuba,[4] no intention of erecting Uruguay into a 'colony in disguise'.[5] Her colonists in Belize certainly overstepped their ancient limits, in advancing to the west and to the south of Spanish treaty lines. But that was all. And the territory into which the Belize settlers advanced was either unoccupied, or occupied solely by Indians.[6] Nor, apart from the acquisition of the Floridas, did the United States seriously contemplate territorial annexation. The Floridas, indeed, she was

[1] *Cf.* Rush to Adams, 10 June 1822, Manning, *op. cit.,* iii, 1467.

[2] S. F. Bemis, *John Quincy Adams and the Foundations of American Foreign Policy* (New York, 1949), pp. 401–2.

[3] See his memorandum of 1 May 1807. Charles Vane, marquess of Londonderry, *Memoirs and Correspondence of Viscount Castlereagh* (12 vols., London, 1848–53), vii, 314 ff. *Cf.* H. S. Ferns, *Britain and Argentina in the Nineteenth Century* (Oxford, 1960), pp. 47–8.

[4] On the Cuban question see Webster, *Britain and the Independence of Latin America,* i, 34–40; Rippy, *op. cit.,* pp. 78–90; H. W. V. Temperley, *The Foreign Policy of Canning, 1822–1827* (London, 1925), pp. 168–77.

[5] Webster, *op. cit.,* i, 66–71.

[6] See my *Diplomatic History of British Honduras, 1638–1901* (London, 1961), pp. 10–19.

determined to have and she would have liked to obtain Texas also. But though Alexander Hamilton had early suggested that the United States should 'squint' at South America,[1] and though many Americans, John Quincy Adams among them, believed that Cuba must one day form a part of the Union, the movement of American expansion was westwards, into the Mississippi Valley, not southwards, into the Caribbean, and there was little likelihood of its taking both directions at once.

Anglo-American commercial rivalry also was in part unreal. The principal British exports to Spanish America were manufactured goods – cottons, woollens, linens, hardware, glassware, china. The principal American exports were foodstuffs – flour, butter, dried and salted provisions – though to these must be added also household furniture, saddlery, coarse cottons and that miscellaneous collection of articles called 'notions'. At various times the United States built up a considerable provision trade, in the supply of flour, for example, to Cuba, the Río de la Plata and Peru.[2] But it was only the low-priced coarse cottons and linens, known as 'domestics', that directly competed with British goods.[3]

A major part of the United States trade to Spanish America, however, was a re-export trade in European commodities, and British consular officials, in the mid-eighteen-twenties, complained that British manufactures brought down to Spanish America from the United States undersold similar articles imported directly from Great Britain. They gave two reasons for this: first, that under the system of sale by auction prevailing in the United States British manufactures were disposed of in America at ridiculously low prices; and,[4] secondly, that American shippers could obtain more favourable freight and charter rates than could British. British ships freighted for Mexico and Peru, they pointed out, might be forced to sail home in ballast, since specie, the usual return cargo, was almost invariably entrusted to the captains of

[1] Griffin, *op. cit.*, p. 45.

[2] T. S. Hood to Planta, Montevideo, 20 Dec. 1824, F.O. 51/1; Woodbine Parish to Canning, Buenos Aires, 5 Dec. 1824, F.O. 6/5; *B.C.R.*, pp. 36–7, 83, 137; and see above, page 135, note 5.

[3] Parish to Canning, 10 Oct. 1825, F.O. 6/9; Parish to Planta, 5 April 1826, F.O. 6/11; *B.C.R.*, pp. 37, 137–9, 237.

[4] *Cf.* T. Tupper to J. P. Hamilton, La Guaira, 16 Jan. 1824, PRO, B[oard of] T[rade Records], 6/37; *B.C.R.*, p. 276, n. 1. For the auction system in the United States see N. S. Buck, *The Development of the Organisation of Anglo-American Trade, 1800–1850* (New Haven, 1925), pp. 137–41, 147–50, 170.

the Royal Navy.[1] The American shipper, on the other hand, could combine carefully selected consignments to the Río de la Plata and Pacific ports with a voyage to the north-west coast for skins and furs and thence to Canton, picking up, on his return, a cargo of dried beef at Buenos Aires for Havana.[2]

I doubt whether this talk of the undercutting of British goods brought from Britain by British goods brought from the United States is to be taken too seriously. But the predominance of American over British shipping in Spanish American ports in the middle 'twenties was certainly remarkable. It was not only from Cuba, which was the 'main focus' of the Latin American trade of the United States, that the complaint came that the Americans were monopolizing the carrying trade.[3] The same fear was expressed from Mexico.[4] And in 1824 American shipping outstripped British not at Havana and Vera Cruz only, but at the Caribbean ports of La Guaira and Maracaibo also.[5] What is more, it did so in the Río de la Plata;[6] and, in 1825, though more British than American vessels called at the Pacific port of Valparaiso, American tonnage was the greater both there and further north at Callao.[7]

What is the significance of these facts? Cuba, still loyal to Spain, undoubtedly fell into the orbit of the United States; American shipping and American trade provided a major part of its wants. The Atlantic and gulf ports of the United States supplied also a considerable proportion of the British manufactures consumed in

---

[1] *Cf.* C. Mackenzie to Canning, Vera Cruz, 7 Oct. 1824, F.O. 50/7; *B.C.R.*, pp. 129, 314. For silver shipments from Peru see *ibid.,* p. 195.

[2] *Cf.* Parish to Canning, 10 Oct. 1825, F.O. 6/9; *B.C.R.*, pp. 38, n. 4, 139–42, 190–1.

[3] Whitaker, *The United States and the Independence of Latin America,* pp. 127, 130; H. T. Kilbee to Planta, Havana, 7 June 1823, F.O. 72/275; 6 Jan. 1824, F.O. 72/304. British shipping arriving at Havana in 1823 was less than 17,000 tons, American more than 100,000, of which 24,000 were engaged in the carrying trade with the ports of other nations. See also *B.C.R.,* p. 47, n. 2.

[4] *B.C.R.,* p. 314.

[5] T. Tupper to Canning, La Guaira, 10 Aug. 1824, B.T. 6/39; R. Sutherland to Henderson, Maracaibo, 7 Aug. 1824, 1 Jan. 1825, F.O. 135/3; *Cf. B.C.R.*, pp. 261–2, 277, 282. American shipping seems to have been slightly in excess of British at Cartagena also. E. Watts to Canning, Cartagena, 7 Jan. 1825, B.T. 6/40.

[6] Comparative Return of Trade at the Port of Buenos Ayres during the years 1822–7, 1 Dec. 1827, F.O. 354/8; T. S. Hood to Planta, Montevideo, 20 Aug. 1824, F.O. 51/1.

[7] *B.C.R.*, pp. 94, n. 2, 124–5. See also Claudio Véliz, *Historia de la Marina Mercante de Chile* (Santiago, 1961), p. 41.

Mexico and Columbia.[1] But the volume of American shipping in the Río de la Plata was a temporary phenomenon, the result of a demand for American flour on account of local shortages of grain;[2] and in the Río de la Plata the value of American exports lagged far behind that of British.[3] British pre-eminence both there and in the old Portuguese colony of Brazil, itself by far the largest market for British goods in South America,[4] was reflected also on the Pacific sea-board. It was the coasting trade as well as the north-western and China trades that helped to swell the volume of American tonnage at Pacific ports. But already in 1818 an American representative had reported that the British in Chile were 'so much more weighty in commercial houses, numbers, wealth, etc., that the American influence and interest' was 'much diminished',[5] and seven years later the American minister at Santiago confessed that 'our trade with Chile is trifling'.[6] 'The power of England is without a rival in America,' wrote a French agent in Colombia in 1823; 'no fleets but hers are to be seen; her merchandizes are bought almost exclusively; her commercial agents, her clerks and brokers, are everywhere to be met with'.[7] The fleets were the ships and squadrons of the Royal Navy, to whose commanders not only the British merchants but the American agents themselves paid tribute.[8] The commercial agents, clerks and brokers represented the eighty or so British commercial houses which had by now established themselves in Spanish American cities,[9] sometimes with inter-locking directorates, as well as travellers and concession-hunters from Britain. And the merchandises were those products of the loom, the kiln, the forge and the factory so eagerly demanded in Spanish America and so varied and extensive that the British

[1] B.C.R., pp. 276, 281, 313, 314; H. G. Ward, Mexico in 1827 (2 vols., London, 1828), i, 435–7.

[2] Cf. Parish to Canning, 5 Dec. 1824, F.O. 6/5; B.C.R., pp. 36–7.

[3] Woodbine Parish, Buenos Ayres and the Provinces of the Rio de la Plata (2nd ed., London, 1852), p. 361, and see also B.C.R., pp. 35–6.

[4] For exports to Brazil see A. K. Manchester, British Preëminence in Brazil, its rise and decline (Chapel Hill, 1933), p. 207, and B.C.R., p. 348.

[5] Manning, op. cit., ii, 943; D. B. Goebel, 'British-American Rivalry in the Chilean Trade, 1817–1820', Journal of Economic History, ii (1942), 198–9.

[6] H. C. Evans, Chile and its Relations with the United States (Durham, N.C., 1927), p. 40.

[7] G. Mollien, Voyage dans la République de Colombie, en 1823 (2 vols., Paris, 1824), i, 281; English edition (London, 1824), pp. 215–16.

[8] Manning, op. cit., i, 568, iii, 1728, 1734.

[9] Sundry British Merchants to Canning, 21 July 1823, F.O. 72/283.

consul-general in Peru could say in 1826: 'there is scarcely an article of any description of manufacture, with the exception of silk piece goods, which is not supplied from our country.'[1]

It was between American recognition of the new Spanish American states in 1822 and their recognition by Britain in 1825 that Anglo-American rivalry reached its height. Not till December 1824, at the battle of Ayacucho, the Yorktown of South America, did the last Spanish viceroy lay down his arms. But by the time that President Monroe, in March 1822, sent his recognition message to Congress, independence was virtually assured. As sea-power as well as land-power slipped from Spanish grasp, only a European army escorted by a European navy could now have reversed the trend.

Already before Castlereagh's death in August 1822 Britain had recognized the flags of Spanish American vessels – a step, incidentally, which the United States had taken seven years earlier; and Canning, succeeding Castlereagh at the Foreign Office in September, believed that recognition of the Spanish American states themselves was quite inevitable. 'If, on the one hand,' he wrote to the Duke of Wellington, 'we shall contribute (as perhaps it must be admitted that we may) to "constitute" the colonies into states by our recognition; on the other hand, it must be recollected that our abstinence will not necessarily retard that constitution, if other powers do not hesitate as long as we.' And what, he asked, would be the alternative – 'the re-establishment of the predominancy of Spain? or the erection of a set of wild buccaneering piratical republics?'[2]

Interestingly enough, Canning ignored the fact, in this private letter to Wellington, that one power, the United States, had already recognized, or had declared its intention of recognizing, the new states.[3] He was to ignore this fact again ten months later,

---

[1] B.C.R., p. 124. Cf. ibid., p. 36, n. 2.

[2] Canning to Wellington, 29 Oct. 1822. *Despatches, Correspondence, and Memoranda of Field Marshal Arthur Duke of Wellington,* edited by his son (5 vols., London, 1867–73), i, 465.

[3] The formal establishment of American diplomatic relations with Colombia took place in June 1822, with Mexico in Dec., and with 'Buenos Ayres' and Chile in 1823. Canning does refer to the action of the United States in his Memorandum for the Cabinet of Nov. 1822, when, exasperated by the depredations committed on British shipping in the West Indies, he argued that the then state of affairs could not be allowed to continue and that the United States had ordered things better. E. J. Stapleton, ed., *Some Official Correspondence of George Canning* (2 vols., London, 1887), i, 51.

when the mistake would be costly. Meanwhile, if he had at first thought to carry through a policy of recognition, he soon found that he lacked the power to do so; and though he had resolved to send out consular agents to those parts of Spanish America where British interests were most extensive, even this step was postponed. Lists of places to which consuls should be sent were drawn up. But not till October 1823 were the consuls themselves appointed, together with commissioners of enquiry to go to Mexico and Colombia.

The episode that followed is one of the most familiar, and one of the most controversial, in the history of Anglo-American relations. In April 1823 a French army invaded Spain. Did Canning fear that intervention in Spain might be followed by an attempt at intervention in Spanish America, that France, in his own words, would put 'at the command of Spain her fleets and armies, to assist the Spanish operations in South America'? An invasion of Spain by land he could not prevent. An invasion of Spanish America by sea he could. 'We have the means,' he wrote, 'of easily and effectually preventing any such projects. . . . There our naval superiority would tell.'[1] But he took precautions.[2] France was warned in a despatch, soon made public, that Britain considered the separation of the Spanish colonies from Spain to have been substantially decided, that their formal recognition by Britain was a matter of time and circumstances, that Britain had no intention of appropriating to herself any portion of the late Spanish possessions, and that she was satisfied that France would make no attempt at appropriation either.[3] And in August he made his famous proposal to Richard Rush that Britain and the United States should go 'hand in hand' in a joint declaration of policy which would be in fact little more than an elaboration, with American agreement, of the warning already given to France.[4]

In 1819 President Monroe had invited Britain to support

[1] Memorandum of February 1823. Stapleton, op. cit., i, 87–88.
[2] Bartlett, op. cit., pp. 66–8; Wellington, Despatches, ii, 139–40.
[3] Canning to Sir Charles Stuart, 31 March 1823, Temperley, op. cit., pp. 84–5.
[4] Manning, op. cit., iii, 1475–95. There was an additional point – that Britain and the United States would not stand in the way of any amicable arrangement between the colonies and Spain. For differing interpretations of Canning's motives see Webster, Britain and the Independence of Latin America, i, 46–7; W. W. Kaufmann, British Policy and the Independence of Latin America, 1804–1828 (New Haven, 1951), pp. 150–5; and Bradford Perkins, Castlereagh and Adams. England and the United States, 1812–1823 (Berkeley and Los Angeles, 1964), pp. 314–16, 318–23.

American policy in a recognition of Buenos Aires;[1] in 1823 Canning invited the United States to support British policy in a warning to Europe and France.[2] Both proposals failed. Britain, in 1819, was still a member of the European alliance; the United States, in 1823, had already recognized the new Spanish American states. Canning ignored this fact, or its importance, and the error was fatal. The United States went its separate way, to give to the world in Monroe's message to Congress of 2 December 1823 its own declaration of principles, and to appear, momentarily, as the guardian of the western hemisphere. Canning turned to the French ambassador in London to secure in the Polignac Memorandum a denial that France entertained any designs hostile to Spanish America, and used this denial also to appear, and perhaps more effectively, as the protector of the new Spanish American states.

Monroe's declaration of principles reached England three weeks later. On the whole it was well received. Brougham, in the House of Commons on 3rd February, declared that it dispersed 'joy, exultation, and gratitude over all the freemen in Europe',[3] and *The Times* rejoiced that the United States had taken so unequivocal a stand and had adopted 'a policy so directly British'.[4] Canning knew better. The stand did indeed reflect an identity of purpose between Britain and the United States in opposition to European intervention in Spanish America. But it reflected also a rivalry and mistrust, never far below the surface, despite the courtesies of official language. Rush himself, interested as he was by Canning's approach, had early questioned Canning's motives,[5] and his distrust grew greater rather than less. John Quincy Adams' private opinion was that Canning hoped 'to obtain some public pledge' from the United States 'ostensibly against the forcible intervention of the Holy Alliance' but 'really or especially against the acquisition by the United States themselves of any part of the Spanish American possessions';[6] and it would be rash to assert that Canning, like Adams, did not have the Cuban question partly in

[1] Manning, *op. cit.*, i, 85–8; Whitaker, *The United States and the Independence of Latin America*. pp. 260–6.

[2] Perkins, *Castlereagh and Adams,* p. 323.

[3] *Parliamentary Debates*, n.s., x, 68.

[4] 6 Jan. 1824.

[5] Dexter Perkins, *The Monroe Doctrine, 1823–1826* (Cambridge, Mass., 1927), p. 82; Whitaker, *The United States and the Independence of Latin America*, pp. 449–53.

[6] Dexter Perkins, *op. cit.*, p. 92.

mind.[1] As for Monroe, he, quite as much as Adams, was anxious not to subordinate American policy to British, not to appear, in Adams' famous phrase, 'as a cock-boat in the wake of the British man-of-war'.[2] And far from being 'British' in its sentiments, his message not only breathed a 'militant republicanism' wholly unacceptable to Canning; still more, it drew that 'line of demarcation' between America and Europe which Canning confessed that he most dreaded. [3]

Canning's counter-attack was quickly launched. The Polignac Memorandum was circulated privately and the newly-appointed consuls for South America, setting sail in January, were instructed to use it to show 'how early and how anxiously Great Britain declared against any project of bringing back the late Spanish colonies under the dominion of the mother country by foreign aid'.[4] In March it was printed and laid before parliament, and soon afterwards it appeared in the Spanish American press. Not till July, however, did Canning win from the cabinet a secret decision to recognize Buenos Aires by means of the negotiation of a commercial treaty, and not till December, a year after the Monroe Doctrine had been promulgated, did he succeed in widening the scope of this decision to include Mexico and Colombia also. Then, indeed, he rejoiced. 'Spanish America is free;' he wrote on 17 December, 'and if we do not mismanage our affairs sadly, she is English . . .';[5] and again, on 8 January, in illustration of his belief that an 'amicable connection' with Mexico, as he had told the cabinet, would 'oppose a powerful barrier' to the influence of the United States: 'The Un. States have gotten the start of us in vain; and we link once more America to Europe.'[6]

'We link once more America to Europe.' But was this link really the result of British recognition of three states, Buenos Aires, Mexico and Colombia, through the negotiation of commercial treaties which Canning, in effect, dictated? Britain did not

[1] *Cf*. Bradford Perkins, *Castlereagh and Adams,* p. 321, for one piece of evidence that he did.   [2] Dexter Perkins, *op. cit.*, p. 74.

[3] Canning to A'Court, 31 Dec. 1823, A. G. Stapleton, *George Canning and his Times* (London, 1859), pp. 394–5.

[4] Planta to Parish, 30 Dec. 1823, F.O. 118/1, enclosing six copies of the Polignac Memorandum. See also Canning's remarks in the House on 3 Feb. 1824, *Parliamentary Debates*, n.s., x, 74.

[5] Canning to Granville, 17 Dec. 1824, A. G. Stapleton, *op. cit.,* p. 411.

[6] Temperley, *op. cit.,* pp. 146–7, 550–4; Canning to Hookham Frere, 8 Jan. 1825, Festing, *op. cit.,* p. 268.

recognize Peru or Chile. Yet 'the English interest in Chile, created', as the American minister in Santiago observed, 'by mining companies, commercial relations, and intermarrying with the natives . . . and supported by the influence of a strong naval force',[1] was quite as marked, in the later eighteen-twenties, as the English interest in Colombia. British recognition was no doubt important to the new states. But the all-important fact was not British recognition, but British power – economic, naval and financial power. Already before the decision to recognize the new states had been announced, loans to the nominal value of more than £13 million had been floated on their behalf in the London capital market, and these included loans to Chile and Peru as well as to Colombia, Mexico and Buenos Aires. According to Sir James Mackintosh, speaking in the House of Commons in June 1824, at least a hundred British merchant houses were by now established in Spanish American cities, and Mackintosh pointed out, as the Liverpool merchants had also pointed out, that more cotton goods were being shipped from Liverpool to Latin America in 1820 than to the United States.[2] The United States had neither the financial and economic resources nor the financial and economic organization to compete on this scale. It was inevitable that the greatest naval, industrial and financial power in the world should count for more with the infant Spanish American states than did the United States.

In England the effect of recognition was to enhance an already eagerly expectant mood. 'British merchants and manufacturers,' wrote Richard Rush in January 1825, 'British capitalists, in short, the whole British publick, are eagerly turning their eyes . . . to the American hemisphere. They are endeavouring to link Britain to these new states, and these new states to Britain, by every tie that excited cupidity can devise, and enormous opulence carry into effect. Nothing was ever like it before, not even the days of the south sea scheme.'[3] As loan after loan had been raised in London, in 1822, in 1824, and now again in 1825, on behalf of the new states, so company after company was formed, to settle the unemployed poor of Great Britain and Ireland on the plains of

[1] Heman Allen to Clay, 5 Nov. 1825, Manning, *op. cit.*, ii, 1106. *Cf.* same to same, 4 April 1826, *ibid.*, ii, 1112.
[2] 15 June 1824. *Parliamentary Debates*, n.s., xi, 1381–8.
[3] Manning, *op. cit.*, iii, 1529.

Argentina, to join the Atlantic and the Pacific by means of a ship-canal – did not Jeremy Bentham himself publish a *Junctiana* proposal? – to fish for pearls in Colombia, to navigate the rivers of South America by steam, for gold mining and silver mining, even for exporting milk-maids to Buenos Aires to make butter. The bubble burst at the end of 1825 and the failure of the mining companies foreshadowed default on the loans. But by this time the total nominal investment of British capital in Latin America amounted to some £25 million sterling.[1]

In Spanish America the effects of recognition were less dramatic though naturally the news was received with enthusiasm. Naturally also it tended to exacerbate Anglo-American jealousies. 'Preparations are making for general illumination and public rejoicing,' wrote the acting American chargé d'affaires in Buenos Aires. 'As to the U.S.,' he complained, 'we are used . . . as rhetorical ornament, a mere figure of speech, and our recognition has been most impudently assimilated, in importance, to a similar measure on the part of one of their smallest provinces; but, among a people as much benighted in ignorance and sensuality as are these people, it cannot be hoped that moral influence can be understood or appreciated.'[2] Similar rejoicings were reported from Colombia,[3] though the irritation of the American minister there took a different form. 'I never saw the English *pride* of *country* show itself more plainly,' he noted in his diary. 'They seem to think that Colombia never was independent before, but that now her prosperity and freedom were *sealed*.'[4]

But though in Buenos Aires the 'Yankees', in the words of Woodbine Parish, tried to persuade 'the natives' that a treaty was 'no recognition' and that the United States were their only 'sincere friends',[5] and though no love was lost between the British and American representatives in Colombia, the bitterest struggle was fought out in Mexico. There, Poinsett had reappeared on the Spanish American scene as the first United States envoy in Mexico City. He had learnt little from his experiences in Chile more than

---

[1] See, on the above paragraph, J. F. Rippy, *British Investments in Latin America, 1822–1949* (Minneapolis, 1959), pp. 17–26, and my *Liberation in South America, 1806–1827* (London, 1952), pp. 138–42.

[2] J. M. Forbes to J. Q. Adams, 17 Dec. 1824, Manning, *op. cit.*, i, 644.

[3] Hamilton to Planta, 8 March 1825, Webster, *op. cit.*, i, 385–6.

[4] *The Diary and Journal of Richard Clough Anderson*, p. 190.

[5] Parish to Planta, 18 Feb. 1825, Webster, *op. cit.*, i, 120.

ten years earlier and, once again, plunged into the turmoil of domestic politics in order to counteract, as he believed, the fatal influence of Great Britain. Henry George Ward, the young British representative, was no less zealous to check-mate the equally fatal designs which he attributed to the United States in general and to Poinsett in particular, and the result was a series of unedifying quarrels, accusations and intrigues. In the end both men were recalled – Ward, in 1827, as a result of disagreements about his expenditure (he contrived to spend £11,000 in two years),[1] Poinsett at the request of the Mexican Government, in 1829.

Poinsett had made no secret of his conviction, duly reported by Ward, that the United States would put itself at the head of an American league or federation, from which Britain would be excluded.[2] This was the sort of danger which Canning had most feared – the danger, as he had told the cabinet in December 1824, that the United States would 'connect itself with all the powers of America in a general trans-atlantic league, of which it would have the sole direction',[3] the danger, in the words of his well-known letter to Hookham Frere, of 'a division of the world into European and American, republican and monarchical; a league of worn-out govts. on the one hand, and of youthful and stirring nations, with the U. States at their head, on the other'.[4] He had thought this danger scotched in 1825. But his fears revived in 1826, partly, perhaps, as a result of Poinsett's indiscretions in Mexico, partly, because of the approaching Panama Congress of American states.

The Panama Congress, an assembly of plenipotentiaries to deliberate on the high matters of peace and war and of international collaboration among the American nations, had long been the cherished dream of Simón Bolívar, now at the height of his power as the liberator of northern South America. He had thought of it originally as a congress of Spanish American states. It was only later that the United States and Brazil were invited to attend. But so also was Britain. Bolívar had no illusions about the relative importance to Spanish America of Britain and the United States. 'All America combined,' he wrote in July 1825, 'is not worth as

[1] Cody, *op. cit.*, pp. 449–55; Rippy, *Rivalry of the United States and Great Britain over Latin America*, pp. 248–302.
[2] Ward to Canning, 27, 30 Sept. 1825, Webster, *op. cit.*, i, 486–7, 489, 490.
[3] Temperley, *op. cit.*, p. 553.
[4] 8 Jan. 1825. Festing, *op. cit.*, pp. 267–8.

much as a British fleet.'[1] And he was convinced that 'our American league', as he called it, could not survive without British support.'[2]

Canning accepted in January 1826 an invitation to send a British representative to Panama, and he appointed in March a young career diplomat, Edward Dawkins, as his commissioner or observer, instructed to note and report on 'the degree of influence in their concerns' which the new states were inclined to allow to the United States. 'The general maxim that our interests and those of the United States are essentially the same, etc. etc.,' he had told Charles Vaughan, the British minister in Washington, in February, 'is one that cannot be too readily admitted, when put forward by the United States. But we must not be the dupes of this conventional language of courtesy. The avowed pretension of the United States to put themselves at the head of the confederacy of all the Americas, and to sway that confederacy against Europe (Great Britain included) is *not* a pretension identified with our interests, or one that we can countenance or tolerate.'[3] And on this point – though there were other points, too, on which British and American policies clashed – Dawkins' instructions were similarly worded. 'You will understand,' wrote Canning, 'that to a league among the states lately colonies of Spain, limited to objects growing out of their common relation to Spain, His Majesty's Government would not object. But any project for putting the United States of North America at the head of an American confederacy as against Europe would be highly displeasing to your Government.'[4]

In the event the United States was not represented at the Panama Congress. One of its delegates died on the way there. The other did not set out until after the Congress had adjourned. But so far as a confederacy of American states was concerned, their absence hardly mattered. There was even less likelihood in 1826 of the United States becoming a member of an American league, whether as its head or not, than there had been of France intervening by force of arms in Spanish America in 1823. These were phantom fears, though it was not unnatural that Canning should entertain

[1] Bolívar to Santander, 10 July 1825, Simón Bolívar, *Obras Completas* (ed. Vicente Lecuna and Esther Barret de Nazaris, 2 vols., Habana, 1947), i, 1129. *Cf.* same to same, 11 March 1825, *ibid.,* i, 1062.
[2] Bolívar to Santander, 28 June 1825, *ibid.,* i, 1120–1. *Cf.* Webster, *op. cit.,* i, 399–400, 402, 532, 541–2.
[3] Canning to Vaughan, 8 Feb. 1826, *ibid.,* ii, 542–3.
[4] Canning to Dawkins, 18 March 1826, No. 1, *ibid.,* i, 404.

them. And as the Polignac Memorandum, in October 1823, had reassured him against the one danger, so Dawkins' report, when he returned to England in October 1826, reassured him against the other. 'The general influence of the United States,' wrote Dawkins, 'is not, in my opinion, to be feared.'[1] And by the side of this judgement of a British agent may be set the opinion of an American agent six months earlier. 'The preponderating influence of England, in the affairs of these countries,' wrote the American minister to Chile, 'is already seen and felt in almost every department . . .'[2]

Canning was never inclined to underrate his own services to the cause of Spanish American independence. 'I delighted in raising these people into States,' he wrote to Granville in October 1825, 'but I shall not let them fancy themselves too fine fellows, as they would be apt to do if not snubbed when they deserve it.'[3] When George IV received the first properly accredited minister from a Spanish American country to Britain, 'Behold!', wrote Canning, 'the New World established, and, if we do not throw it away, ours!'[4] And at the end of 1826 he made his celebrated boast, 'I called the New World into existence to redress the balance of the Old.' He repeated this dictum to Granville, with evident satisfaction, two days later,[5] and it is possible that he believed it. But may not the time and circumstances allow another interpretation? After all, as Dr Johnson observed, 'in lapidary inscriptions a man is not upon oath'.

---

[1] Dawkins to Canning, 15 Oct. 1826, *ibid.*, i, 423.
[2] Heman Allen to Clay, 4 April 1826, Manning, *op. cit.*, ii, 1112.
[3] 11 Oct. 1825, A. G. Stapleton, *op. cit.*, p. 446.
[4] Canning to Granville, 21 Nov. 1825, *ibid.*, p. 447.
[5] Canning to Granville, 14 Dec. 1826, *ibid.*, pp. 546–7.

F

9

Anglo-American Rivalries in
Central America*

Early in the seventeenth century an English or Scottish buccaneer
settled with a few companions at the mouth of a river in a deserted
section of the coast of Central America. The man's name was
Wallace, called 'Valis' or 'Balis' by the Spaniards. The river to
which he gave his name was the Belize river, and the settlement
which he founded ultimately became, in 1862, the colony of
British Honduras.

Such is the legend. In fact little is known of Wallace beyond his
name, and even that is doubtful, and not much about any other of
the early English or Scottish settlers on the westerly shores of the
Bay of Honduras. Almost certainly they were buccaneers turned
logwood-cutters – the two occupations were long interchangeable.
Almost certainly, too, they were operating on the Belize river
some time before 1670, the date of the so-called 'American treaty'
by which Spain recognized England's title to Jamaica and other
de facto possessions in America.[1] And the place later proved attractive to other logwood-cutters moving south from the more
exposed regions of Cape Catoche and the Bay of Campeche.
Captain Nathaniel Uring, who lived on the Belize river for some
months in 1720 and was familiar with the kind of people settled
there, described them as a 'rude drunken Crew', most of whom
had been sailors and some of them pirates;[2] and the Spaniards,
very naturally, repeatedly tried to get rid of them. But they were
difficult to dislodge and could never be driven away for long, and

* [Presidential Address to the Royal Historical Society, December 1967. *Transactions of the Royal Historical Society*, 5th Series, xviii (1968), pp. 174–208].

[1] J. A. Burdon, ed., *A[rchives of] B[ritish] H[onduras]* (3 vols., London, 1931–5),
i, 2–3; J. A. Calderón Quijano, *Belice, 1663 (?) – 1821* (Sevilla, 1944), pp. 33–4, 46–9,
61–2.

[2] *The Voyages and Travels of Captain Nathaniel Uring*, ed. Alfred Dewar (London,
1928), p. 241.

the British government, which indignantly insisted on the liberty of British subjects, however rude and drunken, to cut logwood on these lonely shores, finally wrung from Spain in 1763 a reluctant recognition not only of their right to do this, but of their right also to build the houses and stores which they needed for themselves, their families and their property.

But the Belize settlement was not the only point in Central America at which Britain, or British subjects, had established a hold. Off the southern shores of the Bay of Honduras, and at no great distance from Cape Honduras itself, the island of Ruatan, the largest of the Bay Islands group, had been briefly occupied by colonists – and buccaneers – some years before Cromwell seized Jamaica. It was then more or less deserted for close on a century, but was again briefly occupied and fortified by Britain during the War of Jenkins' Ear.[1] Once more deserted, it became in 1779 a refuge for some of the Belize settlers when their settlement was captured during a further round of Anglo-Spanish hostilities.

Neither Britain nor Spain, however, paid more than occasional attention to Ruatan, despite its excellent harbour and its strategic position. More important, in British eyes, was the Mosquito Shore, by which was usually meant an area stretching eastward from Cape Honduras and then, to an indefinite extent, southward. The Miskito or Mosquito Indians, who gave the Shore their name, were a semi-nomadic tribe who had successfully resisted conquest by the Spaniards and with whom the British had long established friendly relations. 'They have no form of Government among them,' wrote Dampier as of 1681, 'but acknowledge the King of *England* for their Sovereign. They learn our Language, and take the Governour of *Jamaica* to be one of the greatest Princes in the World.'[2] Uring, who was always being shipwrecked and who was stranded among them thirty years later, described them as a 'kind of Monarchy, having a Chief which they call King', as well as several other chiefs of 'great Power and Authority',[3] and these, in later years, enjoyed such hereditary titles as 'Governor', 'Admiral' and 'General', all originally bestowed by the governor

[1] It was given up under the Treaty of Aix-la-Chapelle. See Richard Pares, *War and Trade in the West Indies, 1739–1763* (Oxford, 1936), pp. 103–4.

[2] William Dampier, *A New Voyage Round the World,* ed. Sir Albert Gray (London, 1937), p. 17.

[3] Uring, *op. cit.,* p. 159.

of Jamaica,[1] while the king, whose title also became hereditary, owed his vague pre-eminence to the same authority. Their blood was intermingled with that of shipwrecked negroes and fugitive slaves, and despite some embarrassing habits, such as an addition to slave-raiding expeditions against other Indians and a liking for strong drink, they were useful allies to the British. British traders, wood-cutters and others were settled among them and in 1740 Captain Robert Hodgson the elder, sent over by Governor Trelawny of Jamaica, procured a formal cession of the country from the then King Edward.[2] A small force of troops was later stationed there and in 1749 Hodgson himself was appointed its superintendent. The troops were withdrawn in 1764,[3] but not the superintendent, whose office, subordinate to the government in Jamaica, was almost continuously maintained for another twenty-two years.

With the loss of her North American colonies, however, Britain lost also the superintendency of the Mosquito Shore. By the peace treaty with Spain in 1783, which followed the peace treaty with America, and by the supplementary Convention of London three years later, the rights of the Belize settlers were indeed confirmed. They were even extended. The settlers, it was agreed, could cut not only logwood but mahogany, now far more valuable than logwood, as well as all other woods, and definite boundaries were laid down within which they might operate.[4] But they were strictly forbidden to establish fortifications, industries or plantations; their settlement was to be periodically inspected by Spanish and British officials; and all other places on the continent in general and its adjacent islands were to be evacuated. Ruatan, therefore, was again abandoned, and, to the great disgust of the British settlers, so was the Mosquito Shore. A few British subjects elected to remain there. But early in 1787 some three thousand persons, free and

[1] Account of the Mosquito Indians, by J. Laurie, Black River, 10 Nov. 1774. National Library of Scotland, Robertson-Macdonald Papers. James Laurie, or Lawrie, became the last superintendent of the Mosquito Shore.

[2] E. G. Squier, *The States of Central America* (New York, 1858), p. 744, prints Hodgson's letter to Trelawny of 8 April 1740 containing the details of this interesting ceremony. See also Pares, *op. cit.*, p. 100.

[3] Under the 17th article of the Treaty of Paris in 1763 Britain promised to demolish all fortifications in the Bay of Honduras 'and other places in Spanish territory in that part of the world'.

[4] Between the Hondo and the Belize, according to the Treaty of 1783, extended southwards to the Sibún by the Convention of London in 1786.

slave, left the Shore, and of these more than two thousand went to Belize.[1]

For the next ten years Britain and Spain remained at peace. But war broke out again at the end of 1796 when Spain joined the land-power of France against the sea-power of England. Two years later the captain-general of Yucatán, Lieutenant-General Arturo O'Neill, himself directed an attack on Belize, only to retire frus-trated. This was the last attempt of Spain to dominate the settle-ment by force of arms. Thereafter its inhabitants were inclined to argue that the settlement was theirs by right of conquest. In fact its status was quite unchanged by the Napoleonic wars and the peace treaties which followed them. It remained, as parliament itself described it in 1817, 'a settlement, for certain purposes, in the possession and under the protection of His Majesty', but 'not within the territory and dominion of His Majesty'.[2] But all evidence of Spanish authority had vanished even before Spain, in 1808, had become an ally instead of an enemy of England, and a protest in 1816 against the settlement's fortification was the last assertion of Spanish rights.[3] Thereafter these rights were tacitly though never formally abandoned. Under a superintendent of its own, Belize was now in fact, though not in law, a British colony, and its settlers, moving inland along the Belize and Sibún rivers, and southwards, from one stream to another, in territory never occupied by Spain, had long overstepped its former boundaries. By the eighteen-twenties their activities had been extended first to the Moho and then to the Sarstoon river, and this, they now claimed, was the southern boundary of their settlement.[4]

The Belize settlers, then, while extending their territory, main-tained a *de facto* independence of Spain. And so also did the Mosquito Indians. At Ruatan, it is true, Spain continued to exer-cise a nominal authority.[5] But, except on the San Juan river, she

[1] 573 white and free persons and 1,677 slaves. *A.B.H.*, i, 162, 166.
[2] 57 George III, cap. 53.
[3] Note of 7 Nov. 1816, in Vaughan to Castlereagh, 12 Nov. 1816, P[ublic] R[ecord] O[ffice[, F[oreign] O[ffice Archives], 72/188. For a Note of 1820 also referring to the settlement see my *Diplomatic History of British Honduras, 1638–1901* (London, 1961), pp. 177–8.
[4] *Ibid.*, pp. 13–18, 21–2.
[5] After the suppression in 1796 of a revolt of the Black Caribs in St Vincent a large number of them were transported to Ruatan, whence they spread to the main-land. But Spanish possession was only temporarily disturbed and Spain, in the early eighteen-hundreds, still maintained a small guard of soldiers on the island.

exercised none at all on the Mosquito Shore.[1] And while the Mosquito Indians kept up their traditional hostility to their Spanish American neighbours, the British in Jamaica and Belize kept up their friendly connexions with the Mosquito Indians. Presents were still made to the Mosquito chiefs.[2] The royal princes were educated, or semi-educated, in Jamaica. And King Robert Charles Frederic in 1825, like King George Frederic II in 1816, was crowned in Belize with the rites of the Anglican church and the full panoply of royalty.[3] It was from George Frederic that the Scottish adventurer, Gregor MacGregor, who had fought with Bolívar in Venezuela, obtained in 1820 an enormous grant of land on the Black river, and, styling himself Gregor the First, Sovereign Prince of the Independent State of Poyais, floated a loan of £200,000 on its behalf in the London capital market and deluded a large number of persons into emigrating there. Most of his victims were given temporary or permanent refuge in Belize. He himself, wisely avoiding his principality, died many years later, a Venezuelan general, and in the odour of respectability, at Caracas.[4] His colonization enterprise, if that is the term, had no importance except for the suffering which it caused. But, illustrating MacGregor's rascality and the gullibility of the British public on the one hand, it illustrated on the other the degree to which the Mosquito king purported to exercise an independent authority and the new kinds of danger to which his kingdom was exposed in the first half of the nineteenth century.

[1] The Spaniards had occupied Black River on the northern coast of the Shore after the British evacuation. But they were driven out by the Mosquitos in 1796. M. W. Williams, *Anglo-American Isthmian Diplomacy, 1815–1915* (Washington, 1916), p. 23. Black River was left desolate. Further south the port of San Juan de Nicaragua was officially established in 1796. Whether there was a permanent settlement there is doubtful, though there was a fort inland at Castillo Viejo and at one time a guard-post at the mouth of the San Juan itself.

[2] *A.B.H.*, ii, 314–15. The custom lapsed for a time in the eighteen-twenties.

[3] *Cf.* Orlando W. Roberts, *Narrative of Voyages and Excursions on the East Coast and in the Interior of Central America* ... (Edinburgh, 1827), pp. 146–9; Frederick Crowe, *The Gospel in Central America* (London, 1850), pp. 208–9; John Macgregor, *Commercial Tariffs and Regulations of the Several States of Europe and America* ... *Spanish American Republics,* P[arliamentary] P[apers], H.C., 1847, [769], lxiv, 38–40.

[4] A. Hasbrouck, 'Gregor McGregor and the Colonization of Poyais, between 1820 and 1824', *Hispanic American Historical Review*, vii (1927), 438–59; *A.B.H.,* ii, 274, 275, 276, 278, 282. *Cf.* James Hastie, *Narrative of a Voyage in the Ship Kennersley Castle, from Leith Roads to Poyais* ... (Edinburgh, 1823), and, for the attempts of later speculators to profit by MacGregor's frauds, W. J. Griffith, *Empires in the Wilderness. Foreign Colonization and Development in Guatemala, 1834–1844* (Chapel Hill, 1965), pp. 21–2, 160.

At this point Spanish rule in North and Central America collapsed. The viceroyalty of New Spain and the kingdom or captaincy-general of Guatemala both declared their independence in 1821. Mexico became first an empire and then, in 1823, a republic; and in the same year the provinces of the old kingdom of Guatemala, which Mexico had briefly annexed, proclaimed their independence not merely of old Spain but of New Spain as well and their confederation together as the United Provinces of the Centre of America.

The United Provinces, which thus gave Central America its name, consisted of five states – Costa Rica, San Salvador (the original name), Guatemala, Honduras and Nicaragua. None of them was large. All were poor. But one, Guatemala, which had been the seat of the colonial bureaucracy and was much the wealthiest and most populous of them all, inevitably aroused suspicions that it might seek to assume the mantle of metropolitan Spain, and neither Guatemala nor any of the other states had the slightest intention of subordinating its own private interests to those of the federation as a whole. Never united except in name, the United Provinces were divided from the outset by political, personal, municipal and even ecclesiastical rivalries both within the several states and between them; they were soon engulfed in civil wars; and by 1839 even the shadow of a federation had vanished.

The United Provinces were recognized by the United States in August 1824. But it was not till May 1826 that the first United States chargé d'affaires reached Guatemala City, to remain there for six months only. No successor made his appearance till December 1833. He, it is true, stayed for five years, though he seems to have given very little satisfaction to the State Department. But the next United States representative, John Lloyd Stephens, sent on special mission, returned without having been able to find a government to which he could present his credentials, though he found the ruined cities of the Mayan empire instead, and after one more agent had been appointed – three months were enough for him – the State Department, from 1842 to 1848, ceased to trouble itself about its representation in Central America at all.[1]

This record argues only a moderate concern in Washington with

---

[1] See J. B. Lockey's entertaining essay, 'Diplomatic Futility', *Hispanic American Historical Review*, x (1930), 265–94. An American merchant, Henry Savage, took charge of the United States legation, though without any official rank whatever.

the affairs of Central America; and, despite a desultory interest in plans for a trans-isthmian canal,[1] such was the fact. The region was remote and relatively unknown. United States trade in Central America was negligible. It was British trade, much of it channelled through Belize, that had replaced Spanish trade,[2] even though the United States, in 1825, had signed a treaty of amity and commerce with the United Provinces and Britain had not. Britain had indeed sent an observer to Central America in 1825,[3] and, soon afterwards a consul, who was murdered two years later.[4] But she had refused to recognize the United Provinces, one very good reason being that she doubted, quite rightly, their ability to maintain peace at home and good faith abroad.[5] And even her consular appointments were irregular till the arrival of Frederick Chatfield in June 1834.

Chatfield, a minor official in what was at first a quite unimportant part of the world, found little to admire in Central America except the scenery. But, save for a brief interval, from 1840 to 1842, he remained there for eighteen years. He was rewarded by his elevation to the rank of chargé d'affaires in 1849, when Britain at last recognized a Central American state – Guatemala – and by a virulence of vituperation, for which the arrogance of his temper and conduct was only partly to blame. Above all, he was accused, both then and later, of deliberately encouraging the dissolution of the federal union and the fragmentation of Central America in order to promote the political and territorial hegemony of Great Britain. The charge has persisted till our own day,[6] and Chatfield is still

[1] Gerstle Mack, *The Land Divided. A history of the Panama canal and other isthmian canal projects* (New York, 1944), pp. 125–6, 173–7.

[2] See Robert A. Naylor, 'The British Role in Central America prior to the Clayton-Bulwer Treaty of 1850', *Hispanic American Historical Review*, xl (1960), 361–82. This article summarizes the author's unpublished doctoral dissertation, 'British Commercial Relations in Central America, 1821–1851' (Tulane, 1958).

[3] G. A. Thompson, who had served as secretary to the mission sent by Canning to Mexico. See his *Narrative of an Official Visit to Guatemala from Mexico* (London, 1829).

[4] John O'Reilly, Aug. 1825–Jan. 1828.

[5] See the conditions for recognition laid down by Canning, in C. K. Webster, ed. *Britain and the Independence of Latin America, 1812–1830. Select Documents from the Foreign Office Archives* (2 vols., London, 1938), i, 114, 435, 462, and by Dudley, in 1828, *ibid.*, i, 339.

[6] *Cf.* Williams, *op. cit.*, pp. 31, 38. It is rejected by Naylor, *op. cit.*, and by T. L. Karnes, *The Failure of Union. Central America, 1824–1960* (Chapel Hill, 1961), pp. 112–25. Mario Rodríguez, *A Palmerstonian Diplomat in Central America. Frederick Chatfield, Esq.* (Tucson, Arizona, 1964), p. 366, concurs in the view that Chatfield was not responsible for the dissolution of the federation but believes that he

commonly regarded either as the agent of British imperialism or as its instigator.[1]

Chatfield's opinions are not in doubt. He early dreamt of making the whole of Central America 'subservient to British influence' – his own words.[2] He would have liked to see it peopled, or large parts of it peopled, with British subjects.[3] He hoped that the Guatemalan province of Petén might be united with the British settlement of Belize[4] and that Santo Tomás in the Golfo Dulce could be prevented from becoming a rival port to Belize itself.[5] He proposed in 1839 first that Britain, France and the United States should jointly undertake the superintendence of the area and so put an end to the waging of 'unjust and ruinous wars',[6] and then that Britain should herself intervene to guarantee the fulfilment of treaties and to afford protection to such of the states as asked for her mediation.[7] In the late eighteen-forties he became increasingly fearful of American expansion in Central America. Nothing, he thought, could really stop the 'onward progress' of the 'North Americans'. Indeed, they seemed destined to be the instruments by which Spanish American societies would be emancipated from 'semi-barbarism'. But that was no reason why British interests should not be maintained and extended. Chatfield proposed, therefore, that Britain should establish a 'closer connexion' with Guatemala, as the largest and wealthiest of the five states.[8] She should get possession also, for use as a naval station, of some of the

---

'aligned himself against unionism' once the federation had been dissolved. This, the only biography of Chatfield, is based on extensive research. But much of its argumentation is, in my view, conjectural and its author has been led into a number of highly questionable assumptions and deductions. *Cf.* the suggestion, implicit in his title, that there was a special relationship between Chatfield and Palmerston.

[1] *Cf.* Rodríguez, *op. cit.*, pp. 178, 218, 236, 237, 366.
[2] Chatfield to Palmerston, 7 Nov. 1834, F.O. 15/14.
[3] *Cf.* Chatfield to Backhouse, 13 Oct. 1834, F.O. 15/14; Chatfield to Palmerston, 5 March 1839, F.O. 15/22.
[4] *Cf.* Chatfield to Palmerston, 23 Feb. 1838, enc., F.O. 15/20.
[5] *Cf.* Chatfield to Palmerston, 17 Sept. 1834, F.O. 15/14; 12 Sept., 1835, F.O. 15/16.
[6] *Cf.* Chatfield to Palmerston, 5 June, 5 July 1839, F.O. 15/22.
[7] Chatfield to Palmerston, 20 Aug. 1839, F.O. 15/22. *Cf.* his letter of 19 Nov. 1839, F.O. 15/22: 'sooner or later' Britain must 'interpose for the regulation of these republics'.
[8] Chatfield to Palmerston, 28 Jan. 1847, F.O. 15/45; 28 June 1847, F.O. 15/46, both in part printed in Mark J. Van Aken, 'British Policy Considerations in Central America before 1850 , *Hispanic American Historical Review*, xlii (1962), 55–8.

small islands in the Bay of Fonseca, commanding the most important of the Pacific ports of Central America, as well as of an island in the Nicaraguan harbour of Realejo.[1] With these Pacific islands, with the settlement of Belize, and with what had become the Mosquito protectorate on the Caribbean coast, she would obtain an 'extensive and central hold', more particularly if Guatemala should place herself under British protection, as she seemed to wish.[2] Finally, in 1849, with the support of Captain Aylmer Paynter of HMS *Gorgon* he actually seized upon Tigre, the most important of the islands, in order to prevent, as he said, its temporary cession to the United States.[3]

Chatfield was meddlesome, self-willed and intolerant, and the Foreign Office, on more than one occasion, severely rebuked him. 'Your tone and deportment,' wrote Aberdeen in 1845, 'although they may be energetic and resolute, should never be imperious and threatening, and still less discourteous.' He was to act, Aberdeen added, 'not as an independent person, which you have done in too many instances, but as a subordinate and responsible agent'.[4] But the Foreign Office was far distant and Chatfield was subordinate to no one in Central America. His self-confident zeal was unimpaired by caution and reproof. If he did not always do as he saw done, nevertheless he was not above meeting sharp practice with sharp practice. Nor did he scruple to take a hand in internal politics. But he had been the friend of federation, not its opponent, and not till federation had long ceased to be a reality was he prepared to countenance the recognition of the separate nationality of the several Central American states, believing, so he said, that it was useless to expect them to combine spontaneously for the re-establishment of a general government.[5] There is little in the political history of the period to impugn the validity of this opinion,[6] and while Chatfield undoubtedly opposed any attempts

[1] Chatfield to Palmerston, 29 Jan. 1847, F.O. 15/45; 20 Dec. 1847, F.O. 15/47; 7, 28 March 1848, F.O. 97/88. From Realejo, he wrote in January 1847, a direct line of communication might be maintained with Europe by San Juan de Nicaragua.

[2] Chatfield to Palmerston, 17 Jan. 1848, F.O. 15/51, printed in Aken, *op. cit.*, p. 59; 7 March 1848, F.O. 97/88.

[3] Chatfield to Palmerston, 17 Oct. 1849, F.O. 15/60.

[4] Aberdeen to Chatfield, 1 Oct. 1845, Nos. 6 and 8, F.O. 15/40.

[5] Chatfield to Palmerston, 28 Jan. 1847, F.O. 15/45; 25 April 1846, F.O. 15/42; 28 June 1847, F.O. 15/46.

[6] *Cf.* Karnes, *op. cit.*, pp. 126–37.

of the United States to obtain, as he thought, a political ascendency in Central America by supporting so-called 'unionist' movements or by other means, the charge that he deliberately sought to perpetuate the political fragmentation of the area remains, in the Scottish verdict, 'not proven'.[1]

The British government, for its part, intervened in Central America to protect British subjects and British property. The navy was called upon, on more than one occasion, to support British financial claims by a show of force.[2] But though the Foreign Office was quite prepared to employ gunboat diplomacy in Central America, or anywhere else for that matter, when convinced that such action had a just and necessary basis, it did not use it to obtain special financial or economic privileges. British policy was not one of political domination or control. Chatfield's early hints about populating the area with British subjects, acquiring Petén, and dominating Santo Tomás, were rejected or ignored.[3] Palmerston told him in 1839 that Britain would enter into no arrangements which would bind her to interfere actively and by force in the internal affairs of Central America;[4] and though both Palmerston and the Admiralty would have liked, in 1848, a 'refitting station' for the South American squadron off the Pacific coast of Central America,[5] Chatfield's proposals to take over islands in the Bay of Fonseca and elsewhere in settlement of British financial claims

[1] Van Aken, *op. cit.*, p. 59, prints Palmerston's instruction to Chatfield of 1 November 1848 to the effect that the United States chargé d'affaires was understood to have been told to induce the Central American states to unite into a single state, the better to resist the interference of Great Britain in the affairs of Mosquito, and that Chatfield should take such steps as might be necessary or useful to defeat United States policy in so far as its object was inimical to British interests. But this is evidence of an opposition, not to union as such, but to hostile American policy. Palmerston himself at this time favoured a reunion of the Central American states 'in a friendly league and in connexion with Mosquito and our Honduras'. R. W. Van Alstyne, 'The Central American Policy of Lord Palmerston, 1846–1848', *Hispanic American Historical Review*, vii (1936), p. 351.

[2] Palmerston's attitude on the question of claims is defined in his instruction to Chatfield of 15 July 1840. Rodríguez, *op. cit.*, p. 218.

[3] See, for the indignant repudiation by the Foreign Office and the Colonial Office of the means proposed by Chatfield to dominate Santo Tomás, Griffith, *op. cit.*, pp. 58–9.

[4] Palmerston to Chatfield, 19 Nov. 1839, F.O. 15/22.

[5] Palmerston to Russell, 10 Dec. 1848, PRO, Russell Papers, 30/22/7D; Van Alstyne, *op. cit.*, p. 351 (differently dated). The 'refitting station' Palmerston had in mind was San Juan del Sur. The Admiralty had no base from which the navy might operate in the eastern Pacific, only a storeship at Valparaiso. C. R. Bartlett, *Great Britain and Sea Power, 1815–1853* (Oxford, 1963), p. 182.

were rejected.[1] His suggestion that Guatemala might be placed under British protection was made in vain. A like request from Costa Rica was refused.[2] And when, in October 1849, Chatfield seized Tigre, his action was disavowed and he was told to restore the island to its former condition.[3]

If this was a 'vision of empire', it was a very limited vision. But was there not, on the Caribbean shores of Central America, a different story to be told? Did not Britain consolidate and extend her hold in Belize, at Ruatan and on the Mosquito Shore? She did indeed, and one quite unforeseen result was a direct collision with the United States. But what did these so-called British aggressions amount to? And what purpose did they serve?

Not much need be said of the Belize settlement. Its chief value lay in its mahogany trade, though Belize itself served as a distributing point for British exports throughout Central America. It was the mahogany-cutters who had extended the boundaries of the settlement to the west and to the south of the old Anglo-Spanish treaty lines, and they had done this even before the United Provinces of Central America had declared their independence. But the status of the settlement remained anomalous, and the United Provinces, though unrecognized by Spain, early showed a disposition to regard themselves as the heirs of Spanish rights throughout Central America and to assert a title, therefore, to the Belize settlement itself. To this there was a simple retort. These provinces were not the general assignees of Spanish rights; they had succeeded to those rights only within the territories which they actually occupied. It was 'only with Spain', wrote Palmerston in 1834, that Britain could properly discuss this question; and in

[1] Palmerston to Chatfield, 17 June 1848, F.O. 15/50; 1 May 1849, F.O. 15/56. Chatfield had suggested that the navy should examine and report upon the suitability of establishing a small naval base in the Bay of Fonseca. Palmerston asked the Admiralty to do this, and, when a favourable report was received, called for a map, which he returned without comment. Minute on Chatfield to Palmerston, 20 Dec. 1847, F.O. 15/47. This is slender evidence on which to suggest that at this time Palmerston favoured Chatfield's proposals. Rodríguez, *op. cit.*, pp. 281–4. A similar confidential survey of the Galápagos Islands had been ordered in 1844.

[2] Williams, *op. cit.*, p. 71.

[3] Palmerston to Lawrence, 13 Feb. 1850. W. R. Manning, ed., *Diplomatic Correspondence of the United States. Inter-American Affairs, 1831–1860* (12 vols., Washington, 1936), vii, 352–3. A minute by Palmerston dated 5 March 1850 on Chatfield to Palmerston, 12 Jan. 1850, F.O. 15/64, says: 'H.M.G. do not wish to obtain possession of Tigre island and are only desirous that it should not be alienated to any other power.'

1835 Spain was actually asked, as a matter of courtesy and in formal recognition of a *de facto* right, to cede to Great Britain 'any right of sovereignty which it may be conceived still rests, as regards the British colony of Honduras, in the Crown of Spain'.[1] Nothing came of this proposal, and it is odd that anyone could have thought anything would. But though, in 1840, the superintendent of the settlement, Lieutenant-Colonel Alexander Macdonald, formally proclaimed that the 'Law of England is and shall be the Law of this Settlement or Colony of British Honduras', not till many years later was the British government itself prepared to substitute the title 'colony' for that of 'settlement'. It was content, as Aberdeen put it in 1841, 'practically' to 'govern the Settlement, as we best may', leaving the question of sovereignty on one side,[2] but steadfastly rejecting any claims to it whatever on the part of the neighbouring Spanish American states.

It could not seriously be maintained that the United Provinces or any one of them had been in possession or control of any part of the Belize settlement. In Ruatan, by contrast, there had been some semblance of Central American occupation. The island was represented, from Belize, as the 'key to command' both Belize itself and the Mosquito Shore; fears were expressed lest it should fall into the hands of France; and, at the wishes of the Belize settlers, it was finally linked with Belize in the application made to Spain in 1835.[3] But no attempt to assert British control[4] was made till the late eighteen-thirties, when British subjects from the Cayman Islands had begun to settle there. Some of these complained in 1838 to Colonel Macdonald of interference by the commandant of Trujillo

[1] See my *Diplomatic History*, pp. 29–30, 34–6, 38–40, 181–2. The boundaries of the settlement were defined as the Hondo on the north, the Sarstoon on the south, and as far west as Garbutt's Falls.

[2] *Ibid.*, pp. 46, 49, 60.

[3] Bennett to Horton, 13 June 1825, F.O. 15/4; *A.B.H.*, ii, 368; Cooke to Howick, 13 Aug., 12 Oct. 1831, F.O. 15/11; and see David Waddell, 'Great Britain and the Bay Islands, 1821–61', *Historical Journal*, ii (1959), 61–2.

[4] In June 1830 Major John Anderson, calling at Ruatan, took off some French settlers who said they were starving. They were sent back from Belize in the same vessel in which they arrived when it was discovered they were not under the necessity they had represented, but with a supply of provisions. Dashwood to Backhouse, 3 Nov. 1830, with enclosures, F.O. 15/10. This incident was represented by Squier (*e.g. The States of Central America*, pp. 619–20) and others as a British seizure of the island, subsequently disavowed, and the legend is repeated by Williams, *op. cit.*, p. 37, Dexter Perkins, *The Monroe Doctrine, 1826–1867* (Baltimore, 1933), p. 17, and Karnes, *op. cit.*, p. 109.

and of his hoisting the Central American flag at several places on the island.[1] Macdonald, like Chatfield, was an empire-builder. 'He is a soldier,' wrote an American diplomatic agent in 1842, 'as well as a high-minded, frank and honorable man. He would have made a fit representative of Greece or Rome in the brightest day of their glory.'[2] British subjects, he believed, should be protected; Ruatan was of 'paramount importance' to the security of Belize; and the question of sovereignty over it was still unsettled. With the agreement both of the Colonial Office and of the Foreign Office, he sailed to Ruatan in HMS *Rover* in April 1839, hauled down the Central American flag, and expelled a small guard of soldiers.[3] Palmerston, two years later, seems to have entertained no doubts about the validity of Britain's title to the island. But if the British government was reluctant to declare British sovereignty over Belize, it was, quite rightly, equally reluctant to declare it over Ruatan. Though more immigrant settlers arrived there, they were left to look after themselves, sometimes with the support of magistrates appointed from Belize, sometimes without.[4] And this highly unsatisfactory state of affairs continued till 1852, when Ruatan and its neighbouring islands were formally erected into the Colony of the Bay Islands.

On the Mosquito Shore there was a similarly slow advance. The Belize mahogany-cutters, extending their operations, by agreement with the Mosquito king, to the north coast of present-day Honduras, and complaining loudly, as did the king himself, of Central American attempts at interference, or threats of interference, were partly responsible for raising the vexed problem of the Mosquito protectorate.[5] It was partly raised by Central American pretensions to territorial sovereignty on the shore, both north and south of the San Juan river.[6] And it was partly raised also by the activities of a

[1] Macdonald to Glenelg, with enclosures, 24 Oct. 1838, in Colonial Office to Foreign Office, 31 Dec. 1838, F.O. 15/21.

[2] Manning, *op. cit.*, iii, 163.

[3] Colonial Office to Foreign Office, 31 Dec. 1838; Symonds (HMS *Rover*) to Douglas, 27 May 1839, F.O. 15/22.

[4] Waddell, *op. cit.*, pp. 64–5.

[5] Robert Charles Frederic to King of England, 25 Jan. 1837, F.O. 15/19; Macdonald to Glenelg, 12 Feb. 1837, F.O. 15/19; Macdonald to Chatfield, 20 Feb. 1837, F.O. 252/8; Hyde to Palmerston, 24 Oct. 1837, F.O. 15/19.

[6] Chatfield to Palmerston, 13 Sept., 16 Dec. 1836, F.O. 15/18; 19, 26 Aug. 1837, F.O. 15/19. For the Central American attempt in 1836 to occupy Boca del Toro and the counter-expedition from New Granada, see W. J. Griffith, 'Juan Galindo, Central American Chauvinist', *Hispanic American Historical Review*, xl (1960), p. 44.

group of traders and speculators, of whom the most important were Samuel and Peter Shepherd, who had settled on the Shore early in the century and appear to have had at one time a practical monopoly of its trade. The Shepherds obtained a huge grant of land from the Mosquito king, stretching from a point to the north of Bluefields as far south as Boca del Toro and the Chiriquí lagoon (now a part of the republic of Panama).[1] Naturally they wanted it protected. But there were other holders of grants from King Robert Charles Frederic who also wanted protection. Matthew Willock and his partner, for example, had obtained lands in the neighbourhood of Cape Gracias a Dios which they tried to sell, at enormous profit, to Prince Charles of Prussia, who was interested in a scheme for German colonization there.[2]

Chatfield and Macdonald believed, or at any rate asserted, that the territory of the Mosquito kingdom really did extend as far as the Chiriquí lagoon, though Macdonald thought that the San Juan river was the 'more natural boundary' to the south.[3] They agreed also in wanting to link the Mosquito kingdom closer to Britain. Chatfield, in 1836, thought that it ought properly to be regarded as a 'mediatized district', and in 1837 he told the Central American foreign minister that the Mosquito 'nation' was 'in some respects subject to', as well as in alliance with, Great Britain.[4] Macdonald went further. At the request of the ailing Robert Charles Frederic, who visited him at Belize, he nominated, in February 1840, a board of commissioners, with himself as president, to govern the kingdom in the king's name. He had much to say, in defence of this action, of the need to protect 'an ancient and a most faithful ally' against foreign aggression and of the king's desire to rescue 'his wretchedly ignorant and truly benighted people from their present dark and degraded state', as well as of the advantages to Great Britain of holding the Mosquito Shore under her dominion and particularly that part of it round the mouth of the San Juan. Were the North Americans to get hold of this and create a line of

[1] Christie to Palmerston, 15 May 1849, 16 May 1850, F.O. 53/45; Van Alstyne, *op. cit.*, pp. 341–3.

[2] Gavin B. Henderson, 'German Colonial Projects on the Mosquito Coast, 1844–1848', *English Historical Review*, lix (1944), pp. 261–4; Van Alstyne, *op. cit.*, p. 342.

[3] Chatfield to Palmerston, 13 Sept. 1836, F.O. 15/18; Macdonald to Russell, 25 Aug. 1840, F.O. 15/24. On Mosquito claims to Boca del Toro and the Chiriquí Lagoon, see also the documents printed in *Correspondence respecting the Mosquito Territory, P.P., H.C., 1847–8, [966], lxv, 2–6, 36–40, 47–52.

[4] Chatfield to Palmerston, 13 Sept. 1836, F.O. 15/18; 1 Sept. 1837, F.O. 15/19.

communication by the San Juan and the great Lake of Nicaragua to the Pacific, farewell, said Macdonald, to the 'high commercial footing' that Britain at present enjoyed.[1]

Palmerston, who had told Chatfield, in 1837, not to say that the Mosquito kingdom was 'in some respects subject to' Britain,[2] was impressed by some at least of these arguments. Britain, he felt sure, had a duty to the Mosquito kingdom. 'When a British authority,' he wrote, or rather the Foreign Office wrote for him, 'has with the sanction of the British government placed a crown upon the head of a foreign chief, the British government does seem to be bound in honor to keep that crown, such as it may be, upon the head on which it has been so placed, and to protect in his rights the chief who wears it.' It was highly proper, also, that an attempt should be made 'to impart to a rude and barbarous race of men, some of the elements of social order, some rudiments of political organization, and some instruction in the truths of religion', in short to lay the foundations 'for the introduction of civilization and christianity', as well as for the extension of British trade. And incidentally it was quite possible that a British community might gradually be established all the way along the Caribbean coast from the Río Hondo to Boca del Toro.[3]

Lord John Russell, at the Colonial Office, would have none of this. Macdonald, he thought, had been dilatory, and perhaps disingenuous, in explaining what he had done and why.[4] The commissions issued on behalf of the king had been signed by Macdonald himself. His proceedings amounted to 'little less than taking possession of the Mosquito Shore'. However proper and judicious they might have been if taken under the sole authority of the king, they were taken in fact upon Macdonald's own authority and must be instantly disavowed.

Alarmed at the possible effects of such a disavowal, Macdonald paid a return visit to the king in August 1841, when the king himself appointed a commission, with the same objects as the former commission, consisting of the same persons (except for the omission of two names), and presided over, as before, by Macdonald. Macdonald and the king, in the company also of Peter Shepherd,

[1] Macdonald to Russell, 29 Feb., 25 Aug. 1840, F.O. 15/24.
[2] Palmerston to Chatfield, 15 Dec. 1837, F.O. 15/19.
[3] Minute by Palmerston on Colonial Office to Foreign Office, 27 Nov. 1840; Foreign Office to Colonial Office, 15 Dec. 1840, F.O. 15/24.
[4] Russell to Macdonald, 8 Feb. 1841, F.O. 15/28.

then inspected the whole length of the Mosquito Shore from Cape Gracias a Dios to Boca del Toro, and at the little port which had grown up at San Juan, where there had at one time been a Spanish guard post and there was now a Nicaraguan custom house, deported the Nicaraguan administrator of the customs – a 'shocking ruffian', in Macdonald's opinion.[1] Once again the Colonial Office, now under Lord Stanley, disapproved, and so did the foreign secretary, Lord Aberdeen.[2] Then, in October 1842, the king died, leaving Macdonald and the commissioners as the guardians of his children and vested with authority to provide for the administration of his kingdom. The state of confusion on the Mosquito Shore, the complaints of local British residents that they were unprotected, the rival claims to sovereignty by neighbouring states, now made some determination of its problems imperative. Macdonald, who returned to England in 1843 and was about to leave for Ceylon in charge of the Royal Artillery there, recommended the appointment of a 'political resident', who would give counsel and advice and by his mere presence would help to promote order and justice within the kingdom and to preserve it from aggression from without. Aberdeen accepted this proposal, and in April 1844 Patrick Walker, who had been the colonial secretary at Belize and one of Macdonald's commissioners, and who also had returned to England in 1843, was appointed as resident with the title of agent and consul-general.[3] The Mosquito protectorate, after more than half a century, had again become a reality.

If Macdonald would have been a fit representative of Greece or Rome, Walker, who reached Bluefields in July 1844, was cast in the mould of a devoted district officer. He embraced the cause of the Mosquito Indians with enthusiasm, and the Shepherd brothers, who were later said to have played an important part in the revival of the protectorate,[4] must have been disillusioned indeed. Walker

[1] Macdonald to Russell, 12 July, 8 Sept. 1841, F.O. 15/28; Hall to Palmerston, 18 Oct. 1841, F.O. 15/25; Colonial Office to Foreign Office, 24 Dec. 1841, F.O. 15/28; Manning, *op. cit.*, v, pp. 609–12; Rodríguez, *op. cit.*, pp. 239–44. The custom house was certainly in existence in the early eighteen-thirties.

[2] Colonial Office to Foreign Office, 24 Dec. 1841, F.O. 15/28; Foreign Office to Colonial Office, 2 April 1843, F.O. 15/36. See also Manning, *op. cit.*, iii, 187–8.

[3] Macdonald to Aberdeen, 20 Dec. 1843, F.O. 15/36; Foreign Office Memoranda, 15 Dec. 1843, F.O. 15/36, 6 March 1845, F.O. 53/44; Aberdeen to Walker, 30 April 1844, F.O. 53/1.

[4] Christie to Palmerston, 16 May 1850, F.O. 53/45.

came to the conclusion that their own and other land grants had been fraudulently drawn from the late king when he was drunk. He insisted that they should be cancelled, and, in October 1846, by an act of the newly-established Mosquito council of state, cancelled they were.[1] The young prince, George Augustus Frederic, who was crowned at Belize in May 1845, was taken into Walker's own household and so well-schooled that, in the opinion of the governor of Jamaica, whom he visited in 1847, he could not have been better behaved had he 'been brought up at Windsor or the Tuileries'.[2] And till his death in 1848 Walker was the real ruler of the Mosquito kingdom.

The boundaries of the kingdom had now to be determined. New Granada, Costa Rica, Nicaragua and Honduras all disputed the Mosquito king's claims, and some of them each other's. Chatfield, characteristically, wanted the fullest possible extent of coast-line. Walker, with greater realism, favoured the San Juan river as the southern boundary, though he and Chatfield were agreed that, if the San Juan were to be the boundary, it must be the south bank of the river,[3] giving control of the harbour of San Juan del Norte, a village of some fifty or sixty houses. The Foreign Office debated the problem for more than two years, and Palmerston then decided in favour of the San Juan, for the sake, so he said, of being on indisputable ground.[4] This was in 1847. The neighbouring Spanish American authorities were informed that in the opinion of the British government the territory of the Mosquito king, who was under the protection of the British crown, extended from Cape Honduras to the mouth of the San Juan, and that Her Majesty's government could not see with indifference any attempt to encroach upon it.[5] In October Walker, accompanied by the young king and Captain Granville Loch of HMS *Alarm*, called at San

[1] Walker to Aberdeen, 21 July 1845, F.O. 53/44; Christie to Palmerston, 15 May 1849, F.O. 53/45; Foreign Office Memorandum, 6 March 1845, F.O. 53/44; Henderson, *op. cit.*, pp. 263–4, 267.

[2] Sir Charles Grey to Lord Grey, 22 Nov. 1847, F.O. 53/14.

[3] Chatfield to Aberdeen, 25 April 1846, F.O. 15/42; Walker to Aberdeen, 20 July 1846, F.O. 53/5; Chatfield to Palmerston, 15 April 1847, Walker to Palmerston, 20 May 1847, *Correspondence respecting the Mosquito Territory*, pp. 2–6, 36–40.

[4] Foreign Office Memorandum, 28 April 1845, F.O. 53/44; Minute by Palmerston on Chatfield to Palmerston, 16 Nov. 1847, F.O. 15/47.

[5] Palmerston to Chatfield, 30 June 1847, F.O. 15/44. But Chatfield, in announcing this decision, reserved such claims as the king might have to territory south of the river. Chatfield to Palmerston, 11 Sept. 1847, F.O. 15/47, *Correspondence respecting the Mosquito Territory*, p. 56.

Juan to warn the Nicaraguan authorities there that the Mosquito government intended to 'reassume' sovereignty at the mouth of the San Juan on January 1st next. On that day he again landed, hauled down the Nicaraguan flag and hoisted that of Mosquito, and San Juan, soon afterwards, was renamed Greytown in honour of the governor of Jamaica. The Nicaraguans making a sudden descent upon the place, Walker accompanied Captain Loch in February on a successful punitive expedition against them, but was drowned while attempting to save the life of a friend.

Aberdeen had created the protectorate, Palmerston defined its boundaries. It is tempting to relate these events to others, though of a different order of magnitude, elsewhere on the continent – the movement which resulted in the annexation of Texas to the United States in 1845, the outbreak of the Mexican War in 1846, the American occupation of California in the same year. Chatfield, early in 1847, had sounded the note of alarm at the 'onward progress' of the United States and was full of plans to contain it. Both he and Sir Charles Grey at Jamaica[1] were alive to the importance of the San Juan river as a possible channel of communication across Central America, and Macdonald, in 1840, had expressed his fear lest the San Juan should fall into American hands. With events and warnings such as these, it is natural to assume that British policy in Central America must have been determined by strategic and political considerations as well as by commercial.

Yet very little evidence has so far come to light to suggest that at any time before 1848 the Foreign Office, or for that matter the Colonial Office, were much influenced by fear of American expansion in Central America, that they gave much thought to the strategic situation of the isthmus and to the importance of San Juan as a terminal point in a line of communication to the Pacific, or that they were much alarmed at the prospect of American commercial competition.[2] Considerations such as these had not the slightest importance so far as the Belize settlement was concerned. Ruatan, it is true, was thought to be a possible danger to the security of the Belize settlement should it fall into the hands of

[1] *Cf.* Sir Charles Grey to Lord Grey, 22 Nov. 1847, F.O. 53/14.

[2] Van Aken, *op. cit.,* argues to the contrary. But the three most important documents which he prints reflect Chatfield's views, and these were not necessarily those of the British government. *Cf.* Van Alstyne, *op. cit.,* pp. 347–8, and Naylor, *op. cit.,* p. 381.

some other great power. But there is nothing to show that its acquisition was regarded as a matter of high imperial strategy. Nor is it wise to apply such terms to the establishment of the Mosquito protectorate and the determination of its boundaries. Palmerston, in 1840, had indeed thought that British settlements might in time extend all along the Caribbean shores of Central America. He would have liked to see, in 1848, a reunion of the Central American states 'in a friendly league and in connexion with Mosquito and our Honduras'. And he was not the man to ignore any possible advantages which might result to Britain from the possession by Mosquito rather than by Nicaragua of the port and river of San Juan. But the proposal that the San Juan should be the southern boundary of the kingdom dated from Aberdeen's day;[1] Palmerston appears quite genuinely to have believed that Nicaragua had no good claim to it;[2] and it may be doubted whether, in determining upon it, he was much moved by political speculations or strategic purposes.[3] When, later in the year, W. D. Christie, Walker's successor, suggested that the Mosquito Shore might be converted into a British possession, Palmerston replied that the British government had no wish at present 'to increase the number of the Colonial possessions of the British Crown'. Their desire, he added, was 'to assist the Mosquito State in its advance towards civilization, and to secure it against aggression and encroachment on the part of the neighbouring Spanish American Republics'.[4] It is just possible that he was speaking the truth.

In the United States a different opinion prevailed. Hitherto British pre-eminence in Central America had been unchallenged. The United States had not questioned British rights in Belize. It had taken no notice either of the occupation of Ruatan or of the

[1] Foreign Office Memorandum, 28 April 1845, F.O. 53/44. See also Chatfield to Aberdeen, 25 April 1846, F.O. 15/42.

[2] Palmerston to Grey, 9 March 1848, Palmerston Papers, GC/GR/2407. I am indebted to the Trustees of the Broadlands Archives for their permission to use these papers.

[3] Cf. Van Alstyne, op. cit., pp. 347–8, 351–2. Sir Charles Wood, however, writing in 1856, stated that when there was reason to suppose that a ship canal would be made through Lake Nicaragua it was thought desirable to have some hold on the country through which it passed and that the whole line should not be in the power of one nation. The claims of the Mosquitos to San Juan were then put forward. See Wood to Erskine, 10 June 1856, British Museum, Add. MSS. 49,566, fs. 11–18, cited in Kenneth Bourne, Britain and the Balance of Power in North America, 1815–1908 (London, 1967), pp. 197–8.

[4] Palmerston to Christie, 16 Nov. 1848, F.O. 53/11; Henderson, op. cit., p. 270.

establishment of the Mosquito protectorate. But Greytown was the key to what was thought to be one of the most practicable routes for an inter-oceanic canal, and, at a moment when the 'rising American empire' – to use Professor Van Alstyne's phrase – had acquired New Mexico and California and was turning its attention southwards to Cuba and the strategic routes across Central America, another empire appeared to be seeking to command both the Caribbean shores of Central America and the canal route itself. Despite loud appeals from Nicaragua, however, and a plentiful supply of rumours about British intentions and aggressions, the United States took no hasty action. It merely sent a Kentucky lawyer, Elijah Hise, to Central America to report on the situation there and to encourage both an 'American system of policy' and a 'spirit of reunion' among the Central American states, the better to resist British encroachments.[1] Hise took seven months to reach his destination, though, when he did so, he by no means emulated the caution of his government. In the spring of 1849, however, there was a change of administrations in the United States, and Hise, in June, was superseded by a new agent, Ephraim George Squier.

The news of the great gold discoveries in California had meanwhile precipitated a gold rush across Central America, an easier and safer route than the long trek across the Great Plains and the Rockies and far quicker than the voyage round Cape Horn. Interest in trans-isthmian communications was greatly enhanced. Rival canal companies were formed. One of these, in March 1849, signed a contract with the government of Nicaragua for the utilization of the San Juan river, only to be told that the San Juan belonged to the Mosquito kingdom and could not be disposed of without the consent of its protector, Great Britain; and, at this point, Squier arrived in Nicaragua. He was twenty-eight, a journalist, an amateur archaeologist, and a friend of Parkman; and he owed his appointment, it is said, to the influence of Prescott. He was instructed that the United States would use all moral means to frustrate British designs on the Mosquito Shore and at the port of San Juan. So advised, 'I feel confident,' he wrote in September, 'that I can destroy British influence in these States,

---

[1] Manning, *op. cit.*, iii, 30–5; G. E. Belknap, ed., 'Letters of Bancroft and Buchanan on the Clayton-Bulwer Treaty, 1849, 1850', *American Historical Review*, v (Oct. 1899), 98–9.

and even procure their after expulsion from this part of the continent,' provided, that is, that he could be supported by 'a little display of power';[1] and, power or no power, he set about his task with an arrogance and a complacency worthy of Chatfield himself. Hise, without authority, had signed a treaty with Nicaragua which would have given to the the United States, in return for a guarantee of Nicaraguan territory, a virtual monopoly of the transit route. Squier signed another, less offensive indeed, but which equally ignored the title of the Mosquito kingdom to the San Juan and to Greytown and which incorporated also a new canal contract between Nicaragua and the American Atlantic and Pacific Ship-Canal Company, of which Cornelius Vanderbilt was one of the promoters. Learning, moreover, that Chatfield had placed a lien on the island of Tigre as a security for the payment of debts owed to British subjects, and fearful that he meant to take possession of it, Squier negotiated a further treaty with Honduras for its temporary cession to the United States. Chatfield thereupon seized the island.[2] For this he was rebuked. The island was restored to Honduras, and Squier, in his turn appropriated it a few weeks later. Reproved, like Chatfield, and finally replaced, he returned to Central America in 1853 as a not-too-scrupulous railway promoter, who had meanwhile substituted a war of propaganda against Britain for the diplomatic duel he had fought with Chatfield.[3]

Chatfield had outlasted Squier. Despite what *The Times* described as the 'absurd proceedings of Mr Chatfield and his American competitor, Mr Squires',[4] and despite American complaints of Chatfield's 'haughty and domineering tone',[5] Palmerston declined to recall him, on the ground that, whereas Squier had 'laboured with great activity in infusing into the governments of Central America a spirit of hostility towards Great Britain', Chatfield had confined himself to looking after British interests and had done no injury to the United States.[6] But both Palmerston and the American secretary of state, John M. Clayton, showed a very different spirit

[1] Manning, *op. cit.*, iii, 36–51; M. W. Williams, ed., 'Letters of E. George Squier to John M. Clayton, 1849–1850', *Hispanic American Historical Review*, i (1918), 427.

[2] See Chatfield to Palmerston, 17 Oct. 1849, F.O. 15/60.

[3] On this phase of Squier's career see Charles L. Stansifer, 'E. George Squier and the Honduras Interoceanic Railroad Project', *Hispanic American Historical Review*, xlvi (1966), 1–27.

[4] *The Times,* 13 June 1850.

[5] Bulwer to Palmerston, 28 Jan. 1851, F.O. 5/527.

[6] Memorandum by Palmerston, 17 Feb. 1851, F.O. 5/527.

from that which animated their representatives in Central America. Palmerston, it is true, had no thought of territorial retreat. But neither had he any thought of territorial or political advance, of monopolising the San Juan river, or of controlling a trans-isthmian waterway. Nor did Clayton entertain ideas of this kind; and Clayton was well aware that if a canal were to be built the participation of British capital was essential.

This is the background to the much-analysed and much-criticized Clayton-Bulwer Treaty of 19 April 1850, by which Britain and the United States bound themselves not to seek exclusive control over an inter-oceanic canal, not to occupy, or fortify, or colonize, or exercise dominion over any part of Central America, and not to make use of any protection or alliance which either of them had or might have with a Central American state or people for these forbidden purposes or to obtain special privileges. Its great merit, as Professor Van Alstyne pointed out many years ago, 'lay in the opportunity it furnished for a peaceful and responsible adjustment of the interests of the two countries' in place of the dangerous rivalry growing up between them in Central America.[1] Its great defect was its ambiguity.

The treaty clearly recognized the equivalence of British and American interests in Central America. It clearly imposed a permanent restraint on both American and British territorial expansion in the area. It clearly committed both countries to the support of an inter-oceanic canal to be constructed for the benefit of mankind. But on the controversial matter of existing British claims and engagements in Central America there was no agreement between them, and the vague wording of the non-colonization article of the treaty reflected this fact. Worse, it could be held, in Britain, to refer to future colonization and alliances only, and, in the United States, to apply to present colonization and alliances also.

The treaty signed, Palmerston took care, by means of an exchange of declarations between the British negotiator, Sir Henry Bulwer, and Clayton at the time of ratification, to safeguard, as he thought, Britain's position in Belize and the Bay Islands against any possible misunderstanding. As for the Mosquito protectorate,

[1] R. W. Van Alstyne, 'British Diplomacy and the Clayton-Bulwer Treaty, 1850–1860', *Journal of Modern History*, xi (1939), 162–3. I am much indebted to this valuable article. See also the earlier essay of G. F. Hickson, 'Palmerston and the Clayton-Bulwer Treaty', *Cambridge Historical Journal*, iii (1931), 295–303.

which, at the time, troubled the United States most, this, he believed, was unaffected by the treaty, save that Greytown ought not to remain under British control and should not fall under American.[1] He thought also that the boundaries of the Mosquito kingdom could be defined in treaties with its Spanish American neighbours; effective protection would then have been given to the Indians, and Britain could withdraw from any active interference in their affairs.[2] Greytown he proposed to cede to Costa Rica (due compensation being paid to Mosquito) as a free port, so that while the Pacific terminal of the proposed canal would be under Nicaraguan control, the Atlantic terminal would not. But he finally accepted the American contention that Nicaragua should have both terminals.[3] And the instructions given to the British vice-consul or consul, as he became, at Greytown,[4] as well as to the naval authorities in the West Indies, showed his intention to further what he believed to be the spirit and meaning of the treaty. Meanwhile, Christie, Walker's successor as agent and consul-general on the Mosquito Shore, had returned home on leave in June 1849; he did not go back; no further appointment was made; and in September 1851 the consul-generalship and agency were abolished.[5]

Palmerston's genuine desire[6] to implement the Clayton-Bulwer Treaty was shared by Webster, Clayton's successor in the State Department, and by Granville, Palmerston's successor in the Foreign Office. It was frustrated, so far as the Mosquito protectorate was concerned, principally by the obduracy of Nicaragua, stimulated, according to the British minister in Washington, by the indefatigable E. G. Squier.[7] Nicaragua wanted more than she

---

[1] Palmerston to Bulwer, 28 May 1850, F.O. 115/107; Hunter Miller, ed., *Treaties and other International Acts of the United States of America* (8 vols., Washington, 1931–48), v, 792.

[2] Palmerston to Russell, 5 March 1850, PRO, Russell Papers, 30/22/8D; Van Alstyne, 'British Diplomacy . . .', p. 163.

[3] Van Alstyne, 'British Diplomacy . . .', pp. 163–4. Palmerston to Bulwer, 28 Oct. 1850, 25 June 1851, F.O. 5/510, F.O. 5/526; Bulwer, 'History of the Mosquito Question', p. 33, PRO, Granville Papers, 30/29/19.

[4] Palmerston to Bulwer, 1 Nov. 1850, F.O. 5/510.

[5] Palmerston to Treasury, 24 Sept. 1851, F.O. 53/27.

[6] *Cf.* the extraordinary statement of Mario Rodríguez: 'Great Britain's aggressive [*sic*] policy in Central America came to an end with the dismissal of Lord Palmerston from the Foreign Office. . . .' 'The "Prometheus" and the Clayton-Bulwer Treaty', *Journal of Modern History*, xxxvi (1964), 277–8.

[7] Crampton to Malmesbury, 2 Jan. 1853, F.O. 5/563. And see Van Alstyne, 'British Diplomacy . . .', pp. 167–8.

could get. As a result she got nothing. Greytown, two years after the Clayton-Bulwer Treaty had been signed, was still nominally a part of the Mosquito kingdom, though practically it was a self-governing city. Its town council, till late in March 1852, was presided over by an Englishman who had formerly been the Mosquito king's physician and was now his agent as well as a British consular officer. Most of its inhabitants were North American – and armed.[1] And the municipality had already clashed with and antagonized the Canal Company, or, more precisely, the Accessory Transit Company, which the Canal Company had formed to transport passengers across the isthmus.

Two events added greatly to the irritation and tension engendered by this state of affairs. The first was the establishment in March 1852 of the Colony of the Bay Islands. The second was the defeat of the whigs, who had been responsible for the signing of the Clayton-Bulwer Treaty, in the presidential elections in November. The news of the establishment of the Bay Islands Colony reached Washington late in the year. Naturally it was looked upon as evidence of deep and sinister designs. In fact it seems to have surprised the Foreign Office almost as much as the State Department. Lord Grey, at the Colonial Office in 1850, had held that the inhabitants of Ruatan and its neighbouring islands must either be given some regular form of government or be left free to look elsewhere; that if Britain did not give them the protection which they wanted, the United States would; and therefore that Britain should. But though the wishes of the islanders were consulted during the next two years, there seems to have been no proper consultation between the Colonial Office and the Foreign Office;[2] and the unwisdom, not to say impropriety, of the step was soon evident. The democrats, now returning to power in the United States, were in any event hostile to the Clayton-Bulwer Treaty, which they regarded as contrary to the Monroe Doctrine; the proclamation of a new colony in the Caribbean added fuel to the fires of their discontent; and when, in July 1853, James Buchanan, a former secretary of state, was sent as minister to Britain, he was instructed 'to induce Great Britain to withdraw from all control

[1] Wyke to Malmesbury, 28 May 1852; James Green to Malmesbury, 3 June 1852, P.P. *Correspondence with the United States respecting Central America*, H.C., 1856, [c. 2052], lx, 167–9.

[2] Waddell, *op. cit.*, pp. 66–70, 74. Clarendon, in September 1853, was totally ignorant of the colony's existence. Manning, *op. cit.*, vii, 504.

over the territories and islands of Central America, and, if possible, over the Balize also, and to abstain from intermeddling with the political affairs of the Governments and people in that region of the world'.[1]

A prolonged interchange of views followed between Buchanan and Lord Clarendon, now foreign secretary, in which Buchanan affirmed and Clarendon repudiated the Monroe Doctrine, and Buchanan asserted while Clarendon denied that British claims in Central America had always been unfounded and, after the signing of the Clayton-Bulwer Treaty, were quite unjustifiable. Even when a great European war was impending, or perhaps indeed for this very reason, a dispute with the United States over Central America had to be taken seriously, and the private opinions of Clarendon's colleagues and advisers make interesting reading. No one, plainly, had much regard for the Mosquito protectorate. Bulwer thought it a 'rotten affair'; Addington, the permanent under-secretary at the Foreign Office, a 'millstone round our necks'; Palmerston, of 'no earthly advantage' to Britain. In Russell's view the Indians were 'wretched savages', in Aberdeen's their territory had been extended 'beyond all just bounds'. But no one was prepared to abandon them altogether. For one thing, British prestige, as Bulwer pointed out, would be seriously damaged. For another, a duty to the Mosquito Indians had been incurred and Britain was bound to discharge it. The only question was how. Greytown, it was agreed, was a separate problem. As for Ruatan, Palmerston alone seems to have had no doubts about the legality of Britain's title. Bulwer and Addington believed it to be weak and Aberdeen a 'manifest usurpation', worthy of the United States itself.[2] No one, again, seems to have been ready to sacrifice the Belize settlement or to agree to a contraction of its boundaries, as the United States had demanded, and the mistaken impression that there was a disposition to give way on all these points arises from the attribution to Clarendon of a note written late in 1854 by Buchanan

[1] Manning, *op. cit.*, vii, 86–7.

[2] Bulwer to Clarendon, 24 Jan., March 1854, Bodleian Library, Oxford, MSS. Clarendon, dep. c. 24; Addington to Clarendon, 5 March 1854, *ibid.*; Palmerston to Clarendon, 22 April 1854, *ibid.*, dep. c. 15; Russell to Clarendon, 14, 24 April 1854, *ibid.*; Aberdeen to Clarendon, 17 April 1854, *ibid.*, dep. c. 14; Aberdeen to Clarendon, 5 Nov. 1854, R. W. Van Alstyne, 'Anglo-American Relations, 1853–1857. British Statesmen on the Clayton-Bulwer Treaty and American Expansion', *American Historical Review*, xlii (1936–7), p. 498.

which he may have hoped, but can hardly have seriously believed, that Clarendon would adopt.[1] Addington asked for, and got, a decided repudiation of the Monroe Doctrine. He made the point also that 'a very conciliatory tone is highly desirable with the United States, but it may be carried so far as rather to excite nausea than affection'.[2]

The Clarendon-Buchanan exchange concluded with an offer on the part of Britain to submit the interpretation of the Clayton-Bulwer Treaty to arbitration, an offer which was renewed a year later. Meanwhile anarchy prevailed in Central America. Squier, 'an active and intriguing Yankee', who openly professed, wrote Chatfield's successor, the most bitter hostility to Britain, had again made his appearance, and his language was echoed by that of the new American minister, Solon Borland.[3] A further quarrel at Greytown between the municipality and the Accessory Transit Company ended in the bombardment and destruction of the town by an American warship in July 1854. And though there was an outburst of indignation in the United States as well as in Britain at what Clarendon described as an outrage unparalleled in the annals of modern times, the Administration refused either to disavow the action or to compensate those British subjects whose property had been destroyed. 'Perhaps the least degrading course,' wrote Clarendon, a year later, 'would be to let the matter drop at least till we have taken Sebastopol.'[4] But before Sebastopol could be taken not only had one American filibuster, Colonel Kinney, landed at Greytown, but another, William Walker, who had already led raids on Mexican territory from the United States, had descended on Nicaragua, then in the throes of civil war. There, in October 1855, he captured the town of Granada, set up a provisional government, which was actually recognized by the United States in May 1856, and had himself 'elected' president. Antagonizing the Transit Company, and faced by a coalition of the other

[1] The Note is printed by Van Alstyne, 'Anglo-American Relations . . .', pp. 496–7, attributed to Clarendon and dated c. August 1854. It was in fact written some time in November. For Buchanan's authorship see Waddell, *op. cit.*, p. 70, n. The permanent under-secretary at the Foreign Office described it as 'a most impudent' production. Hammond to Clarendon, 28 Nov. 1854, MSS. Clarendon, dep. c. 25. Rodríguez, 'The "Prometheus" . . .', p. 276, and *A Palmerstonian Diplomat*, p. 363, repeats the error.

[2] Addington to Clarendon, 5 March 1854, MSS. Clarendon, dep. c. 24.

[3] Wyke to Clarendon, 27 Nov. 1853, F.O. 15/79.

[4] Clarendon to Palmerston, 31 July 1855, Palmerston Papers, GC/CL/675/1.

Central American republics, he was indeed driven out in 1857, but twice attempted to return before meeting his death in Honduras in 1860.

Such a state of affairs was intolerable. It is some index to Central American fears, not now of Britain but of the United States, that Guatemala, in 1855, suggested that Britain and France should either secretly or openly take her under their protection, that Costa Rica, in 1856, asked both for arms and for the protection of the great European maritime powers, and that a similar cry for help came from the former Nicaraguan minister in Washington.[1] 'The sword of Damocles,' he observed, hung 'by a hair over the heads of the Spanish-American peoples.' And in Spain, which had her own reasons for distrusting the United States, there were high hopes that the American recognition of Walker's government would bring about a war between the United States and Britain, 'the thing of all others', wrote the British minister in Madrid, 'that would give most pleasure' to the Spanish government.[2]

Palmerston had been anxious to take a firm line with the United States over the bombardment of Greytown in 1854. He was all for warlike preparations a year later, when the Crimean 'recruitment crisis' was looming up in the United States.[3] His 'first impulse', the Duke of Argyll remarked, 'was always to move fleets', and in June 1856 he wanted a fleet to be sent to Greytown. But though the ships were sent, the naval officers were under strict orders only to protect British lives and property. Public opinion in Britain, it had rapidly become clear, was not prepared to run the risk of a war with the United States over Central America.[4] Nor was the United States prepared for an open breach with Britain. Once again, therefore, a serious effort was made to obtain a diplomatic settlement of the Central American question. It very nearly succeeded. By the Dallas-Clarendon Treaty of October Britain was to have her way over the Belize settlement. An arrangement agreeable to both parties was reached over Greytown and the Mosquito protectorate, which was to become an Indian reserve within the limits of Nicaragua. And, in accordance with American wishes and a

---

[1] Wyke to Clarendon, 28 Nov. 1855, F.O. 15/85; *British and Foreign State Papers,* xlvi, 784–803; Marcoleta to Clarendon, Paris, 4 Sept. 1856, F.O. 15/92.

[2] Howden to Clarendon, 1 June 1856, F.O. 72/893.

[3] Bourne, *op. cit.,* pp. 182–3, 186–7.

[3] George Douglas, Eighth Duke of Argyll, *Autobiography and Memoirs* (2 vols., London, 1906), ii, 47, 49; Bourne, *op. cit.,* pp. 196–200.

recently-signed but unratified Anglo-Honduran convention, the Bay Islands were to be made over to Honduras. The islands, however, were to become a 'free' or self-governing territory, and the United States Senate, when ratifying the treaty (by a single vote) in March 1857, amended this provision. The British government revised the amendment, and Buchanan, now president of the United States, rejected the revision. The treaty therefore failed.

Here, then, was the whole vexed question back in its original state. Each side doubted the good faith of the other. Palmerston, now prime minister, regarded Buchanan, and Buchanan regarded Palmerston, with much the same suspicion and distrust that Canning and John Quincy Adams had felt for one another thirty years earlier. The Clayton-Bulwer Treaty, instead of solving the Central American question, merely seemed to have exacerbated it. The treaty itself was little more than a dead letter. It was greatly disliked in the United States, and in Britain also the question was now asked whether it should not be abandoned.

Its most vigorous champion was Lord Napier, the new British minister in Washington. The treaty enshrined, said Napier, two great principles – the territorial neutrality of the isthmus, and equal transit rights across it; and, looking to Britain's future communications with western Canada, Australia and China, these were worth the sacrifice of every British possession in Central America.[1] Napier urged, therefore, that an envoy should at once be sent to Central America to settle all outstanding problems, in accordance with the American construction of the Clayton-Bulwer treaty but by direct negotiations with the Central American states themselves. Otherwise the treaty, he thought, would be abrogated by Act of Congress; the United States would be left with a free hand in Central America; and all guarantees would vanish.[2]

Palmerston agreed with the recommendation that direct negotiations should be begun with the Central American states themselves. But the instructions given to Sir William Gore Ouseley, the envoy appointed, were not quite what Napier had asked for. Ouseley was to act in conformity, not with the broad American construction of the Clayton-Bulwer Treaty, but with the gloss

[1] *Cf.* Napier to Clarendon, 7 June 1857, F.O. 5/672, 23 June 1857, MSS. Clarendon, dep. c. 81; to Malmesbury, 31 July, 31 Dec. 1858, F.O. 5/693, F.O. 5/695.
[2] Napier to Clarendon, 23 June 1857, MSS. Clarendon, dep. c. 81.

upon it provided by the Dallas-Clarendon Treaty;[1] and though Palmerston, like Napier, was anxious to preserve the treaty, his reasons differed from Napier's. The treaty, he told Clarendon, was valuable 'for the very reason' which made 'the Yankees so anxious to get rid of it', namely that it prevented them from taking possession of any part of Central America. The treaty once abrogated, they would soon occupy the whole. No doubt Britain would benefit commercially by 'having the whole American continent occupied by an active enterprising race like the Anglo-Saxons instead of the sleepy Spaniards', but, practically, this would endanger the security of the West Indian islands, and while a hundred years hence the Americans would doubtless have got far down 'towards Cape Horn', that was no reason why Britain should not try to keep her own.[2]

To forestall a possible American denunciation of the treaty, Ouseley was sent first to Washington, where he was to explain the nature of his mission before going on to Central America.[3] Ouseley's opinions, however, were the exact opposite of Napier's. For Napier the Clayton-Bulwer Treaty was a positive good; for Ouseley it was a positive evil. Britain, he held, was being asked to surrender substantial advantages of position, political and military, for no real equivalent. He feared that the United States, one way or another, would evade her obligations under the treaty and possibly abrogate it altogether once Britain had withdrawn from Central America; and in his opinion it would be better that the treaty should be abrogated at once so that Britain could retain her possessions, and, with them, a position of strength.[4]

Napier, Palmerston and Clarendon had no illusions about Britain's alleged advantages of position in Central America, for the simple reason that they were well aware that Englishmen cared nothing for such questions as the Bay Islands and Mosquito and would certainly not be prepared to fight for them in any collision

[1] Palmerston to Clarendon, 7 July, 30 Sept. 1857, MSS. Clarendon, dep. c. 69; Clarendon to Ouseley, 30 Oct. 1857, P.P. *Further Correspondence with the Government of the United States respecting Central America*, H.C., 1860, [c. 2748], lxviii, 48–51; Napier to Cass, 30 Nov. 1857, Manning, *op. cit.*, vii, 720–3.

[2] Palmerston to Clarendon, 7 July, 30 Sept., 22 Dec. 1857, MSS. Clarendon, dep. c. 69.

[3] Clarendon to Palmerston, 13 Oct. 1857, Palmerston Papers, GC/CL/1106/1.

[4] Napier to Clarendon, 30 Nov., 14 Dec. 1857, MSS. Clarendon, dep. c. 81; Ouseley to Clarendon, 14 Dec. 1857, *ibid.*, 22 Jan. 1858, *ibid.*, dep. c. 83. *Cf.* Ouseley to Malmesbury, 31 March, 6 July, 1858, F.O. 15/98.

with the United States.[1] But Clarendon, who shared Napier's opinion that Britain had no real interest in Central America 'beyond the freedom and independence of the transit',[2] shared Ouseley's fear that the United States might indeed evade her obligations under the treaty and that Britain might lose everything and gain nothing. Like Ouseley, therefore, he concluded that it might be better to abrogate the treaty at once, Britain retaining both Belize and the Bay Islands; and Palmerston was at any rate sufficiently convinced by these arguments to agree that an approach should be made to Buchanan to see what arrangement he would be prepared to substitute for the treaty should Britain concur in abrogation.[3]

As Britain drew near to making a formal offer of abrogation by mutual consent, however, the United States drew back, suspicious of Britain's motives and alarmed lest she should be left with too extensive a territorial hold in Central America.[4] 'The manifestation of a disposition to abrogate the treaty,' Napier later wrote, 'has been most conducive to its maintenance.'[5] In the end it was the method of direct negotiation in Central America that triumphed, though Ouseley proved an incompetent negotiator and had to be replaced; and the settlement closely followed the lines of the Dallas-Clarendon Treaty. The Mosquito king became a hereditary chief on a Mosquito reserve within the limits of Nicaragua (with an allowance of $1,500 a year). Greytown was surrendered to Nicaragua as a free port. The Bay Islands, much to the indignation of the Colonial Office, who were not consulted, and to the dismay of their inhabitants, were given to Honduras. Britain retained Belize with its extended boundaries and erected it in 1862 into the colony of British Honduras.

So ended the stormiest episode in the history of Anglo-American relations in Latin America between the promulgation of the Mon-

---

[1] Napier to Clarendon, 23 June 1857, MSS. Clarendon, dep. c. 81; Palmerston to Clarendon, 15 Dec. 1857, *ibid.*, dep. c. 69; Clarendon to Palmerston, 30 Dec. 1857, Palmerston Papers, GC/CL/1131, printed in Kenneth Bourne, 'The Clayton-Bulwer Treaty and the Decline of British Opposition to the Territorial Expansion of the United States, 1857–60', *Journal of Modern History*, xxiii (1961), 289–90.

[2] Clarendon to Palmerston, 25 Sept. 1857, Palmerston Papers, GC/CL/1098.

[3] Palmerston to Clarendon, 31 Dec. 1857, printed in Bourne, 'The Clayton-Bulwer Treaty . . .', pp. 290–1.

[4] *Cf.* Ouseley to Malmesbury, 20 March 1858, F.O. 15/98, and Williams, *op. cit.*, p. 251.

[5] Napier to Malmesbury, 31 Dec. 1858, F.O. 5/695.

roe Doctrine in 1823 and the crisis which arose over the Anglo-Venezuelan dispute in 1895–6. British policy in Central America had always been more haphazard than contemporaries supposed or posterity has allowed. It was, too, in the decade of the eighteen-fifties, at a time when Britain's own, but earlier, high-handed behaviour at Ruatan and San Juan was more than matched by that of the United States and its citizens at Greytown and in Nicaragua, remarkably restrained. Britain, of course, had major preoccupations in Europe, the Near East and India. No British statesman readily gave to American problems the attention he lavished on European: America, north as well as south, was still on the perphery of international affairs. As for Central America, no one outside 'the sphere of diplomatic employment', as Napier justly remarked, either knew or cared anything about it.[1] To the country at large it was certainly not worth a quarrel with the United States. American cotton and American trade counted for more than the whole of Central America put together, let alone the Bay Islands and Mosquito.

This was not all. The British government had watched without enthusiasm the onward sweep of the United States in Texas and California. But it had scant respect for the countries of Central America. 'Of all the ignorant, bigoted states in the world,' wrote the permanent under-secretary at the Foreign Office in 1853, 'Nicaragua is about the worst.'[2] And in the fifties the conviction grew that the southward expansion of the United States on the North American continent was not only inevitable, but, in some respects, advantageous. Palmerston himself expressed such an opinion in 1857, though he wished the process to be delayed as long as possible. Napier, in the following year, could write of the mission of the United States to achieve the regeneration of the former Spanish colonies. And Lord Malmesbury and Lord John Russell, at the Foreign Office, were prepared to contemplate the territorial expansion of the United States, if not with pleasure, at least with resignation.[3]

Finally, as Palmerston said, the Americans were 'on the spot, strong' and 'deeply interested': Britain was 'far away, weak from

[1] Napier to Clarendon, 23 June 1857, MSS. Clarendon, dep. c. 81.
[2] Addington to Clarendon, 16 Nov. 1853, MSS. Clarendon, dep. c. 11.
[3] Williams, *op. cit.*, p. 268 n.; J. F. Rippy, *Latin America in World Politics* (New York, 1931), pp. 103–4, 108; Bourne, *Britain and the Balance of Power*, pp. 200–5.

distance', and 'controlled by the indifference of the nation to the question discussed'.[1] In the face of American determination, therefore, Britain in part gave way. She had recognized in 1850 that the United States was on a footing of equality with herself in Central America. In 1860 she was beginning to recognize that the footing was one of superiority. But this did not imply any acceptance of the Monroe Doctrine, with its division of the world into spheres and hemispheres. It was not the Monroe Doctrine but the Clayton-Bulwer Treaty that determined the final settlement. The treaty, not the doctrine, became what Malmesbury called the 'acceptable and practical rule' for the relations of England and the United States in Central America;[2] and so it remained till the end of the century. By then, Britain's old preeminence had not only been successfully challenged in Central America; the time had come to challenge it in South America also.

---

[1] Palmerston to Clarendon, 31 Dec. 1857.
[2] Malmesbury to Napier, 8 Dec. 1858, F.O. 5/689.

10

Anglo-American Rivalries and the Venezuela Crisis of 1895*

Historians should be grateful to President Cleveland. It was his insistence on the arbitration of the dispute between Britain and Venezuela over the boundary of British Guiana that led to an intensive search in Spanish, Dutch, British and other archives for the evidence of European activities between the Amazon and the Orinoco during the three centuries after the discovery of America. The documents so found and printed are essential for any understanding of the historical background of the Anglo-Venezuelan dispute and of great interest to the colonial historian in general.[1] But gratitude is tempered with dismay when, to the immense range of sources, printed and unprinted, for the study of the Anglo-Venezuelan dispute proper, there is added the formidable volume of materials in American and British archives, both public and private, relating to the Anglo-American crisis to which, in 1895, the Anglo-Venezuelan dispute gave rise. Fortunately, even the more recently available collections of papers have already been put to exellent use;[2] and in attempting to review this controversy,

---

* [Presidential Address to the Royal Historical Society, December 1966. *Transactions of the Royal Historical Society*, 5th Series, xvii (1967), 131–64.]

[1] See more particularly *British Guiana Boundary. Arbitration with the United States of Venezuela. Appendix to the Case on behalf of the Government of Her Britannic Majesty* (7 vols., London, 1898), *Appendix to the Counter-Case* (London, 1898), hereinafter cited as *B.G.B.; Report and Accompanying Papers of the Commission appointed by the President of the United States 'to investigate and report upon the true divisional line between the Republic of Venezuela and British Guiana'* (9 vols., Washington, 1896–7), vol. ii; Joseph Strickland, S.J., *Documents and Maps on the Boundary Question between Venezuela and British Guayana from the Capuchin Archives in Rome* (Rome, 1896).

[2] A. E. Campbell, *Great Britain and the United States, 1895–1903* (London, 1960); E. R. May, *Imperial Democracy. The Emergence of America as a Great Power* (New York, 1961); J. A. S. Grenville, *Lord Salisbury and Foreign Policy. The Close of the Nineteenth Century* (London, 1964); J. A. S. Grenville and G. B. Young, *Politics, Strategy, and American Diplomacy. Studies in Foreign Policy, 1873–1917* (New Haven and London, 1966).

its historical background and origins, and the crisis to which it led, as a whole, I wish, first, to acknowledge my obligation to those British and American scholars who have done so much to elucidate the diplomacy of the eighteen-nineties, and, secondly, to express my hope that the interest of the subject may suffice to excuse the hardihood of the enterprise. The Venezuela crisis of 1895 was one of the most momentous episodes in the history of Anglo-American relations in general and of Anglo-American rivalries in Latin America in particular. It was, also, as Professor W. L. Burn once remarked, one of those major shocks which compel the theory of international relations to adjust itself to new facts. Both in Britain and the United States it belongs to another and a vanished age. But the controversy itself has not even yet been buried in Venezuela.

The Spaniards, who, already before the sixteenth century closed, had roamed the New World from the Grand Canyon of the Colorado to the south of South America, were the first to sail along the shores of the Guianas. They sailed also up, and down, the Orinoco, and in search of the land of the Cinnamon and of the golden city of Manoa they explored the vast inland world between the highlands of Guiana and the great coastal ranges of the Andes. But the Guianas themselves remained almost wholly neglected and unexplored.[1] San José de Oruña in Trinidad and Santo Tomé de Guayana on the Orinoco were the outposts of Spain at the end of the century,[2] and while it was left to the English to produce the first printed accounts of what soon came to be called 'the wild

[1] The fable of a Spanish ascent of the Essequibo in 1553 was long ago exploded. See G. L. Burr, 'The Guiana Boundary. A postscript to the work of the American Commission', *American Historical Review*, vi (Oct. 1900), 51, n. 1. But it is still repeated. A Spanish expedition did land between the Essequibo and the Oyapok in 1576. The sole survivor of those who did not abandon the landing party turned up many years later in Margarita with the story that he had visited Manoa and that it had taken him from dawn to dusk to cross the city from its gates to the palace of the Inca. V. T. Harlow, ed., *The Discoverie of the Large and Bewtiful Empire of Guiana by Sir Walter Ralegh* (London, 1928), pp. lxvii, lxxviii. See also, for a Venezuelan view of Spanish enterprise in the sixteenth century in the area which was to become British, French and Dutch Guiana, Pablo Ojer, S.J., *La Formación del Oriente Venezolano. I. Creación de las Gobernaciones* (Caracas, 1966), more particularly pp. 181, 202–3, 209, 291–3, 571, 576.

[2] *Cf.* Antonio Berrío to the King, Margarita, 1 Jan. 1593, printed in Harlow, *op. cit.*, pp. 102–3: 'From the mouth of the River Amazon to that of the Orinoco the map indicates more than four hundred leagues in all this latitude and more than one thousand five hundred in longitude, in which there is not a single Spanish habitation.' Berrío, who enjoyed the title of 'Gobernador del Dorado', founded both San José de Oruña and Santo Tomé, where he died in 1597.

coast' between the Amazon and the Orinoco,[1] it was left to the Dutch to make the first permanent settlements upon it.

The earliest of these settlements was on the Essequibo river. It owed its survival, if not its origin, to the Dutch West India Company, which obtained its charter in 1621, less than a year after the Pilgrim Fathers, who had themselves thought of voyaging to Guiana, landed at Plymouth Rock.[2] Other settlements followed, to the east of the Essequibo, on the Berbice, and, later, to the west of it, on the Pomeroon and on the Moruka. These last were dispersed by an English invasion in 1665. The Essequibo settlement, however, quickly recovered. By the beginning of the eighteenth century it was the centre of a far-flung trading network, north, south and west.[3] The Spanish outpost of Santo Tomé, by contrast, which had more than once been sacked and whose site had more than once been moved, was still no more than a poverty-stricken village. It contained in 1720, so the governor of Cumaná asserted, only 'twenty or twenty-five houses, occupied by the same number of residents, deprived of all human assistance, and with no means whatever to clear the dense forests which surrounded the place'.[4]

There is ample evidence of Spanish jealousy of the continued prosperity, indeed of the continued existence, of the Dutch in Guiana in the eighteenth century, and of Spanish ambitions to destroy or contain them.[5] But Spanish ambitions squared ill with Spanish resources, more particularly with 'the destitute, miserable, and backward state' of Spanish Guayana, to use the words of its governor in 1788.[6] Santo Tomé was indeed rehabilitated and,

---

[1] By Raleigh, Keymis and Masham, 1596 and 1598.

[2] For the early history of Dutch settlement, both before and after the foundation of the West India Company, see Burr, *op. cit.*, George Edmundson, 'The Dutch in Western Guiana', *English Historical Review*, xvi (Oct. 1901), 640–75, and Storm van's Gravesande, *The Rise of British Guiana*, compiled from his despatches by C. A. Harris and J. A. J. de Villiers (2 vols., Hakluyt Society, 1911), i, 10–21, 146–53.

[3] *Cf.* for its references to trade on the Upper Essequibo, the Upper Mazaruni, the Upper Cuyuní and the Orinoco, the interesting Official Diary kept at Fort Kijkoveral, July 1699 to June 1701, *B.G.B., Appendix to Counter-Case*, pp. 47–158.

[4] Report on the Transfer of the City of Guayana to the Angostura of the Orinoco by Don José Diguja, Governor of Cumaná, 15 Dec. 1763, *B.G.B., Appendix*, iii, 10. For the history of Santo Tomé, see V. T. Harlow, ed., *Ralegh's Last Voyage* (London, 1932), pp. 357–67, and Ojer, *op. cit.*, pp. 512, 568, 572.

[5] *Cf.* the secret instructions given to José de Iturriaga, 8 Oct. 1753, to try to dislodge foreigners on the coast of Guayana and to incite negro rebellions against the Dutch to the end that Portugal and Spain might divide the territory between them. *B.G.B., Appendix*, ii, 86–8.

[6] Report of Miguel Marmión, Guayana, 10 July 1788, *ibid.*, v, 59.

moved up-river, entered on a new lease of life at the famous Orinoco 'narrows' under the name of Angostura. Dutch fishermen down-stream, and Dutch traders and their Indian allies in the coastal region to the south and east of the river and on the waters of the Cuyuní, were subjected from time to time to Spanish harassment.[1] But save in the area between the Cuyuní and the Caroní, where the Catalonian Capuchins established their mission villages – no mean achievement indeed – settlement or colonization by the Spaniards there was none.[2] The Dutch, for their part, opened the Demerara region to settlement and encouraged the immigration of English planters from Barbados and other islands. They cemented alliances with the Indian tribes of the interior, presenting their chiefs with staves of office ornamented with large silver knobs and the seal of the West India Company. They maintained trading posts on the Upper Essequibo, on the Cuyuní, and, in the coastal zone, on the Moruka, and their sphere of influence extended to the Boca Grande of the Orinoco on the one hand, and, up the Cuyuní, to the neighbourhood of the Franciscan missions on the other.[3] But no boundaries between the Dutch and Spanish possessions were ever defined and none was established when early in the nineteenth century the Dutch colonies of Berbice, Demerara, and Essequibo finally passed into British hands.

For the next half-century, Spanish, or Venezuelan, Guayana, as it became with the revolt of Spain's American colonies, stagnated. Angostura, renamed Ciudad Bolívar in commemoration of its association with the great liberator of northern South America,[4] was an exception. As the chief riverine port it was a city of modest

[1] *Cf.* Resolution of States-General, 31 July 1759, *ibid.,* ii, 176; Court of Policy, Essequibo, to West India Company, May 1769, *ibid.,* iv, 12. The Spaniards, on the other hand, complained of attacks by the Carib Indians, said to be in alliance with the Dutch, on the Capuchin missions.

[2] Despite contemporary rumours and later assertions to the contrary, the mission settlements never reached the Cuyuní itself. But there is some evidence that a Spanish fort was at least begun at the confluence of the Cuyuní and the Corumo in the 1790's. The project was approved by the crown in 1791. *Ibid.,* v, 63, 130–2.

[3] For a list of postholders see *ibid.,* vii, 152 ff.; for a brief account of the Cuyuní posts, Burr, *op. cit.,* pp. 61–2; for Dutch claims to the Cuyuní, the Moruka, the Pomeroon and the Waini, the Remonstrance of the States-General to the Court of Spain, 2 Aug. 1769, *B.G.B., Appendix,* iv, 29 ff.; and for the contention that the Barima was the dividing line between Dutch and Spanish territory, *ibid.,* ii, 197 (1760), 200, 201 (1761); iii, 131 (1766), 141 (1767). See also Storm van's Gravesande, *op. cit.,* i, 239, 369; ii, 374, 376, 388, 430, 431, 460 ff., 503, 516, 528, 601.

[4] It was Bolívar's temporary capital from 1817 to 1820 and it was to the Congress of Angostura in 1819 that he delivered his most celebrated oration.

prosperity, the link between the vast interior plains of the Orinoco and the outside world. But, apart from its capital city, Venezuelan Guayana fell ever deeper into decay. The mission villages had been ruined, their pastors massacred almost to a man during the revolutionary wars. 'There are no missions,' reported a Venezuelan inspector in 1847, only their 'eloquent and pitiful remains'. 'In the thirty years,' he added, 'which have passed since the freedom of Guayana . . . that province has disappeared'.[1] Nor did it revive till gold was discovered or re-discovered in the old mission area late in the eighteen-forties and in the eighteen-fifties.

Demerara, Essequibo and Berbice, meanwhile, had been united in 1831 into the colony of British Guiana. The sources of its great rivers and much of its physical geography were still unknown, and in 1835 a young German naturalist, Robert Schomburgk, undertook a mission of exploration under the auspices of the Royal Geographical Society. Schomburgk spent nearly four years in British Guiana, mostly in its more southerly regions, and on the completion of his work wrote a letter to the governor pointing out the 'paramount necessity' of determining the frontiers of the colony by survey. With the letter he sent a sketch map on which was drawn a line boundary representing what he supposed to be the western boundary claimed by the Dutch, and the map and extracts from the accompanying correspondence were published as a Parliamentary Paper in 1840.[2]

Schomburgk returned to British Guiana in 1841, commissioned now to survey its boundaries. The task took him two and a half years, and the result, the famous Schomburgk line, was delineated and defined in a series of maps and reports sent home to the Colonial Office. So far as the frontier with Venezuela was concerned, the line, in Schomburgk's view, did not embrace all the territory which he now believed Britain might legitimately

[1] Report of Andrés Level, 5 July 1847, *B.G.B., Appendix*, vi, 152, 153, 162.
[2] *Papers relative to British Guiana*, H.C., 1840, xxxiv, (288). The map was also printed in Schomburgk's *Description of British Guiana, Geographical and Statistical . . .* (London, 1840). The boundary line, which Schomburgk describes in a letter to Governor Light on 16 July 1839, ran from a point on the Orinoco near the mouth of the Amacuro to a point on the Cuyuní and thence in a southwesterly direction towards the Mazaruni. It was the line – an arbitrary line – which Arrowsmith had engraved on his maps of Colombia of 1832 and 1834. See Clements Markham to Mallet-Prevost, draft, May 1896, in Markham to Sanderson, 13 May 1896, P[ublic] R[ecord] O[ffice], F[oreign] O[ffice Records] 80/371. Given this line Schomburgk calculated the area of British Guiana to be 76,000 square miles.

claim.[1] But it had the merit, as he repeatedly insisted, of following natural divisions instead of imaginary lines.[2] And, as Sir Clements Markham later explained to Mr Mallet-Prevost, it was intended to divide territory which had been in Spanish or Venezuelan occupaton from that which had not and in which the Dutch had established posts or settlements.[3] Such was the theory. And the Schomburgk line was to form the basis both of British claims and of the later boundary of British Guiana.

It might have been expected that Schomburgk's survey would be followed by the negotiation of boundary treaties with neighbouring countries, and such a treaty was indeed proposed by Venezuela so soon as she was informed of Schomburgk's appointment. She proposed it again late in 1841, protesting also against the erection by Schomburgk of two boundary posts at points on the south bank of the delta of the Orinoco.[4] And in 1844 she put forward the claim that the Essequibo was the dividing line between British and Venezuelan territory.[5] But when, in this same year, Lord Aberdeen formally proposed to the Venezuelan government a line of boundary so far modifying Schomburgk's line as to leave the mouth of the Orinoco, and much adjoining territory, completely under Venezuelan control,[6] his offer was ignored. Thereafter, for more than thirty years, the frontier question slept. Schomburgk's maps remained in manuscript. The general course

[1] Territory, that is, watered by rivers, such as the Yuruari, which ultimately flowed into the Essequibo. The boundary line would thus approach 'the very heart of Venezuelan Guiana'. But the rivers, he thought, were of less importance to Great Britain than Punta Barima. Schomburgk to Governor Light, 23 Jan. 1843, *B.G.B., Appendix*, vii, 50.

[2] Schomburgk to Light, 23 Oct. 1841; Memorandum by Schomburgk, 30 Nov. 1841; Schomburgk to Stanley, 1 Nov. 1844, *ibid.*, pp. 31–3, 37, 57.

[3] Markham to Mallet-Prevost, May 1896, F.O. 80/371. Like the line of 1840 the Schomburgk line placed in British territory the south bank of the Boca Grande of the Orinoco upstream to the Amacuro. But it followed a more circuitous course to the Cuyuní, struck the river at a higher point (at the confluence of the Acarabisi), and then continued along the Cuyuní from east to west and thence to its source.

[4] At Punta Barima and at the mouth of the Amacuro. Aberdeen agreed to remove them, without prejudice to British claims. Aberdeen to Alejo Fortique, 31 Jan. 1842, *B.G.B., Appendix*, vii, 80.

[5] Fortique to Aberdeen, 31 Jan. 1844, *ibid.*, pp. 86–7.

[6] Aberdeen to Fortique, 30 March 1844, *ibid.*, pp. 88–90. The line ran from the mouth of the Moruka to a point on the Acarabisi, thence conforming to Schomburgk's line. Palmerston, in 1850, stated that since Aberdeen's proposal had not been accepted, it would not be renewed. Palmerston to B. H. Wilson, 30 Aug. 1850. P[*arliamentary*] P[*apers*], Venezuela, No. 1, H.C., 1896 [c. 7972], xcvii, 260.

of his line was not unknown to the Venezuelan government.[1] But to the world at large the only boundary stamped with Schomburgk's authority was the line which had been drawn on the highly inaccurate sketch map published in 1840, and this was sometimes assumed by mapmakers and others to be Schomburgk's own line. It was reproduced, with slight variations, on later maps, including, such was official incompetence or indifference, a map prepared at the instance of the colonial authorities in 1875 and published in the following year.[2] And it is perhaps not surprising that when in 1886 the true Schomburgk line was at last made public Britain should have been accused, in President Cleveland's words, of extending 'in some mysterious way' the frontier which Schomburgk had drawn.[3]

It is not necessary to examine in detail the barren diplomatic interchanges between Britain and Venezuela about the frontiers of British Guiana. Both parties declared in 1850 that they would not occupy or encroach upon any part of the territory in dispute between them.[4] But where that territory began or ended none stayed to say. Nor did argument again begin till 1876. Meanwhile, in the eighteen-sixties and eighteen-seventies, what had been the old mission area of Spanish Guayana underwent an economic transformation. Where once the Franciscan fathers had established their mission villages, there now appeared, in the Yuruari basin, the rough mining settlements of the Caratal goldfield, their huts and houses thatched with the leaves of the *carata* palm. El Callao mine, whose first shaft was sunk in 1871, was for a time one of the richest gold mines in the world; from the goldfields as a whole

[1] It had known, for example, of Schomburgk's activities in 1841 south of the Orinoco. Aberdeen's line in 1844 coincided with Schomburgk's line from the Acarabisi onwards, and Lord Granville in 1881 provided the Venezuelan government with a map which showed the Schomburgk line with certain variations in the coastal area resulting from his own modification of Schomburgk's boundary, all to the advantage of Venezuela. *B.G.B., Appendix,* vii, 99–100.

[2] Clements Markham to Mallet-Prevost, May 1896, F.O. 80/371. This is Stanford's map of British Guiana, which had a note on it stating that the 'boundaries indicated in this map are those laid down by the late Sir Robert Schomburgk who was engaged in exploring the Colony during the years 1835 to 1839 . . .' The boundary was afterwards altered and the note erased. See below, p. 194, note 3.

[3] Grover Cleveland, *Presidential Problems* (New York, 1904), p. 221.

[4] *B.G.B., Appendix,* vi, 185–88. For Anglo-Venezuelan relations in the eighteen-forties, and the use which was made in Venezuelan domestic politics of the bogy of British imperialism, see George E. Carl, 'Orígines del Conflicto de Límites entre Venezuela y La Guayana Británica, 1840–1850', *Boletín Histórico* (Caracas, Fundación John Boulton, 1966), iv (Núm. 12), pp. 253–73.

more than one million ounces were extracted between 1860 and 1883; and before the boom years ended in 1886 so great had been the influx of immigrants from the British Isles and from the British West Indies, as well as from British Guiana, that the mining field, in one visitor's opinion, had 'more the appearance of an English Colony than a part of the Spanish-speaking Republic of Venezuela'.[1]

'English colony' or not, there was never any serious challenge to Venezuelan title to the mining district. Lord Salisbury indeed declared in 1880 that Britain could rightfully claim the whole of the basin of the Cuyuní (of which the Yuruari and the mining field formed a part), and this had been Schomburgk's opinion too.[2] But, like Schomburgk, Salisbury had no intention of pressing such a claim. It was a paper claim, maintained, indeed, to the very end, but put forward, apparently, to counter the revival of the equally, or still more, extravagant pretension of Venezuela, reiterated on three occasions between 1876 and 1879, that her frontier lay along the Essequibo.[3] And Lord Salisbury made it clear that, given the great difference between these claims, each side would have to make very considerable concessions to the other.

But all attempts to find an agreed frontier failed.[4] In the eighteen-eighties, as in the eighteen-forties, Britain was ready to concede to

[1] Report by Vice-Consul Reddan on the Gold Mines etc. of Venezuela, July 1884, *P.P., H.C.*, 1884 [c. 4172], lxxxiii, 102, 145. I should like here to express my indebtedness to Dr David Robinson, who kindly allowed me to read his unpublished doctoral dissertation on 'Geographical Change in Venezuelan Guayana, 1600–1880', and who has also drawn the map to illustrate this paper. J. H. Reddan was vice-consul at Ciudad Bolívar.

[2] Salisbury to Rojas, 10 Jan. 1880, *B.G.B., Appendix,* vii, 96–7. For Schomburgk's opinion see above, p. 191, note 1.

[3] Calcaño to Derby, 14 Nov. 1876; Rojas to Derby, 13 Feb. 1877; Rojas to Salisbury, 19 May 1879, *ibid.,* pp. 90–6.

[4] The Venezuelan minister, J. M. Rojas, revived in 1880 Aberdeen's suggestion that the frontier should begin at the mouth of the Moruka and then proposed a line running from a mile to the north of the Moruka to the 60th meridian and thence due south. Rojas to Granville, 23 Sept. 1880, 21 Feb. 1881, *ibid.,* pp. 97–8. For this he was severely rebuked by his own government, though most accounts of the controversy ignore this fact. E. B. Nuñez, *Tres Momentos en la Controversia de Límites de Guayana* (2nd edn, Caracas, 1962), p. 32. Lord Granville made a counter-proposal, which lacked, in the later opinion of President Cleveland, 'almost every feature of concession', but which, surrendering the Boca Grande of the Orinoco to Venezuela, was very similar to the line determined upon by the Tribunal of Arbitration in 1899. Granville to Rojas, 15 Sept. 1881, *B.G.B., Appendix,* vii, 99; Cleveland, *Presidential Problems,* p. 206. And Lord Rosebery, in 1886, proposed a more generous line than Lord Granville's, while stipulating that the Orinoco should be entirely free to commerce and navigation. Rosebery to Guzman Blanco, 20 July 1886, *B.G.B., Appendix,* vii, 116–17.

Venezuela complete command of the mouth of the Orinoco and to forego also her claims to territory west of the Schomburgk line. She was even prepared to agree to the arbitration of her title to some of the territory to the east of it.[1] Venezuela, on the other hand, having shown, as it seemed, a momentary disposition in 1880 to recede from her extravagant demands, reverted to them instead, insisted that her frontier was indeed the Essequibo, and formally granted to citizens of the United States colonization concessions which appeared to cover almost the whole of the territory between the Essequibo and the Boca Grande of the Orinoco.[2] The concessionaires had to be warned and steps taken to protect British interests. Finally, in October 1886, Britain proclaimed the Schomburgk line to be the provisional frontier of British Guiana,[3] and Venezuela, in February 1887, severed diplomatic relations with Britain.[4] Proposals for their renewal, and for the simultanous settlement of the boundary dispute, were put forward in 1890 and again in 1893, but put forward in vain;[5] and, in the meantime, both

[1] That is, between Granville's line and Rojas's line. Rosebery to Guzman Blanco, 20 July 1886, *cit.* p. 193, note 4.

[2] See the concessions to C. C. Fitzgerald, 22 Sept. 1883, and to Herbert Gordan, 21 May 1884, *ibid.*, vi, 219–22, 237. The Fitzgerald concession was made over to the Manoa Company of New York, one of whose agents, Robert Wells, was arrested and tried by the special magistrate for the Pomeroon district in 1884 for maltreating an Indian (hanging him up by his heels) on territory claimed by Britain. On the ill-fortunes of this company see C. G. Jackson, 'The Manoa Company', *Inter-American Economic Affairs*, xiii, no. 4 (1960), 12–45.

[3] Stanford's map of British Guiana of 1875 (see above, p. 192, note 3) was now revised and reissued and Schomburgk's earlier estimate of the area of the colony (see above, p. 190, note 2) was also revised to take into account all the territory properly embraced within the Schomburgk line.

[4] By way of an ultimatum she demanded the evacuation by Britain of all territory between the Orinoco and the Pomeroon.

[5] In the course of the discussions in 1890 Britain offered not to press her extreme claims west of the Schomburgk line, to recognize outright Venezuelan title to the 'valuable districts in the neighbourhood of Guacipati' (the northerly part of the mining field), and to submit all other claims west of the line to arbitration. See the memoranda of Sir Thomas Sanderson in *B.G.B., Appendix*, vii, 137, 140. But privately and unofficially it was again suggested that she would be prepared to surrender her claims to the south bank of the Boca Grande of the Orinoco in return for compensation elsewhere. Foreign Office to Colonial Office, 31 July 1890, F.O. 80/339. See also Michelena to Rosebery, 29 Sept. 1893, F.O. 80/355; *Libro Amarillo, 1894* (Caracas), p. 98; *P.P.*, Venezuela, No. 1, H.C., 1896 [c. 7972], xcvii, 440; Memorandum on the Boundary Question, by José Andrade, 31 March 1894, *Papers relating to the Foreign Relations of the United States, 1894* (Washington, 1895), p. 834. In 1895 the Venezuelans complained that Rosebery ignored this suggestion in the 1893 discussions. Pulido to Andrade, 17 April 1895, *Foreign Relations, 1895*, ii, 1482–3. The governor of British Guiana had in fact objected to it on the ground that the Barima River, which flowed

sides took further steps to safeguard their rights and claims. By 1892 rival police or military stations faced each other high up on the Cuyuní, at the mouth of the Yuruán river, the highway from the Cuyuní to the Caratal mining fields, and faced each other also on opposite banks of the Amacuro in the delta of the Orinoco.

In the summer of 1894, then, the boundary dispute between Britain and Venezuela was already more than half a century old and diplomatic relations between the two countries had been severed for more than seven years. At this point Venezuela appealed to public opinion in the United States. She had already sought the diplomatic support of her sister Latin American republics.[1] Year in, year out, moreover, though her own relations with the United States were none too friendly, she had laid her complaints before the State Department.[2] She had invoked the 'doctrine of the immortal Monroe'; she had asserted that what was in question was the control of the Orinoco, though plainly it was not; and she had declared that Britain's 'insatiate thirst for conquest' knew no bounds. But the United States had refused to excite herself in the matter. She had tendered her good offices to Britain. In a note which the American minister in London never delivered[3] (though the fact was to escape both President Cleveland and his secretary of state, Richard Olney), she had expressed her 'grave disquietude' at British territorial claims. And she had suggested that Britain might refer the dispute to arbitration. But despite evident signs of uneasiness, she did little more,[4] until, by a turn of fortune and a handsome fee, Venezuela secured the services, as her special agent in the United States, of William Lindsay Scruggs.

Scruggs was a former United States minister both to Colombia and to Venezuela. Though, as Minister to Colombia, he had acted

into the Boca Grande, was the highway to and from the Northwest district of the colony and that this outlet might be closed if the Orinoco were entirely under Venezuelan control. Colonial Office to Foreign Office, 28 Jan. 1891, F.O. 80/343, 30 Dec. 1891, F.O. 80/344.

[1] *Libro Amarillo, 1894,* pp. 43–5.

[2] The first of these appeals was made in 1876, the second in 1880. Thereafter they were frequent. See, more particularly, C. C. Tansill, *The Foreign Policy of Thomas F. Bayard, 1885–1897* (New York, 1940), pp. 625–63, and Dexter Perkins, *The Monroe Doctrine, 1867–1907* (Baltimore, 1937), pp. 51–60.

[3] Bayard to Phelps, 17 Feb. 1888, Henry James, *Richard Olney and his Public Services* (Boston and New York, 1923), pp. 221–2.

[4] James G. Blaine, who resigned as secretary of state in June 1892, had shown strong symptoms of impatience in 1891. Tansill, *op. cit.,* p. 648.

as arbitrator in a dispute between Colombia and Great Britain, as minister to Venezuela he had shown no great concern over the dispute between Britain and Venezuela. Nor did he have a high opinion of Venezuelan politicians. 'There has not been an honest and clean administration of government in Venezuela for thirty years,' he wrote in 1892. Holding this opinion, a few months later he was dismissed by the president of the United States for bribing the president of Venezuela.[1] The State Department does not always keep its secrets. But this secret was not disclosed till Professor Grenville and Professor Young uncovered it seventy-four years later. Scruggs returned to his home town of Atlanta, ostensibly having resigned. But he was not long unemployed. By the autumn of 1894 he was in the pay of Venezuela and engaged in writing a pamphlet which he published in October, its title: *British Aggressions in Venezuela, or the Monroe Doctrine on Trial.*

What purported to be the historical facts in Scrugg's pamphlet were supplied by the Venezuelan minister in Washington, José Andrade. But historical facts mattered little either to Andrade or to Scruggs. Their object was to show that a weak but progressive Latin American republic was threatened with dismemberment by the ruthless aggressions of a stronger power, Britain; that the principles of 'autonomous government' on the American continent and of American public law were alike imperilled; that Britain threatened to plant herself on the Orinoco; that the consequences of her success would be alarming both to the United States and to South America; and that the United States had a 'moral duty to interfere'.

As a skilful propagandist Scruggs ensured that his pamphlet should be widely and judiciously distributed, to state governors, to Congressmen and journalists, to public libraries and to clubs.[2] As a skilful propagandist also, he took care to obtain the attention of Congress as well as of the press. It was Scruggs who wrote the resolution which he persuaded Leonidas Livingston, of Atlanta, to present to the House of Representatives in January 1895 recommending that the Anglo-Venezuelan dispute should be referred to friendly arbitration. It was Scruggs who wrote the speech with which Livingston supported this resolution in Febru-

[1] Grenville and Young, *Politics, Strategy, and American Diplomacy*, pp. 127–8, 132–3.
[2] See his *The Colombian and Venezuelan Republics, with notes on other parts of Central and South America* (London, 1900), p. 296.

ary. And it was Scruggs who 'induced' Senator Henry Cabot Lodge to 'study' the dispute – his own words – with the result that Lodge wrote, in June, a masterly philippic in the *North American Review*, reproducing some of Scruggs's historical errors and adding others of his own. Finally, Scruggs twice interviewed President Cleveland, once in January, when the president asked him for one or more additional copies of his pamphlet, and again in May, when, after a discussion lasting for two hours, Cleveland promised to look into the question personally.[1]

Not everyone, of course, was disposed to swallow Scruggs – and Andrade – whole. The secretary of state, Walter Q. Gresham, his predecessor, Thomas F. Bayard, now the ambassador in London, the State Department itself, certainly did not do so.[2] But in the spring of 1895 there was an increasing readiness to accept Venezuelan propaganda at its face value. Neither the Foreign Office nor the Colonial Office had ever bothered itself much about public opinion in the United States, or, indeed, about any opinion in the United States, so far as the Anglo-Venezuelan dispute was concerned. Lord Rosebery, in 1892, had protested against the publication of a highly tendentious article in the *Bulletin* of the Commercial Bureau of the American Republics, at that time almost a branch of the State Department.[3] But no one had troubled to explain exactly what were the bases of British claims, to clear up the confusions and misunderstandings about the Schomburgk line, or to keep the United States informed about the behind-the-scenes negotiations with Venezuela. When, early in 1895, the Foreign Office was told of the willingness of the United States to lend its good offices to a settlement of the Anglo-Venezuelan dispute by arbitration, Lord Kimberley, at that time Foreign secretary, did point out that though Britain held firm to the Schomburgk line, she was prepared to make large abatements from her claims to the west of it. But it never occurred to him to explain

[1] Grenville and Young, *op. cit.*, pp. 142–5, 225–6, 152–3. The second interview took place on May 1. It was followed by the well-known meeting (wrongly ascribed to April) between Cleveland and his friend, D. M. Dickinson. *Ibid.*, pp. 150–2. Thereafter, Dickinson, in a speech at Detroit, which Cleveland subsequently endorsed, launched a violent tirade against British policy.

[2] *Ibid.*, pp. 145–6; Tansill, *op. cit.*, pp. 664, n., 695, 697–8.

[3] 34th *Bulletin*, 1892; Rosebery to Herbert, 27 Aug. 1892, *P.P.*, United States, No. 1, H.C., 1896 [c. 7926], xcvii, 4. It is possible that the author was the Bureau's Director, W. E. Curtis, who later wrote *Venezuela. A Land Where it's always Summer* (London, 1896).

also that she had repeatedly, and even as late as 1890, offered to surrender her claims to Punta Barima at the mouth of the Orinoco, and that a major reason why she was no longer willing to do this was because she was anxious to maintain the free navigation of that part of the river into which the Barima itself flowed and feared (with some justification) that Venezuela might seek to close it.[1]

For British casualness. British indifference to opinion in the United States, British reticence, there was now a penalty to be paid. Twisting the lion's tail was an old game, not confined to the American Irish. But there was more to the rising tide of criticism and hostility in the United States than a predisposition to believe the worst of Britain. The propaganda which Scruggs so successfully employed appealed precisely to that blend of idealism and self-interest which had inspired the original Monroe Doctrine in the eighteen-twenties and was to give it renewed vitality in the eighteen-nineties.

It is true, of course, that most Americans, like most Englishmen, knew very little about the Monroe Doctrine and cared still less about Venezuela. But that the political system of the New World was different from the political system of the Old, that America ought to be wholly American, and that European influence in the western hemisphere was dangerous to the peace and security of the United States, these were axioms as self-evident in the eighteen-nineties as they had been to Adams, Monroe and many others, in the eighteen-twenties. Then, indeed, the balance of economic and naval power had been heavily weighted in favour of British influence in Latin America. It was still so weighted in the eighteen-nineties. Never had the flow of British capital to Latin

[1] See above, p. 194, note 5. Kimberley to Pauncefote, 23 Feb. 1895, F.O. 80/361; *P.P., United States*, No. 1, H.C., 1896, pp. 5–6, and *cf.* Bayard to Gresham, 5 April 1895, Tansill, *op. cit.,* 696, note 160; Cleveland, *Presidential Problems*, pp. 251–5, where Kimberley's remarks are transformed into an 'ultimatum', and Allan Nevins, *Grover Cleveland, A study in courage* (New York, 1933), pp. 631–2: 'The news that Kimberley was asserting an informal claim [to the Orinoco] was profoundly alarming'. But there was nothing new in British claims. Nor, in the view of the Colonial Office, was 'the control of the mouth of the Orinoco' really in question. 'Point Barima,' argued C. A. Harris, 'can hardly be said to command the main mouth of the river; and Great Britain, if actuated by motives of aggression, could at any time with equal ease command the passage by her ships of war.' Memorandum in reply to the note of the United States Secretary of State on the Venezuelan Boundary, 2 Sept. 1895, F.O. 80/363. For Venezuelan threats to the free navigation of the Orinoco see Walter LaFaber, *The New Empire. An Interpretation of American Expansion, 1860–1898* (Ithaca, 1963), p. 252.

America been so great as in the decade of the 'eighties, and never had European economic penetration, led by Britain, been so extensive. But American capital now also looked abroad. American industry had developed to the point at which it needed foreign markets. Long before the economic collapse of 1893 had enhanced its attractiveness, James G. Blaine had preached the doctrine that 'while the great powers of Europe are steadily enlarging their colonial domination in Asia and Africa it is the especial province of this country to improve and expand its trade with the nations of America'.[1] Officials in Latin America, such as John E. Bacon, had deplored the decline of the American merchant marine. Publicists, such as H. R. Helper, had advocated the construction of a Pan-American railway. Congress itself, in 1884, sent a commercial mission to Latin America, of which W. E. Curtis, later the director of the Commercial Bureau of the American Republics, was at first the secretary. Five years later Blaine had the satisfaction of presiding over the first International Conference of American States, whose purposes, certainly, were as much commercial as political. And when, in 1895, the National Association of Manufacturers was formed, it was to Latin America that the Association looked and in Venezuela, indeed, that it established its first sample warehouse.[2] 'We are a great nation,' declared Senator Lodge in December 1895, 'and we have a great nation's duties and responsibilities. The path which we should follow lies clear before us. We must be the leaders in the Western Hemisphere. We must protect our coasts and hold the commerce of that hemisphere.'[3]

If this was the task, as Lodge saw it, then in Latin America the United States came face to face with Europe and with Britain in particular. It was not that British claims in the western hemisphere were 'multiplying', as one argument runs,[4] erroneously, I think, though British economic interests, in banking and railways, in public utilities and in the export industries certainly were. But

[1] LaFaber, op. cit., p. 105.

[2] Ibid., pp. 191–4. See also his article, 'The Background of Cleveland's Venezuelan Policy: A reinterpretation', American Historical Review, xlvi (July 1961), 947–67, and A. P. Whitaker, The Western Hemisphere Idea: its rise and decline (Ithaca, 1954), pp. 74–85.

[3] Henry Cabot Lodge, Speeches and Addresses, 1884–1909 (Boston and New York, 1909), pp. 238–9. Cf. his speech of 2 March 1895: 'We are a great people; we control this continent; we are dominant in this hemisphere.' Ibid., pp. 185–6.

[4] LaFaber, The New Empire, pp. 243, 246, and 'Background of Cleveland's Venezuelan Policy', p. 958.

Americans feared that these claims were multiplying. 'We have no intention,' said Lord Salisbury in 1891, 'of constituting ourselves a Providence in any South American quarrel. We have been pressed, earnestly pressed, to undertake the part of arbitrator, of compulsory arbitrator in quarrels on the west coast of South America, in the Chilian quarrels [Salisbury was referring to the civil war of 1891], and to throw down our warder in order that the tournament may cease. We have been earnestly pressed, also, on the east of the continent to undertake the regeneration of Argentine finance. On neither of these subjects are Her Majesty's Government in the least degree disposed to encroach on the functions of Providence.' Britain's task, Salisbury continued, was 'to look after British interests, to assert them and to defend them if they are unjustly attacked', not to interfere in the troubles or quarrels of other nations.[1]

This was merely to reaffirm traditional policy, the policy laid down by Castlereagh and Canning. But it was not the view of British policy which Blaine had taken in 1882 when he described the War of the Pacific as 'an English war on Peru, with Chile as the instrument'.[2] It was not Gresham's view when, in 1894, during the great Brazilian naval revolt, he took measures to put a stop to the attempted blockade of Rio de Janiero, in the belief that a rebel victory would be contrary to American economic interests and half-suspecting that Britain was encouraging the revolt in order to obtain, among other things, the restoration of the Brazilian monarchy.[3] Yet, however much British and American sympathies may have been enlisted on opposite sides in these disputes, so far as the British government is concerned not the slightest evidence has yet been produced from the British archives to justify Blaine's conviction or Gresham's suspicions.[4]

[1] *The Times,* 30 July 1891. I owe this reference to H. S. Ferns, *Britain and Argentina in the Nineteenth Century* (Oxford, 1960), p. 465.

[2] See the interesting discussion by V. G. Kiernan, 'Foreign Interests in the War of the Pacific', *Hispanic American Historical Review*, xxv (1955), 14–36, which disposes of Blaine's contention so far as the British government is concerned.

[3] LaFaber, *The New Empire,* pp. 210–17, and 'United States Depression Diplomacy and the Brazilian Revolution, 1893–1894', *Hispanic American Historical Review,* xl (1960), 107–18. Professor LaFaber appears to share Gresham's suspicions.

[4] A Foreign Office Minute of 1 Jan. 1894 in F.O. 13/733, on a complaint about the harm done to British shipping by the rebel naval operations, observes: 'H.M. Govt. much regret this lamentable state of affairs, [but] have no right or intention to interfere in the quarrel,' and adds that 'it would not be proper for H.M. Govt. to attempt to influence or decide' the course of the revolution.

There were occasions, however, when British interests did seem to need to be asserted or defended, and in 1895 such an occasion occurred in Central America. This was an area in which the United States, because of her interest in an American-controlled isthmian canal, was peculiarly sensitive to the dangers of European influence. It was an area also in which Britain possessed a colony – British Honduras – and had at one time exercised a protectorate. The protectorate, over the Mosquito Indians of the region known as the Mosquito Shore, had become a reserve within the republic of Nicaragua, its self-governing status being more clearly defined as the result of an arbitral award by the emperor of Austria in 1881.

It was perhaps natural that in disputes with the Nicaraguan government the inhabitants of the reserve – some of whom were British, and, at a later stage, many others American – should have tended to look to Britain, and equally natural that the United States should have begun to fear that Britain was seeking to restore the protectorate. Lord Salisbury, in 1889, denied any such intention, and Salisbury's denial was repeated in 1894 by Lord Kimberley after Nicaraguan intervention in the reserve had led to protests and disorders, the dispatch of an American warship (it struck a reef and was lost on the way), and the landing of British marines at Bluefields. The marines were soon withdrawn; when further disorders took place, it was American, not British, sailors who were landed; and, by the end of the year, the reserve had been formally incorporated into Nicaragua, allegedly at the wish of the Mosquitos themselves and to the rather sanctimonious relief of the Foreign Office. But the whole affair had roused great uneasiness in the United States. During the disturbances, moreover, two Americans and a number of British subjects, including a vice-consul, had been seized by the Nicaraguans, roughly handled and removed from the reserve. The Americans were quickly released, but not the British. Britain thereupon demanded redress and an indemnity of £15,000, and when this also was delayed British marines, in April 1895, occupied the port of Corinto.

This was battleship diplomacy; it was not unknown to the United States; and Gresham, the secretary of state, though he thought that the British demands were harsh, thought also that they must be met. But public opinion was violently outraged. The Cleveland administration was vigorously attacked for its supineness in the face of British brutality and aggression; and Scruggs, in his campaign on behalf of Venezuela, found a powerful if un-expected ally in the Royal Navy.[1]

At this point Gresham was taken ill and died. He was succeeded on June 8 by the attorney-general, Richard Olney, a hard-headed corporation lawyer, to whom Scruggs at once sent a copy of his pamphlet. Gresham, though he had been impelled to write to Bayard in March in words which, Professor May has suggested, may have been the President's rather than his own, that Britain's attitude was unjust and that the time was coming when the United States would have 'to call a halt', had been well aware of Venezuelan efforts to mould opinion and the press. He had firmly stated his opinion also that Venezuela should resume diplomatic relations with Britain.[2] And there seems no reason to suppose that the instruction which he was preparing to send to the American ambassador in London would at all have resembled the dispatch which Olney did send on July 20 with the warm approval of Cleveland but without, apparently, any real discussion within the State Department and not much with the cabinet.[3]

Olney's note reviewed the history both of the Anglo-Venezuelan dispute and of the Monroe Doctrine, arriving at the conclusion that the dispute was 'in any view far within the scope and spirit' of the doctrine. It asserted that any permanent political union between a European and an American state was 'unnatural and inexpedient', and in illustration of this dictum drew a picture of the dangers to which South America and the United States would be exposed by the transfer of European political systems to the western hemisphere. In contrast to Canning's famous statement, seventy years earlier, that 'Spanish America is free; and if we do not mismanage our affairs sadly, she is English', it declared that 'today the United States is practically sovereign on this continent,

---

[1] The Nicaraguan affair is dealt with by M. W. Williams, *Anglo-American Isthmian Diplomacy, 1815–1915* (Washington, 1916), pp. 288–99; R. L. Morrow, 'A Conflict between the Commercial Interests of the United States and its Foreign Policy', *Hispanic American Historical Review*, x (1930), 2–13; Tansill, *op. cit.*, pp. 668–90; and LaFaber, *The New Empire*, pp. 218–28. See also, for American opinion, N. M. Blake, 'Background of Cleveland's Venezuelan Policy', *American Historical Review*, xlvii (Jan. 1942), 263–6.

[2] Tansill, *op. cit.*, pp. 695–6; May, *Imperial Democracy*, p. 39; Grenville and Young, *op. cit.*, pp. 145–8.

[3] *Cf.* Matilda Gresham, *Life of Walter Quintin Gresham, 1832–1895* (2 vols., Chicago, 1919), ii, 795. But see LaFaber, *op. cit.*, p. 255. James, *op. cit.*, p. 111, points out that it does not appear that Olney's assistants in the State Department saw the note. It was read over to members of the cabinet. For the text see *Foreign Relations, 1895*, i, 545–62.

and its fiat is law upon the subjects to which it confines its interposition'. Finally, it demanded that Britain should agree to submit
the Venezuelan boundary question in its entirety to arbitration
and that, if she were unwilling to do this, the President should be
informed in time for him to lay the whole subject before Congress
in his next annual message.

Olney's despatch represented the triumph of Scruggs and of
Venezuela in the sense that by July 1895 both the president and
the secretary of state had been brought to believe that Britain
was in the wrong, that the vital interests of the United States were
involved, and that the United States must intervene. In this they
were in accord with the public mind and were doubtless not
indifferent to the pleasures of popular support. But here Scrugg's
triumph and Venezuela's ended. Not a word was said to Venezuela
about the note, though its proposals affected her deeply. What
seems to have been uppermost in Olney's mind, indeed, was not
the interests of Venezuela but the interests of the United States,
the vindication of the Monroe Doctrine,[1] and, I would add, of the
paramount position of the United States in the western hemisphere.
From this point of view he was neither anti-English nor pro-
Venezuelan. He was simply pro-American. He never recognized, or
at any rate never admitted, the flagrant inaccuracies of his celebrated note. Neither did Cleveland, who, much pleased with the
note at the time, saw no flaws in it six years later when writing his
own account of the dispute.[2] But Olney did admit that his language
was sometimes 'of the bumptious order' and gave the excuse that
'in English eyes the United States was then so completely a negligible quantity that it was believed only words the equivalent of
blows would be really effective'.[3]

But words the equivalent of blows had not the slightest effect on
Lord Salisbury as prime minister and in charge of the Foreign
Office or on Mr Joseph Chamberlain at the Colonial Office.
Chamberlain, who had now got the idea into his head that there was
a gold-bearing region in the colony close to and 'probably over'

[1] See, more particularly, the able argument of G. B. Young, 'Intervention under
the Monroe Doctrine: The Olney Corollary', *Political Science Quarterly*, lvii (1942),
247–80; Grenville, *Lord Salisbury and Foreign Policy*, p. 58; and Grenville and Young,
op. cit., pp. 166, 175–6.

[2] Cleveland to Olney, 3 March 1901, Allan Nevins, ed., *Letters of Grover Cleveland,
1850–1908* (New York, 1933), pp. 546–7.

[3] Olney to Knox, 29 Jan. 1912, James, *op. cit.*, p. 140.

the Schomburgk line, as he said, which might turn out to be another Transvaal or West Australia,[1] was all for belligerence. The United States, he thought, should be told that the Monroe Doctrine had nothing whatever to do with the boundary dispute, and, moreover, that Britain was herself an American power with a territorial area greater than that of the United States.[2] He was eager also to teach the Venezuelans a lesson. In January 1895 the British police station at Yuruán, high up the Cuyuní, had been attacked and British subjects had been arrested and ill-treated. True, the station had been quickly re-occupied. But such a state of affairs, in Chamberlain's opinion, was 'almost intolerable', and he wanted, therefore, a strong note to be sent to Venezuela demanding redress and the fullest possible compensation under the threat of force.[3] And though at least one voice was raised in the Foreign Office to protest that the Colonial Office was 'too bloody-minded about the business',[4] on October 14 the note was sent, together with an instruction to the governor of British Guiana to repel any additional act of Venezuelan aggression beyond the Schomburgk line. If further evidence were wanted of Chamberlain's lack of understanding of Olney's note, of the Monroe Doctrine, and of the temper of American opinion, it is afforded by his extraordinary suggestion, early in December, that Britain should propose to France an exchange of the Caribbean island of Dominica for Dahomey and its hinterland. Equally remarkable, Lord Salisbury actually made the proposal.[5]

Chamberlain's comments on Olney's note were sent to the Foreign Office early in September, together with a memorandum drawn up in the Colonial Office by C. A. Harris which concluded that there was no reply that Britain could return to Olney 'except that she declines to submit to any arbitration the bogus claims of Venezuela to the greater part of a British Colony'.[6] A month

---

[1] Chamberlain to Salisbury, 4 Sept. 1895, S[alisbury] P[apers], Correspondence from Chamberlain, 1887–1897. (I am much indebted to the Marquess of Salisbury and to the librarian of Christ Church, Oxford, for the permission given me to make use of these papers.) See also Grenville, *op. cit.*, p. 63.

[2] Colonial Office to Foreign Office, 11 Sept. 1895, F.O. 80/363.

[3] Colonial Office to Foreign Office, 30 Aug. 1895, F.O. 80/362.

[4] Minute of 30 Aug. 1895, F.O. 80/362.

[5] The idea was Lord Selborne's. Chamberlain to Salisbury, 8 Dec. 1895, S.P., Correspondence from Chamberlain; May, *op. cit.*, pp. 45–6. France was also to surrender her fishing rights off Newfoundland.

[6] Memorandum in reply to the note of the United States Secretary of State on the

later, the law officers of the crown, whose advice had also been sought, gave it as their opinion that Olney's interpretation of the Monroe Doctrine was 'absolutely incompatible with international law'.[1] Not till the end of November, however, was Salisbury's reply ready, and then, sent by sea in the form of two despatches to Sir Julian Pauncefote, the British ambassador in Washington, it arrived too late for the president's annual message at the opening of Congress.[2]

'It is surprising,' Pauncefote once complained from Washington, 'how few public men in this country can carry on a discussion like a gentleman; they write like rival attorneys or newspaper editors. I cannot rely on Mr Olney any more than on his predecessors.'[3] No one could accuse Lord Salisbury of such behaviour. The tone of his reply was studiously courteous. But it strongly reminded one contemporary American historian of the condescension with which Sir Leicester Dedlock in *Bleak House* submitted to an interview with Mr Rouncewell, the ironmaster.[4] And not only did Lord Salisbury in effect rebuke Olney for his interference, correct his errors and reject his proposals; he directly challenged his interpretation of the Monroe Doctrine. 'Mr Olney's principle,' wrote Salisbury, 'that American questions are for American decision, even if it receive any countenance from the language of President Monroe (which it does not), cannot be sustained by any reasoning drawn from the law of nations. The Government of the United States is not entitled to affirm as a universal proposition, with reference to a number of independent States for whose conduct it assumes no responsibility, that its interests are necessarily concerned in whatever may befall those States, simply because they are situated in the Western Hemisphere.'[5]

Venezuelan Boundary, 2 Sept. 1895, in Colonial Office to Foreign Office, 11 Sept. 1895, F.O. 80/363. Harris later edited the despatches of Storm van's Gravesande for the Hakluyt Society.

[1] Law Officers to Salisbury, 12 Oct. 1895, F.O. 80/363.

[2] As Professor Grenville has shown, there seems no reason to suppose that the delay was deliberate. Salisbury was preoccupied with the Turkish crisis. Moreover, having prepared one despatch only, dealing with the Monroe Doctrine, he was then asked by the cabinet to prepare a second, dealing with the frontier dispute. Grenville, *op. cit.,* p. 62. And the Foreign Office seems to have mistaken the date on which the President would deliver his message.

[3] Pauncefote to Salisbury, 24 July 1896, S.P., America, 1895–1898, A/139.

[4] H. T. Peck, *Twenty Years of the Republic* (New York, 1906), p. 422.

[5] *Foreign Relations, 1895,* i, 563–76.

The explosion that followed was not surprising. In August the second assistant secretary of state in Washington had reported that the 'newspaper men' were 'wild' over the discovery that Britain had recently taken possession of the uninhabited island of Trinidade, some six hundred miles off the coast of Brazil, for use as a cable station.[1] Pauncefote, in October, when the news of Britain's ultimatum to Venezuela over the Yuruán incident had arrived, 'found the Press raging and lying outrageously about Venezuela'.[2] 'The Venezuelan trouble,' he wrote again in November, 'has occupied the Press and the Jingoes almost exclusively, and the most fantastic speculations are indulged in by the "irresponsible chatterers" as to what may be the outcome of the matter and as to the tone and character of the British reply to what they term "Olney's ultimatum",'[3] rumours of which had long been circulating. And though, when the reply did arrive, Pauncefote thought it 'superb',[4] Olney and Cleveland, who had awaited it with increasing impatience, were outraged; and Olney, at any rate, not at all sensitive to the feelings of others, deeply felt what he later described as 'the seeming if not intentional, contumely' with which, as he thought, his own note had been received.[5]

The Presidential Message of 17 December, drafted by Olney, sent to his Boston office, not to the State Department, to be typed, and revised by Cleveland, sitting up till sunrise, was partly the result of hot temper; it was partly the only acceptable alternative to surrender. It resoundingly reaffirmed the Monroe Doctrine and its application to the Anglo-Venezuelan dispute. It asked Congress to appropriate funds for a Commission which should seek to determine the true line of division between Venezuela and British Guiana, and it declared that when the Commission's report had been made and accepted, it would be the duty of the United States 'to resist by every means in its power as a willful aggression upon its rights and interests the appropriation by Great Britain of any lands or the exercise of governmental jurisdiction over any territory

[1] LaFaber, *op. cit.*, p. 246. Brazil protested, Britain gave way.
[2] Pauncefote to Salisbury, 25 Oct. 1895, S. P. A/139.
[3] Pauncefote to Salisbury, 8 Nov. 1895, *ibid.* See also, for American excitement, Blake, *op. cit.*, pp. 270–2, and Tansill, *op. cit.*, p. 709, n., and pp. 710–13.
[4] Pauncefote to Barrington, 17 Dec. 1895, S.P., A/139.
[5] Olney to Chamberlain, 28 Sept. 1896, C[hamberlain] P[apers], Birmingham University Library, J.C. 7/5/1A/23. (For permission to make use of these papers I am much indebted to the Librarian.) Olney's letter is printed in A. L. P. Dennis, *Adventures in American Diplomacy, 1896–1906* (New York, 1928), p. 59.

which after investigation' the United States had 'determined of right' belonged to Venezuela.

On the face of it Cleveland's message was virtually an ultimatum. It sounded the 'note of war'.[1] 'Nothing is heard', wrote Pauncefote to Salisbury, three days later, 'but the voice of the Jingo bellowing out defiance to England.'[2] Only a few observers, ex-Governor Long of Massachusetts, for example, and Pauncefote himself, noted the velvet glove beneath the gauntlet of mail. The proposed Commission, thought Long, provided a way out, 'through which the whole bubble can fizzle and effervesce',[3] and Pauncefote, in similar terms, thought it a 'fine safety valve'.[4] As modern historians have noted, Cleveland nowhere bound himself to accept the Commission's report. No word was said of the principles on which it would act or of the length of time at its disposal. And, once again, Venezuela was not consulted.[5] It was not the qualifications or omissions, however, it was the belligerent phrases of the message that caught the public eye. 'Annihilation stares you in the face,' wrote a Kentucky business man to Salisbury on December 18,[6] and Olney had some reason for saying later that the 'American heart' was stirred as it had not been since the Civil War.[7] But the panic of December 20 on the New York stock exchange was a moderating influence,[8] and Pauncefote soon discerned a 'strong undercurrent' of opinion flowing, as he wrote, 'in opposition' to the apparently 'warlike attitude of the president'.[9] By the beginning of the New Year the immediate sense of crisis was already beginning to fade. Pauncefote could note with relief that 'a wave of reason is passing over this country after the extraordinary exhibition of "dementia" which we have witnessed'.[10]

[1] Pauncefote to Salisbury, 24 Dec. 1895, F.O. 80/364.

[2] Pauncefote to Salisbury, 20 Dec. 1895, S.P., A/139. See also Campbell, *Great Britain and the United States*, p. 16.

[3] Enclosure in W. L. Broadbent to Salisbury, 19 Dec. 1895, F.O. 80/364.

[4] Pauncefote to Salisbury, 3 Jan. 1896, S.P., A/139.

[5] See S. F. Bemis, *A Diplomatic History of the United States* (London, 1937), p. 419; Young, *op. cit.*, pp. 259–61; Grenville, *op. cit.*, pp. 66–7; Grenville and Young, *op. cit.*, pp. 167–8.

[6] D. C. Crutcher to Salisbury, 18 Dec. 1895, F.O. 80/364.

[7] Olney to Chamberlain, 28 Sept. 1896, C.P.

[8] For divided opinions in the business and financial world see LaFaber, *op. cit.*, pp. 270–6.

[9] Pauncefote to Salisbury, 24 Dec. 1895, F.O. 80/364. For Cleveland's critics see Perkins, *op. cit.*, pp. 194–9; Tansill, *op. cit.*, pp. 726–8; and May, *op. cit.*, pp. 56–8.

[10] Pauncefote to Salisbury, 3 Jan. 1896, S.P., A/139.

Electrifying the United States, Cleveland's message startled and shocked Great Britain. Lord Salisbury, indeed, remained unmoved. The whole affair, he thought, would 'fizzle out'.[1] And Chamberlain, though gravely concerned, showed no disposition to give way.[2] It was neither a British nor an American interest, he wrote, that European powers should move into America; and, so far, Britain might support the American contention. But an 'unnatural and altogether unprecedented extension' of the Monroe Doctrine she could not accept.[3] His under-secretary, Lord Selborne, on the other hand, expressed a general bewilderment when he confessed that 'the hatred', as it seemed to him, 'of England by Americans is to me quite unaccountable. We expect the French to hate us and are quite prepared to reciprocate the compliment if necessary; but the Americans, No!';[4] and Sir William Harcourt's insistence, as joint-leader of the Opposition, that there must be no war with America, accurately reflected, after the first outburst of indignation, the tenor of British opinion.[5] It is no doubt true that the Kaiser's telegram to President Kruger on January 3 congratulating him on the defeat of Dr Jameson's 'armed bands' in South Africa helped to deflect this current of indignation from the United States to Germany. But it may be questioned whether under almost any circumstances British opinion would have tolerated a war with the United States. And, of course, Olney and Cleveland, for their part, did not want war with England.

A passage, now familiar, in Chamberlain's diary reveals what happened next. For many years Britain had been willing to agree to the arbitration of all territory to the west of the Schomburgk line, and Chamberlain, indeed, in August 1895, had wanted to insist on it.[6] This was still Lord Salisbury's view. But at his cabinet

[1] Goschen to Salisbury, 19 Dec. 1895, A. D. Elliot, *The Life of George Joachim Goschen, First Viscount Goschen, 1831–1907* (2 vols., London, 1911), ii, 204.

[2] *Cf.* J. L. Garvin [and Julian Amery], *The Life of Joseph Chamberlain* (4 vols., London, 1932–51), iii, 72.

[3] Chamberlain to Selborne, 20 Dec. 1895, C.P., J.C. 7/5/1B/4.

[4] Selborne to Chamberlain, 18 Dec. 1895, C.P., J.C. 7/5/1B/2.

[5] Chamberlain's Diary, 9 Jan. 1896, *ibid.*, J.C. 7/5/1B/14. *Cf.* Garvin, *op. cit.*, iii, 160–1, and A. G. Gardiner, *The Life of Sir William Harcourt* (2 vols., London, 1923), ii, 397. A. J. Balfour, on 15 January, publicly declared that 'a war with the United States' carried with it something of 'the unnatural horror of a civil war'. *Ibid.*, ii, 397–8.

[6] Colonial Office to Foreign Office, 30 Aug. 1895, F.O. 80/362.

meeting on January 11 he found that 'the great majority – if not all the cabinet – would be glad of any honourable settlement', and, though he himself was ready to resign rather than 'to yield unconditionally to American threats', he did not reject a proposal that the United States should be asked whether she would consent to an arbitration 'limited to the territory on either side of the Schomburgk line at present unsettled'.[1]

With this decision Britain in effect recognized the right of the United States to intervene in the Anglo-Venezuelan dispute. She abandoned also her insistence on the Schomburgk line. But months of unofficial as well as official discussions followed before an agreement could be reached. President Cleveland's Boundary Commission, and the distinguished investigators whom it employed, such as Justin Winsor, John Franklin Jameson and George Lincoln Burr, were not long in getting to work and were given friendly assistance in England. Burr, at a later date, was even allowed the use of Chamberlain's own room in the Colonial Office while Chamberlain was away in the United States.[2] And while Chamberlain, in London, reversed his earlier instructions and ordered the colonial authorities in British Guiana to avoid any action that might have the appearance of aggression,[3] Olney, in Washington, insisted that Venezuela should make amends to England for the incident which had occurred at Yuruán in January[4] and rebuked her for allowing a further frontier incident to occur in June.[5]

Of the Anglo-American negotiations themselves three points deserve to be particularly noted. First, the United States, with British concurrence, acted on Venezuela's behalf, but Venezuela herself was not consulted, or, rather, as Professor Young pointed out some years ago, she was not consulted till the very end of the negotiations, and then only perfunctorily.[6] Venezuela, said Olney

---

[1] Chamberlain's Diary, 11 Jan. 1896, C.P.; Garvin, *op. cit.*, iii, 161–2; May, *op. cit.*, p. 50; Grenville, *op. cit.*, p. 68.

[2] R. H. Bainton, *George Lincoln Burr* (Ithaca, 1943), p. 78.

[3] Colonial Office to Foreign Office, 18 Jan. 1896, F.O. 80/367, 1 May 1896, F.O. 80/371.

[4] Pauncefote to Salisbury, 31 Jan. 1896, S.P., A/139; Denning (Mexico) to Salisbury, 7 Feb. 1896, F.O. 80/368; Pauncefote to Salisbury, 18 Feb. 1896, F.O. 80/368, 20 May 1896, F.O. 80/371.

[5] Olney to Andrade, 25 June 1896, in Pauncefote to Salisbury, 30 June 1896, F.O. 80/372.

[6] *Libro Amarillo, 1897*, p. xxxi; Young, *op. cit.*, pp. 275–6.

on one occasion, 'has got to do exactly what we tell her';¹ he revealed not the slightest wish that she should be represented by one of her own citizens on the Tribunal of Arbitration which he proposed should be set up; and when a final agreement was reached in Washington her president was simply given to understand that it was 'very just and fair' and that he 'had better expedite its completion' or it would be 'bad for his country'. So, at least, Pauncefote reported.²

Secondly, Olney wanted arbitration to be complete and unrestricted, to embrace, that is, all the territory that Britain claimed on the one hand and Venezuela on the other, though, from the first, he was ready to concede that due weight should be given to long-continued occupation.³ Salisbury and Chamberlain, on the other hand, were determined to safeguard what they called 'settled areas'. Britain, wrote Salisbury in January, was 'contending for men – not for land, for the rights of settlers' who had been 'encouraged to invest in such property and to tie up their fortunes in it'; and Chamberlain, on the following day, used almost identical words.⁴ In their opinion, therefore, settled districts must be excluded from the terms of arbitration. 'There would be almost as much ground,' said Salisbury in March, 'for giving up the West Indian island of Trinidad.'⁵ But the questions remained: what constituted a settled area, and was settlement, at any period, however recent, sufficient to give title?

The way out of these difficulties was suggested by Olney. He proposed, first, that in determining the boundary line such weight and effect should be given to occupation as 'reason, justice, the

¹ Sir Stafford Northcote to Salisbury, 16 March 1896, on an interview with Olney. S.P., Northcote, H.S. See also Grenville and Young, *op. cit.,* pp. 175–6. Northcote also interviewed Cleveland, who observed that 'there was no active feeling of sympathy in the U.S. with the Venezuelans themselves – that it was a question of U.S. dignity in maintaining the position they had taken up of arbitration in some shape'. Northcote to Salisbury, 22 March 1896, S.P.

² Pauncefote to Salisbury, 13 Nov. 1896, S.P., A/139.

³ *Cf.* Olney to Bayard, 14, 22 Jan., 8 Feb. 1896, James, *op. cit.,* pp. 229, 233–6. For a detailed account of the negotiations see Tansill, *op. cit.,* pp. 740 ff., and T. C. Smith, 'Secretary Olney's Real Credit in the Venezuelan Affair' [May, 1933], Massachusetts Historical Society, *Proceedings,* lxv (1940), pp. 112–47.

⁴ Salisbury to Chamberlain, 31 Jan. 1896, C.P., J.C. 5/67/44; Grenville, *op. cit.,* p. 63; Chamberlain to Playfair, 1 Feb. 1896, C.P., J.C. 7/5/1B/27. *Cf.* Salisbury to Pauncefote, 7 Feb. 1896, S.P., Private, America, A/140; 22 May, F.O. 80/371, 3 July, F.O. 80/373; to Chamberlain, 12 Aug., C.P., J.C. 5/67/54.

⁵ Salisbury to Pauncefote, Tel., 3 March 1896, F.O. 80/369.

rules of international law and the equities' of any particular case might seem to require.[1] This proposal satisfied Salisbury's attorney-general, Sir Richard Webster,[2] and it was embodied as a rule governing the arbitrators in the final Treaty of Arbitration. But it failed to satisfy Salisbury himself. The claims of Venezuela, he wrote, were 'so far reaching' that they impeached 'titles which have been unquestioned for many generations' and brought into dispute 'interests and rights' which could not 'properly be disposed of by an unrestricted arbitration'.[3] Olney admitted the objection. But could it not be agreed, he asked, that while arbitration should be unrestricted, there should be an instruction to the arbitrators that territory which had been in the 'exclusive, notorious, and actual use and occupation of either party for even two generations', or say for sixty years, should be held to belong to that party?[4] And this principle was also finally accepted, though the term of sixty years was shortened to fifty.

Such rules obviously disposed of Venezuela's extreme pretensions.[5] But, as Chamberlain pointed out, in the 'thirties and 'forties there had been substantially no settled districts 'away from the coast or in the immediate vicinity of the left bank of the Essequibo'.[6] And British claims did not rest on settlement alone. They rested also 'upon an effective occupation' by means 'of trading posts at strategic points, general administration and use of the territory between these points, and permanent connection with the native tribes covering the area so administered'.[7] In September Chamberlain himself paid a visit to the United States. Historians have generally regarded it as unimportant, and so, on the whole, it was. But it was now – and this is my third point – that, in interviews and correspondence with Olney, he put forward the view that the arbitrators must take into account not only long-continued

---

[1] Olney to Pauncefote, 12 June 1896, F.O. 80/372; *Foreign Relations, 1896*, pp. 249–52. *Cf.* his earlier letter to Bayard, 8 Feb. 1896, James, *op. cit.*, p. 235.

[2] Later Lord Alverstone. Memorandum by Richard E. Webster, 24 July 1896, S.P., Cabinet Papers, Box 4.

[3] Salisbury to Pauncefote, 3 July 1896, F.O. 80/373; *Foreign Relations, 1896*, pp. 252–3. *Cf.* Salisbury to Chamberlain, 12 Aug. 1896, C.P., J.C. 5/67/54.

[4] Olney to Pauncefote, 13 July 1896, F.O. 80/373; *Foreign Relations, 1896*, pp. 253–4. *Cf.* Smith, *op. cit.*, p. 138.

[5] Pauncefote to Salisbury, 15 July 1896, F.O. 80/373; Chamberlain to Salisbury, 21 Aug. 1896, S.P., Correspondence from Chamberlain.

[6] Chamberlain to Salisbury, 4 July 1896, S.P., Correspondence from Chamberlain.

[7] Wingfield to Sanderson, 5 Aug. 1896, F.O. 80/373.

occupation in the sense of settlement, but also long-continued political control of territory neither actually used nor occupied.[1]

Olney seems to have recognized – so Chamberlain's letters imply – that there was force in this proposal. And Chamberlain, on his return to England, pursued it. He wrote it, rather against the inclination of the attorney-general, into the draft which formed the basis of Pauncefote's final negotiations with Olney;[2] and the safeguard that exclusive political control of a district, as well as actual settlement of it, during a defined term, should be deemed sufficient to constitute title was incorporated into the heads of the proposed treaty of arbitration between Venezuela and Great Britain as agreed between Britain and the United States and signed by Olney and Pauncefote on 12 November 1896.

The heads of agreement laid down the terms and rules of arbitration and provided for an arbitral tribunal, two of whose members, representing Venezuela, were to be chosen by the Supreme Court of the United States, two by the judges of the supreme court of justice in Great Britain, and a fifth member, who was to preside, selected by these four jointly. Given the rules which were to guide the arbitrators, Britain, as the event was to prove, had little to fear from arbitration, and Lord Salisbury, in a speech at the Guildhall on November 9, was able to refer to the controversy as though it were at an end.[3]

But though Britain and the United States had made the agreement, the parties to it were to be Britain and Venezuela, and it still remained for Venezuela to acquiesce. Nearly a year earlier Cleveland's special message to Congress had been greeted in Venezuela with enthusiasm. There had been processions, banquets, speeches. And these rejoicings were echoed elsewhere. It is true that President Montt of Chile, a country whose relations with the United States had long been unfriendly, bluntly remarked that 'the United States would make Venezuela pay dearly for any action taken on her account';[4] that ex-President Pellegrini of Argentina declared the Monroe Doctrine to be an anachronism;[5]

[1] Chamberlain to Olney, 9 Sept. 1896; to Salisbury, 9, 17 Sept. 1896, S.P., Correspondence from Chamberlain. Tansill, *op. cit.*, p. 772, prints parts of the letter to Olney but without comment.

[2] Sanderson to Webster, 15 Oct.; Sanderson to Pauncefote, 16 Oct.; Webster to Sanderson, 19 Oct. 1896, F.O. 80/375.

[3] *The Times,* 10 Nov. 1896; James, *op. cit.,* p. 133.

[4] Kennedy (Valparaiso) to Salisbury, 26 Feb. 1896, F.O. 80/368.

[5] Perkins, *op. cit.,* pp. 212–13.

and that the president of Brazil observed that he believed in South America 'for the South Americans, not for the Americans of the North'.[1] On the other hand, both Houses of Congress in Brazil passed resolutions of congratulation on the message; demonstrations of support took place in Colombia and Panama; and friendly comment appeared in Ecuador, Guatemala and Peru.[2]

There were no rejoicings of any kind in November and December 1896. On the contrary, the terms of the proposed treaty were read in Venezuela with disapprobation amounting to dismay.[3] The press and the politicians strongly criticized the fifty-year rule and the way in which the arbitrators were to be selected. President Crespo even referred to a sense of 'national humiliation'.[4] And it was as a concession to wounded feelings that the terms of the treaty were so far modified as to permit the president himself to nominate an arbitrator.[5] Even so, it was distinctly understood that he should not name a Venezuelan, and his choice in fact fell on the Chief Justice of the United States.

This concession made, the treaty was signed in February 1897 and ratifications were exchanged in June. A distinguished panel of jurists was then set up, two American, two British, and one Russian. President Cleveland's Boundary Commission, meanwhile, had suspended its investigations as early as November 1896 (though it still had to produce a voluminous report), and its secretary, Mallet-Prevost, became one of the counsel retained by the Venezuelan government. Pauncefote thought that the 'wretched Scruggs', as he called him,[6] would be another. But in this he was mistaken: Scruggs was rapidly falling from grace in Venezuela as well as in the United States. In October 1899, sitting at Paris, the Tribunal made its award. The line of boundary which it approved more or less followed the Schomburgk line. But Venezuela was given a small portion of disputed territory at either end, Punta Barima on the Orinoco on the one hand, and the extreme upper Cuyuní on the other. In return she was compelled

[1] Phipps (Rio de Janeiro) to Salisbury, 9 March 1896, F.O. 128/223.

[2] Perkins, *op. cit.*, pp. 210–11; Consul Mallet (Panama) to Salisbury, 24 Dec. 1895, F.O. 80/364; W. S. Robertson, 'Hispanic American Appreciations of the Monroe Doctrine', *Hispanic American Historical Review*, iii (1920), 1–16.

[3] *Cf. Libro Amarillo, 1897*, p. xxxii; Young, *op. cit.*, pp. 276–7.

[4] Olney to Pauncefote, 11 Dec. 1896, S.P., A/139; Pauncefote to Salisbury, 28 Dec. 1896, F.O. 80/376.

[5] Pauncefote to Salisbury, 5 Jan. 1897, F.O. 80/379.

[6] Pauncefote to Salisbury, 22 Jan. 1897, S.P., A/139.

to recognize the free navigation both of the Barima and of the Amacuro.[1]

For the most part, then, the British case was vindicated. But this was the least important result of the Anglo-Venezuelan dispute. Pauncefote could argue in November 1896 that Britain had 'accepted nothing but the good offices of the United States and the use of her judicial officers to carry out an arbitration with Venezuela which otherwise would have been impossible'.[2] But this was special pleading. Hitherto Great Britain had paid but little respect to the Monroe Doctrine. It could be viewed, Lord Clarendon had said in 1854, only 'as the dictum of the distinguished personage who delivered it', not 'as an international axiom which ought to regulate the conduct of European states';[3] and Clarendon's words were almost literally repeated by Lord Salisbury in his note of November 1895. A few days later Britain was presented with the alternative either of directly challenging the Monroe Doctrine or of accepting, in large measure, the interpretation of it then current in the United States. The disparity in military and naval power between the two countries was still enormous. But, for many reasons,[4] Britain did not choose to take up the challenge, and her refusal to do so meant that no effective opposition to the doctrine could be offered by any other power. The Monroe Doctrine, it could be argued, was not merely strengthened, possibly it was preserved, by the refusal of the greatest naval power in the world to oppose it to the point of war.

But that refusal entailed other consequences. In 1826 British trade, British capital, British diplomacy and British naval power had won for Great Britain a pre-eminent position in Latin America. In 1896 American diplomacy, American trade and American capital were beginning to win that pre-eminence for the

[1] The line was demarcated by a joint Anglo-Venezuelan commission between 1901 and 1905. The allegations made by Mallet-Prevost in a memorandum written in 1944 and published in 1949, after his death, that the Tribunal acted under political pressure and that the award was the result of a bargain between Britain and Russia, are effectively disposed of by C. J. Child, 'The Venezuela-British Guiana Boundary Arbitration of 1899', *American Journal of International Law*, 44, No. 4 (1950), pp. 682–93.

[2] Pauncefote to Salisbury, 13 Nov. 1896, S.P., A/139.

[3] 2 May 1854. W. R. Manning, ed., *Diplomatic Correspondence of the United States. Inter-American Affairs, 1831–1860* (12 vols., Washington, 1932–9), vii, 541.

[4] For Britain's increasing isolation in Europe and the world see Grenville and Young, *op. cit.*, pp. 170–1.

United States, at least in the more northerly parts of the region. British trade and British capital were still the more important. But in the Venezuela crisis Britain recognized in effect that it was not Great Britain but the United States which occupied a special position in relation to Latin America. The years that followed saw the withdrawal of the British West Indies squadron and the rapid growth of the American navy. They saw, in 1901, by the second Hay-Pauncefote Treaty, the recognition by Britain of American supremacy in the Caribbean. They saw, finally, the full emergence of the United States as a world power and the complete and cordial acceptance by Britain of the principles of 1823 as currently interpreted in the United States. 'We welcome,' said Mr Balfour, as prime minister, in February 1903, 'any increase of the influence of the United States of America upon the great Western Hemisphere,' and in the debate on the king's speech at the opening of parliament the government spokesman boldly asserted that 'the principle of the Monroe Doctrine has always received the unwavering support of successive Ministries in this country'.[1] Politicians' memories are notoriously fallible. But, as it is related that the Duke of Wellington remarked to the person who addressed him as 'Mr Jones, I believe', 'Sir, if you believe that, you will believe anything.'

[1] *The Times*, 14 Feb. 1903; *Parliamentary Debates*, 4th Series, cxviii, 60 (John Gretton); Perkins, *op. cit.*, pp. 360–1.

11

The Caudillo Tradition*

Constitutional theory and political practice almost invariably differ. But it cannot be denied that in Latin America, or at least in large parts of that area, the discrepancies between them have been peculiarly marked. The theory is that of democratic representative government, and while many Latin Americans may reject this theory in their hearts, believing, indeed, that it is quite unsuited to Latin American conditions, few among their statesmen venture to repudiate it with their lips.[1] Its principles are extolled even by those who least respect them.[2] The constitution of every Latin American state is framed in their light. And, though there have been deviations from the norm, the long history of constitution-making in Latin America reveals, as Mr Kingsley Davis has remarked, a 'persistent effort to give greater reality to the democratic ideal'[3] and to block, by legal prescription, every nook and cranny of possible abuse.

Yet it is an ideal world that most of these documents describe. They are statements of aspirations, not of facts. The facts are different. The government of the Dominican Republic, says Article 2 of the 1947 constitution of that state, 'is essentially civil, republican, democratic, and representative'. And the same words are repeated in Article 111. But everyone knows that the government of the Dominican Republic is, and has been for more than a

---

* [First published in *Soldiers and Governments,* ed. M. Howard (London, 1957), pp. 149–65.]

[1] President Vargas of Brazil, during his long dictatorship from 1930 to 1945, and General Higinio Morínigo of Paraguay were among the few.

[2] Thus Colonel Perón: 'considero indispensable ratificar nuestra fe en las instituciones democráticas y republicanas que nos gobiernan.' *Doctrina Peronista* (Buenos Aires, 1948), p. 17.

[3] Kingsley Davis, 'Political Ambivalence in Latin America', in A. N. Christensen, ed., *The Evolution of Latin American Government* (New York, 1951), p. 226, reprinted from *Journal of Legal and Political Sociology,* i (1942), 127–50.

quarter of a century, the personal government of one man, Generalissimo Rafael Leonidas Trujillo,[1] the doyen of Latin American dictators, and, to quote the titles which a grateful country has bestowed upon him, the 'Benefactor of the Fatherland' and the 'Restorer of the Financial Independence of the Republic'. Article 335 of the 1939 constitution of Nicaragua (replaced by a new constitution in 1948) states that 'The army, composed of the national guard and the police, is . . . intended to guarantee the independence of the nation, the integrity of its territory, internal peace, and the security of individual rights.' It was in fact used to put General Anastasio Somoza into power in 1937 and to keep him there till his assassination in September 1956.[2] The 1938 constitution of Bolivia, revised in 1945, lays it down in Article 4 that 'The people shall not deliberate or govern except by means of their representatives and by the authorities created by law. Any armed force or association of persons usurping the rights of the people commits the crime of sedition.'[3] The crime was successfully committed on five occasions between 1938 and 1952,[4] and neither the government which promulgated the constitution nor the government which revised it came into power by legal means.

These are not isolated examples. It is true that except for Juan Vicente Gómez, who was the master of Venezuela for twenty-seven years, no Latin American dictator in recent times has enjoyed so long a period of absolute power as Generalissimo Trujillo or even as President Somoza. It is true also that the disorders which have plagued Bolivia have been matched, in South America, only by what have been euphemistically described as 'alterations of the legal order' in Paraguay and by the multiplicity of so-called revolutions and *coups d'état* in Ecuador – a country which counted fourteen presidents between 1931 and

[1] The statement is unaffected by the fact that General Trujillo allowed the presidency to be held by Dr Jacinto Peynado from 1938–40, by Manuel de Jesús Troncoso de la Concha from 1940–2, and by his brother, Héctor Trujillo, from 1952–6. [He himself was assassinated in 1961.]
[2] General Somoza permitted Dr Leonardo Argüello to become his successor in May 1947, but, Dr Argüello proving insufficiently compliant, he was removed and replaced by the General's uncle, who died in 1950.
[3] In citing Latin American constitutions, I have followed the texts in R. H. Fitzgibbon, *The Constitutions of the Americas* (Chicago, 1948).
[4] In 1939, 1943, 1946, 1951 and 1952.

H

1940 and four within the span of four weeks in 1947.[1] But resort to fraud or force has long been, and still is, an accepted method of changing a Latin American government or of prolonging it in power. The approximation of political practice to constitutional theory, evident in Uruguay, Costa Rica and Chile,[2] is the exception rather than the rule. Personal governments or military governments have flourished in large states as well as in small, in Brazil and Argentina (despite the fig-leaves with which Colonel Perón attempted to cover his dictatorial nakedness) as well as in Nicaragua, Guatemala or the Dominican Republic. And so strong is the revolutionary tradition that since the end of the Second World War there are only five of these twenty republics in which a de facto régime has not succumbed to military pressure or armed rebellion.[3] Four heads of government, in these post-war years, have been assassinated.[4] One president has committed suicide.[5] And while the largest of all the republics, Brazil, has returned to the constitutional path, Colombia, abandoning the traditions of almost half a century, has left it.[6]

Names are misleading. A revolution, as the term is employed in Latin America, does not necessarily imply some violent convulsion of society or of the state. It is an extra-legal method of replacing one government by another; and it may well be thought that the significance of a good many Latin American revolutions has been that they have no significance, except as evidence of a particular set of social, economic, and political conditions. The masses of the people were not affected, their life was unchanged.

[1] See G. I. Blanksten, *Ecuador. Constitutions and Caudillos* (Berkeley and Los Angeles, 1951), pp. 10–11, 32, 55–7. It is worthy of note that President Galo Plaza, inaugurated in 1948, completed his constitutional term, and his successor, Dr José María Velasco Ibarra, long the stormy petrel of Ecuadorean politics, was equally fortunate.

[2] Chile's constitutional life was gravely disturbed between 1924 and 1932, and Costa Rica's in 1948. Uruguay experienced a *coup d'état*, carried out by President Terra, in 1933, and popular government was briefly suspended by President Baldomir in 1942.

[3] The Dominican Republic, Chile, Mexico, Nicaragua and Uruguay. For the removal of a puppet president in Nicaragua see above, p. 217, note 2.

[4] President Gualberto Villarroel of Bolivia in 1946; Delgado Chalbaud, who headed the military junta in Venezuela in 1950; José Remón, of Panama, in 1955; and Anastasio Somoza, of Nicaragua, in 1956.

[5] Getulio Vargas, who shot himself on 24 August 1954.

[6] [Despite the continuance of violence and guerrilla warfare, constitutional government was restored in Colombia by the nineteen-sixties. The Trujillo régime in the Dominican Republic was overthrown in 1961 when Trujillo himself became the fifth Latin American president to be assassinated since 1946.]

Of other revolutions, especially in more recent years, the repercussions may be wider and the implications far-reaching. The *coups d'état* which brought Dr Vargas to power in Brazil in the nineteen-thirties and Colonel Perón in Argentina in the nineteen-forties accelerated the rise of social and political forces, hitherto submerged, which can never again be ignored. The changes of régime in Guatemala in 1945 and in Bolivia in 1952 could plainly not be dismissed as a mere substitution of the 'outs' for the 'ins'. But only one Latin American revolution in modern times – the great upheaval which began in Mexico in 1910 – can sustain comparison with the French Revolution of the eighteenth century or the Russian Revolution in the twentieth.[1]

The fact remains that force plays a major role in Latin American politics. Nor is it merely exhibited in the recurrent drama of *coups d'état* and rebellions, or in occasional displays of mass violence. The free functioning of political parties, the honest conduct of elections, and a willingness to abide by their result, are certainly among the essentials of a democratic system. But they have not been distinguishing features of Latin American political life. Politics, in most of the republics, are power politics. 'The grim jest,' to use the words of Professor Fitzgibbon, that in each of 'the more strongly governed states' of Central America there have been two parties, 'the one in power and the one in jail,'[2] had only too much truth in the decade of the nineteen-thirties and may even evoke a wry smile now. Mr Cecil Jane, in a well-known book published in 1929, rashly observed that 'The Argentine is today one of the most stable and well-ordered states not only in America but in the world; it is one in which revolution is as improbable as it is in England.'[3] A revolution took place in the following year, and whatever the vagaries of electoral practices before 1930, since 1930 free and honest elections in Argentina have been unknown, unless the two Peronista elections of 1946 and 1951 are to be regarded as dubious exceptions.[4] In Brazil, where the army acted

---

[1] /See above, 'Tradition and Revolt in Latin America', pp. 15–16. The Mexican Revolution stood alone till the decade of the 'fifties, which saw the beginning of violent social revolution both in Bolivia (1952) and in Cuba (1959).]

[2] R. H. Fitzgibbon, 'Executive Power in Central America', in Christensen, *op. cit.*, pp. 410–11, reprinted from *Journal of Politics*, iii (1941), 297–307.

[3] Cecil Jane, *Liberty and Despotism in Spanish America* (Oxford, 1929), p. 173.

[4] [As of 1957. Colonel Perón was overthrown in 1955. Military rule followed till 1958 and was temporarily renewed in 1962 and again in 1966.]

after 1945 as the guardian of the constitution, President Vargas, in the previous fifteen years, dispensed with elections altogether but promulgated two constitutions, of which the last was so ingeniously constructed that no one could tell whether it was ever in operation or not. And, in Mexico, it may, or may not, be taken as evidence of the popularity of the régime which the Mexican Revolution has created, that though elections are regularly fought they are as regularly won by the Partido Revolucionario Institucional, that is, by the government.

Nor is this all. 'Away with the cant of "measures, not men!",' said Canning in 1802, 'the idle supposition that it is the harness and not the horses that draw the chariot along! No, Sir; if the comparison must be made, if the distinction must be taken, men are everything, measures comparatively nothing.'[1] This was, and to some extent is, the Latin American view too. 'The history of the South American Republics,' wrote Francisco García Calderón, 'may be reduced to the biographies of their representative men,'[2] and partial as this interpretation is, it serves to underline the extreme importance of the part played by the individual in Latin American politics. The 'representative men' in the nineteenth century were the caudillos, the 'monarchs in republican dress', the 'natural' leaders, the men 'with a mission', as Professor Blanksten describes them.[3] This 'species of political saurian', says Dr Uslar Pietri, was 'doomed to extinction by the changes in the economic, social, and cultural environment'.[4] But the caudillo tradition survives. Political creeds exist, and some of them are increasingly important. But personalities have always mattered more than programmes, and parties are as much the expression of personal loyalties as of political principles. And as the caudillo was above the law, so also is his modern counterpart impatient of restraints upon the free exercise of his will. 'If that is the law,' said Queen Victoria on a famous occasion, 'the law must be altered.' And in Latin America, as convenience dictates, altered it is, or ignored. The tradition of legality is embodied in the written constitutions of the Latin American states; their unwritten constitutions reflect, all too often, a disrespect for law.

[1] *The Speeches of the Right Honourable George Canning* (6 vols., London, 1828), ii, 61.
[2] Francisco García Calderón, *Latin America: its rise and progress* (London, 1913), p. 99.
[3] Blanksten, *op. cit.*, pp. 34–5.
[4] G. S. Wise, *Caudillo. A portrait of Antonio Guzmán Blanco* (New York, 1951), p. v.

Like the fifteenth-century Italian despot, the nineteenth-century caudillo was an expression of the needs and conditions of his time. But caudillismo was older than the 'age of the caudillos'. Its roots lay deep in the colonial past and in the structure, the character and the traditions of Spanish American society. Spain's empire in the New World had been an absolutism, a paternal absolutism, it is true, but an absolutism none the less. Its principle was the principle of authority. Loyalty to the crown was the cement which held the vast, heterogeneous structure together, and, after three hundred years of Spanish imperial rule, it still needed the shock of the Napoleonic invasions of the Iberian peninsula and the consequent crisis of the Spanish monarchy to precipitate the revolutions which led to independence. But the Spaniards are a highly individualistic people. Anarchy, says Salvador de Madariaga, is their 'natural state'.[1] And in the Indies Spaniards and Spanish Americans were distant indeed from Spain. They were used to authority. But they were used also to ignoring authority. 'Obedezco, pero no cumplo', 'I obey, but I do not execute.' Who but a Spaniard could have devised so ingenious a formula for nullifying the royal will, as nullified it so frequently was? It was not merely in civic tumults nor even in occasional rebellions that what Pedro Henríquez-Ureña calls 'the latent anarchy of the colonial régime' was revealed.[2] The comment of Antonio de Ulloa, visiting Peru in the seventeen-forties, comes forcibly to mind. 'Here . . .', he reported, 'everyone considers himself a sovereign.'[3]

The principle of authority destroyed, loyalty to the crown dissolved, it was the anarchical element that prevailed. The collapse of the empire was the collapse of the state, whose ally, the church, was itself gravely compromised. It was in vain that the architects of a new order attempted to establish a rational pattern of freedom in constitutions which, too often, borrowed eclectically from abroad, and conformed too rarely to political and social realities at home. Once the old basis of political obligation had been undermined, there was no firm foundation, as General O'Leary noted in his famous memoirs, on which political institutions could be

[1] Salvador de Madariaga, *The Rise of the Spanish American Empire* (London, 1947), p. 283.
[2] Pedro Henríquez-Ureña, *Literary Currents in Spanish America* (Cambridge, Mass., 1946), p. 112.
[3] Jorge Juan and Antonio de Ulloa, *Noticias Secretas de América* (2 parts, London, 1826), p. 436.

built.[1] There were exceptions. In Chile the landed gentry early drew together to give the country stability and to open the way for the slow unfolding of its economic life. And Brazil was always a case apart. But in most of the new republics of Spanish America there was little cohesive force, little sense of *communitas*, to weld into a whole the diverse elements of which society was composed; and while the masses were sunk in poverty and ignorance the dominant social class had yet to learn to govern itself before it could govern others. Politically at least these states were not the adult heirs of imperial Spain; they were her orphan children,[2] their homelands ravaged, their prosperity destroyed, their economic life disrupted the enormous catastrophe of civil war. 'Many tyrants will arise upon my tomb,' wrote Bolívar in 1826,[3] and the prophecy was fulfilled. The constitutionalists, as Professor Morse remarks, those who 'avowed the existence in fact of a state-community', were 'swept away before the winds of personalism'.[4] Authority revived not in the impersonal state but in the person of the caudillo. Dictatorship became the norm of government, revolution the method of changing it. 'We convulsed a continent for our independence,' says Martin Decoud in Conrad's *Nostromo*, 'only to become the passive prey of a democratic parody.'

A military class enjoying special privileges, the so-called *fuero militar,* had made its appearance in Spanish America before the wars of independence began. But it was the wars that fastened militarism on so many of the new republics. A relatively large standing army, such as was retained in Mexico, too often proved a menace rather than a protection to the state whose security it was designed to serve. Military loyalties became distinct from civic loyalties, and military interests from civil interests. 'The presence of a fortunate soldier,' San Martín had said in his famous farewell proclamation to the people of Peru, '. . . is dangerous to newly constituted states.'[5] But it was the soldiers, who, in their

[1] *Memorias del General Daniel Florencio O'Leary. Narración* (3 vols., Caracas, 1952), i, 20.

[2] 'La verdad es que las colonias hispanas, a diferencia de las inglesas del continente, no consiguen su emancipación por la mayor edad, sino por la orfandad'. Jaime Eyzaguirre, *Fisonomía Histórica de Chile* (Mexico, 1948), p. 98.

[3] Vicente Lecuna, ed., *Cartas del Libertador* (12 vols., Caracas and New York, 1929–59), v, 292.

[4] R. M. Morse, 'Toward a Theory of Spanish American Government', *Journal of the History of Ideas*, xv (1954), 79–80.

[5] R. A. Humphreys, *Liberation in South America, 1806–1827* (London, 1952), p. 114; *Documentos del Archivo de San Martín* (12 vols., Buenos Aires, 1910–11), x, 356.

own view, were the indispensable men. Most of the early presidents-dictators, and of the lesser local and provincial caudillos as well, were military leaders, veterans of the revolutionary armies, ambitious local commanders, and, in Argentina, gaucho chieftains of the plains. A civilian autocrat, such as the formidable Dr José Gaspar Rodríguez de Francia, whose ruthless reign in Paraguay attracted, inevitably, the half-admiring attention of Carlyle, was the exception rather than the rule.

The caudillos ruled by force. And, mostly, they fell by force. Some, like the infamous Carlos Solano López of Paraguay, were destroyed in war. Some, like the theocratic Gabriel García Moreno of Ecuador, one of the most remarkable of the later civilian caudillos, were assassinated. Some, like Rosas, the greatest and the worst of the Argentine tyrants, ended their days in exile. But few died peacefully in power. Dr Francia in Paraguay and Rafael Carrera in Guatemala were notable exceptions. And few, once they had tasted power, voluntarily relinquished it. Most of them had some basis of general support in one or another segment of the population, and most, also, were capable of inspiring a passionate loyalty among their immediate followers. In Argentina Darwin was told that a man who had murdered another, 'when arrested and questioned concerning his motive, answered, "He spoke disrespectfully of General Rosas, so I killed him." ' 'At the end of a week,' adds Darwin, 'the murderer was at liberty.'[1] Nor were the caudillos all of one sort. There were autocrats who waded through blood to presidential thrones, ignorant adventurers, like Mariano Melgarejo of Bolivia, who perpetrated unspeakable crimes. And there were astute and cynical despots who had nothing to learn from the pages of Machiavelli.[2] But not all the caudillos were tyrants. Among them were sincere and high-minded men, not without honour or undeserving of honour in the countries which they ruled; and even among the worst there were some who, by breaking and moulding lesser despots to their will, helped to substitute a larger conception of the state as a nation for the

[1] Charles Darwin, *Journal of Researches into the Natural History and Geology of the Countries visited during the voyage of H.M.S. 'Beagle' round the world* (9th ed., London, 1890), p. 53.

[2] 'On nearly every page of Machiavelli,' observes Professor Morse, 'appears practical advice which almost seems distilled from the careers of scores of Spanish American caudillos,' *op. cit.,* p. 81. For the caudillos in general see C. E. Chapman, 'The Age of the Caudillos: a chapter in Hispanic American history', *Hispanic American Historical Review*, xii (1932), 281–300.

agglomération of personal and local loyalties which had hindered its action and restrained its growth.

When the 'age of the caudillos' ended, if ended it has, is a matter of debate. In some of the Spanish American states the struggle for stability, the problem of how to reconcile freedom with order, had not been resolved even when the nineteenth century closed. In some it has not been resolved today. But the turbulent years of the first half-century were certainly the worst. Slowly, however, the temper of politics began to change. The cruder forms of military despotism began to vanish. Civilian oligarchies took control and a new type of presidential autocrat arose. In Argentina the unity of the nation and its constitutional organization were at last attained by the eighteen-sixties. And thereafter the face of the great pampa, where the gauchos had fought and the Indians roamed, was transformed. The great currents of European capital and immigration, the coming of the railway net-work, the invention of wire-fencing and of the refrigerator and the refrigerator ship, all spelt the advent of a new age. In Brazil the monarchy which had served the country so long and so well, which had preserved its unity and had given to it a political education, was displaced by a federal republic. But though a military conspiracy destroyed the empire, its fall was bloodless and its legacy to Brazil was a tradition of constitutionalism. Mexico, after the great reform movement of the mid-nineteenth century and the tragic episodes of foreign intervention and the empire of Maximilian, finally found peace and stability under the long dictatorship of Porfirio Díaz; and Díaz was indeed the new type of caudillo. The régime rested, no doubt, on military force. But it was grounded also on economic interests, business interests as well as landed interests. Díaz could refer to his legislators as 'my herd of tame horses'.[1] Like Aristotle's tyrants he preferred foreigners to citizens. But the Pax Porfiriana offered substantial rewards – the approval of foreign powers, the economic prosperity of the supporting groups, and the modernization of Mexico.

What were the results of this great transformation? Bryce summed them up in what is perhaps the best of all travel books on South America, published in 1912. There were, he found, three classes of states in Latin America. First, there were 'true republics in the European sense', countries, that is, in which

[1] L. B. Simpson, *Many Mexicos* (3rd ed., Berkeley and Los Angeles, 1952), p. 263.

authority had been obtained under constitutional forms, not by armed force, and where the machinery of constitutional government functioned with regularity and reasonable fairness. Secondly, there were the 'petty despotisms', more or less oppressive and corrupt, and created and maintained by military force. And, thirdly, there was a fairly large intermediary class, a group in which the machinery of constitutional government indeed existed but worked more or less irregularly and imperfectly. In the first class Bryce placed two countries only – the 'aristocratic republic' of Chile, whose history had always been distinctive, and Argentina. Mexico, he believed, belonged to the intermediary class and Haiti was by far the worst of the despotic.[1] At this point Bryce ceased to particularize.

Such, then, was the situation at the opening of the present century. But again a great transformation scene occurred. Uruguay embarked on the great experiment of state socialism. The state entered into commerce and industry; it assumed new social responsibilities; its political machinery was overhauled. And what had formerly been one of the most backward and turbulent of the Latin American republics was transformed, within a few years, into one of the most vigorous and most progressive. Colombia, a land where dictators had never flourished long, but whose political life had been fevered in the extreme, substituted ballots for bullets, developed a two-party system, and won for itself by the nineteen-thirties a reputation for maturity and stability which was seemingly well-deserved.[2] The little state of Costa Rica in Central America, with the advantages of a comparatively homogeneous population, a high degree of literacy and a fairly wide distribution of property, grew into a 'true republic', in Bryce's sense of the word, an oasis of democracy amidst a desert of Central American dictators. And in Mexico the Pax Porfiriana was broken. Díaz was driven from office. The pent-up passions of the people, the suppressed desires for social and economic liberation, burst into conflagration, and Mexico became the scene of the first genuine social revolution in the New World.

The observations upon which Lord Bryce's book had been founded were made in 1910. What changes had been wrought in

---

[1] James Bryce, *South America. Observations and Impressions* (rev. ed., New York, 1920), pp. 526, 541–3.

[2] *Cf.* C. H. Haring, *South American Progress* (Cambridge, Mass., 1934), p. 183.

the political pattern of the Latin American republics twenty-five years later, and what variations have subsequently occurred? In the first place, it seemed fairly obvious, in the decade of the nineteen-thirties, that Costa Rica and Colombia ought now properly to be included in the category of what Bryce called 'bona fide' republics, republics, that is, in which the constitutional machinery was 'a reality and not a sham'. The high-handed proceedings of President Gabriel Terra raised doubts about Uruguay. But whereas in Uruguay and Costa Rica the structure of democratic government was strengthened rather than weakened in succeeding years, though at the cost of a brief civil war in the latter country in 1948, in Colombia it crumbled, and there, in 1953, a military government was installed.

Secondly, of the two states which Bryce had labelled 'constitutional' republics in 1910, namely Argentina and Chile, Argentina's claim to that title was already far more equivocal than Chile's. It is true that Chile's evolutionary constitutional development had been rudely interrupted in 1924–5, when the army entered politics, and not till 1932, after an embarrassing sequence of *coups d'état*, were normal political procedures fully restored. But restored they were, and though the stresses and strains of political life are acute, Chile has held fast to the democratic ideal. In Argentina, on the other hand, where the army also entered politics in 1930, the revolution of that year entrenched a conservative oligarchy in power, and by force and fraud it remained in power until a series of barrack-room revolutions in 1943 and 1944 prepared the way for the Peronista dictatorship.

Finally, as an example of his 'intermediary' class of states, neither true constitutional republics on the one hand nor mere autocracies or military despotisms on the other, Bryce, in 1910, selected Mexico. Brazil, perhaps, would have been a better choice. But Brazil, in 1930, abandoned constitutionalism altogether. Only in the years after the Second World War was it slowly and haltingly restored. As for Mexico, whose social revolution seemed to have run its course by the early nineteen-thirties but was now, on the contrary, to enter upon its most active phase, it could not be denied that the government was in fact a dictatorship clothed in legal forms and that the army was its chief source of power.[1] And

[1] *Cf.* Frank Tannenbaum, *Mexico: the Struggle for Peace and Bread* (New York, 1950), p. 83.

whatever the political as well as the social gains that the Revolution has made, Mexico must still be classed among the 'intermediary' states.

Despite, then, the bright democratic faith that burns in the majority of the constitutions of the Latin American states, democracy in Latin America is a plant of slow growth, whose shoots easily wither and decay.[1] Nor could it be otherwise. Democracy, says the famous Mexican constitution of 1917, should be considered 'not solely as a juridical structure and a political system, but as a system of life based on the continuous economic, social and cultural improvement of the people'.[2] There is the rub. There can be no political democracy without a measure of social democracy. And the social structure of the majority of the Latin American states is still profoundly undemocratic. The illiteracy and poverty so evident in most of the republics, the great cultural cleavages in the societies of the Indian and mestizo states, the glaring social inequalities, the land system which has concentrated political as well as social power in the hands of small minorities, these are not the foundations on which the structure of democratic government is easily built. And they have been combined with a tradition of authoritarianism in church and state on the one hand, and, on the other, with a highly personalist interpretation of politics.

It is true that the social landscape has been changing, rapidly changing in Argentina and Mexico and Brazil, but much more slowly in Peru, or Bolivia, or Ecuador. The great technological revolution of modern times, the rapid expansion of the cities, the rise of a middle class and of the urban industrial and labouring classes, all are threats to the traditional social order. And while the functions of the state have themselves been enormously expanded to meet new responsibilities, new elements have entered into political calculations. President Alessandri recognized them in Chile in the nineteen-twenties. Dr Vargas appealed to them in Brazil in the nineteen-thirties. And Colonel Perón exploited them in Argentina in the nineteen-forties. But social change is one thing, social solidarity is quite another. And the integration which Uruguay has achieved on one side of the Río de la Plata, Argentina has failed to achieve on the other.

[1] See the very interesting discussions in W. W. Pierson, ed., 'Pathology of Democracy in Latin America: a symposium', *American Political Science Review*, xliv (1950), 99–149. [2] Article 3.

The rule of an oligarchy or the rule of a dictator, these have been the traditional forms of Latin American government. They are still the prevailing forms today. There have been enlightened oligarchies, and unenlightened oligarchies, dictatorships serving limited interests, sometimes, indeed, little more than personal interests, and dictatorships which have looked to a general interest. But whatever the ends proposed or the interests served, régimes of force have been as common in the twentieth century as they were in the nineteenth century. The terms upon which political power may for long be held have, in most countries, changed, or are in process of change. The sphere of government has been greatly enlarged. New doctrines – doctrines which undergo a sea-change as they cross the Atlantic – have been imported from abroad. The twin forces of nationalism and socialism have newly been released. But the caudillo tradition survives. The dictator of the twentieth century, whether he belongs, like President Somoza, to a type that is vanishing, or whether, like Colonel Perón, he adopts all the trappings of modernity, is the heir of the nineteenth-century caudillo, and his lineage, perhaps, is older still. Was it not Gonzalo Pizarro whom the citizens of Lima saluted, in 1546, as 'Liberator, and Protector of the people'?[1]

A study of the social origins – usually comparatively humble – and of the early careers of the twentieth-century caudillos, if caudillos they may be called, would make fascinating reading. It would range from the ex-private of marines in the Dominican Republic, later Generalissimo Trujillo, to the ex-professor of law in the University of Guayaquil, Dr José María Velasco Ibarra, formerly president of Ecuador. Dr Vargas would occupy a distinguished place, and so would Colonel Perón. But soldiers would be more prominently represented than civilians. For the army, if not the only road to power, is still a major road to power, and the roll of colonels and generals who have exchanged military for political command is long.

[1] W. H. Prescott, *History of the Conquest of Peru* (5th ed., 3 vols., London, 1857), iii, 113.

The Study of Latin American History*

It is with more than the ordinary degree of trepidation, proper no doubt to feel, and decent to avow, on occasions such as this, that I address you today on the study of Latin American history. The chair is new; the professor, confronted with the rapidly growing literature of the history of twenty countries in at least four languages, is uncomfortably aware of his own limitations; and the subject, certainly in this country, is undeveloped. More than a hundred and seventy years ago William Robertson, the Historiographer-Royal of Scotland and the principal of the University of Edinburgh, published in London his *History of America*, still to be read with pleasure and profit. And from Principal Robertson, whom Gibbon termed, with gracious condescension, 'the first historian of the present age',[1] from Principal Robertson to Mr F. A. Kirkpatrick there have not been wanting in Britain distinguished students of Latin America. But they have been extraordinarily few. Remove the names of Southey at the beginning of the nineteenth century and of Sir Clements Markham at the end, of Cecil Jane and Cunninghame Graham and Pelham Box in our own day, and not many are left, at least among historians. Mr Kirkpatrick himself has had to tread the path of the pioneer, as had E. G. Bourne, Bernard Moses and W. R. Shepherd in the United States, and I am grateful for the opportunity to pay to him my tribute of admiration and respect. All scholars in this country must be in his debt, and all must build on foundations which he has helped to lay. But, while in the United States the range of scholarship has widened until it has brought the entire evolution

---

* [An inaugural lecture delivered at University College, London, on 4 November 1948 (London, 1948).]
[1] *The Memoirs of the Life of Edward Gibbon* (ed. G. B. Hill, London, 1900), p. 296.

of Latin America from the fifteenth to the twentieth century under investigation, that has not been so in England.

There are, it is true, signs of an awakening interest and of a realization that here is a gap to be filled;[1] and in other universities than ours there is reason to hope that Latin American history may soon take its place beside that other infant intruder in the history schools, the history of the United States. But it is fitting, I think, that the first Chair of Latin American history to be established in this country should be within the University of London and at University College.[2] It is fitting, not because the natural bent of this college is towards the exploration of 'fresh woods and pastures new', though that is true. Nor because a Chair of Latin American history here is the proper complement to that Chair of American history of whose holder I am proud to consider myself in some sense a pupil, though that also is true. It is fitting, I suggest, because those same liberal opinions which launched this college on its adventure of freedom at home made England, even under a tory government, the friend of freedom abroad. The formal announcement of the plans for the new University of London and the recognition by Britain of the new states of Spanish America occurred in the same year; and the founders of our college, or some at least among the most important of them, were themselves deeply interested in that second birth of a new world which seemed, in the first quarter of the nineteenth century, to hold within itself so high a destiny.

Consider the members of the first Council of this college in 1826. Distinguished even in that distinguished company was James Mill, whose meeting with Bentham, in 1808, had been of such transcendent importance to both. But Mill was the friend not only of Bentham but of the great precursor of Spanish American independence, Francisco de Miranda; and if Miranda inspired, Mill wrote the famous article in the *Edinburgh Review*, in 1809, on the emancipation of Spanish America, in which the future historian of British India saluted the 'brilliant prospects' opening up

[1] [Not, however, till 1962 was a Committee on Latin American Studies set up by the University Grants Committee. Its proposals for the establishment of five Centres of Latin American Studies, at Cambridge, Glasgow, Liverpool, London and Oxford, were accepted by Her Majesty's Government, and since 1965 all of these have come into existence. See the *Report of the Committee on Latin American Studies* (London, HMSO, 1965).]

[2] [The second Chair was established at Oxford in 1967.]

for mankind in South America.[1] With Mill, the radical, sat Brougham, the whig: and Brougham, the grand-nephew of Principal Robertson, had early turned his versatile genius to the cause of Spanish American independence. There, also, were Mackintosh and Lansdowne: Mackintosh, who had termed the Foreign Enlistment Bill of 1819 a bill 'to repress the rising liberty of the South Americans',[2] and who had proposed to call in the New World to redress the balance of the Old long before Canning coined his famous phrase;[3] Lansdowne, who had played in the Lords much the same part on behalf of Spanish America as Mackintosh played in the Commons. There, finally, were Alexander Baring and Isaac Lyon Goldsmid, whose names, surely, are as important in the financial history of Argentina and Brazil as they are in that of Europe. We need feel no surprise that the Council, with these men among its members, should have expressed the hope, in its first *Statement*, that the 'future legislators, governors and leading men' of Latin America might find in Gower Street a congenial place for education.[4] The deplorable tendency of South Americans to migrate to Paris was, alas, already evident. But here, as General William Miller explained, here, in Gower Street, they would 'imbibe sound principles and correct notions', and here they would avoid the dangerous contagion of 'Parisian vices and buffoonery'.[5]

One other name I must mention. Jeremy Bentham was not one of the founders of our college. He was a proprietor, no more. But, as Professor Bellot has observed, 'the intellectual debt of the university to him and the close association with him of some of the most prominent among the promoters is beyond dispute'.[6] His Auto-Ikon and his manuscripts are among our most treasured possessions.

Bentham's interest in Spanish America was first aroused by that plausible scoundrel and ex-vice-president of the United States,

---

[1] *Edinburgh Review*, xiii (Jan. 1809), 277 ff. See Alexander Bain, *James Mill* (London, 1882), pp. 97, 106, and W. S. Robertson, *The Life of Miranda* (2 vols., Chapel Hill, 1929), ii, 48–52.

[2] 13 May 1819. *Parliamentary Debates*, xl, 367.

[3] 15 June 1824, *ibid.*, n.s., xi, 1392.

[4] *Statement by the Council of the University of London, explanatory of the nature and objects of the Institution* (London, 1827), p. 10.

[5] William Miller to Sir Robert Wilson, 15 Jan. 1827, College Correspondence, No. 543.

[6] H. Hale Bellot, *University College, London, 1826–1926* (London, 1929), p. 25.

Aaron Burr. On a summer morning in 1804 Burr shot and killed Alexander Hamilton. Ostracized at home, he then engaged in romantic designs to detach the western states of America from the Union and Mexico from Spain, was arrested and tried for treason, and, though acquitted, sought refuge in France and England. Here he met Bentham. He meant, says Bentham, 'to make himself Emperor of Mexico. He told me I should be the legislator, and he would send a ship of war for me.'[1] This was fantasy. But Bentham's imagination was fired, and, in 1808, he seriously thought of removing to Mexico City.[2] We have among the college manuscripts a characteristic list of desiderata and of information to be obtained in preparation for so arduous a journey – distances by road in Mexico, cost of freight, packet boats, travelling carriages, age at which women marry, libraries, whether any clothes, vermin and bugs, etc. – the list is long.[3] But the enterprise proved too difficult. Bentham, at this point, met Miranda. Under Miranda's influence his thoughts were diverted from Mexico to South America, and in 1810 it was to another country 'still more charming', he wrote, 'the province of Venezuela', that he proposed to go. 'It will be,' he added, 'to do a little business in the way of my trade – to draw up a body of laws for the people there, they having, together with a number of the other Spanish American colonies, taken advantage of the times, and shaken off the Spanish yoke . . .'[4] As usual, his thoughts were transferred to paper. 'Carracas,' he heads it, 'Necessity of an all comprehensive Code,' and he adds a characteristic argument to show the advantages to be derived from the choice of Jeremy Bentham as the codifier.[5]

Once again his hopes were dashed; but from this time onwards it seems to have been the duty of every South American in London to pay his respects at Queen's Square Place. Bolívar himself was there in 1810, viewed by, but not, apparently, viewing its master;[6] and in 1820, when the great liberator had already become famous, and might become – was it not possible? – a disciple,

---

[1] John Bowring, ed., *The Works of Jeremy Bentham* (11 vols., Edinburgh, 1843), x, 432.

[2] *Ibid.*, x, 439–48.

[3] Bentham MSS., lx, 6–11.

[4] *Works*, x, 457.

[5] Bentham MSS., xii, 1–4; xxi, 1–6.

[6] Bentham to Rivadavia, 20 Feb. 1819, British Museum, Add. MSS., 33, 545, f. 348. See also a draft of a letter from Bentham to Bolívar, 24 Jan. 1820, Bentham MSS., x, 3–6.

Bentham began a correspondence with him which continued, amidst professions of mutual admiration, until 1827. At this point a conservative reaction secured the prohibition of the use of the *Traités de Legislation* in Colombian schools and colleges, and Bentham's opinion of the Liberator suffered a decided change,[1] a change, it may be added, which Bolívar's rival, Santander, did nothing to reverse when he visited Bentham in 1830.[2]

Rivadavia, one of the commanding figures in the early history of Argentina, also met Bentham, in 1818, I think, and we have Bowring's testimony that 'of the representatives of South America in this country, Rivadavia was the man of whom Bentham thought the most highly'.[3] It is not surprising. For Rivadavia not only referred to Bentham as the 'Newton of Legislation', not only began to translate the *Traités* into Spanish,[4] but, still more flattering, he ascribed to Bentham much of the merit for those notable reforms which, as a secretary of state, he had begun to introduce, with such startling effect, in Buenos Aires.[5] It was, moreover, the Buenos Aires government which announced the intention of constructing a new prison, 'in the form proposed by Mr Bentham under the name of Panopticon'.[6] And if, in Buenos Aires, Rivadavia was a professed pupil, in Central America, José del Valle, statesman, publicist, philosopher, was, more than a pupil, a son. 'My ever dear father,' he writes to Bentham;[7] Bentham remembered him in his will; and on Bentham's death the Federal Congress of Central America, at del Valle's motion, went into mourning.[8]

I wish I could conclude from all this that Bentham's influence in Latin America was profound. It is true that some 40,000 copies of his works, edited by Dumont, and translated into Spanish, were said to have been sold for the Spanish American market by

[1] *Works*, x, 552, 565; xi, 33.
[2] Santander to Bentham, 10 July 1830, Add. MSS., 33, 546, f. 444. See also *Works*, xi, 53.
[3] *Works*, x, 500.
[4] J. B. to Bolívar, 24 Jan. 1820, Bentham MSS., x, 3–6; Rivadavia to Bentham, 25 Aug. 1818, Add. MSS., 33, 545, f. 312.
[5] Rivadavia to Bentham, 26 Aug. 1822, Add. MSS., 33, 545, f. 596; *Works*, iv, 592–3.
[6] *Argos de Buenos Aires*, 6 July 1825.
[7] Del Valle to Bentham, 31 May 1830, Add. MSS., 33, 546, f. 418; *Works*, xi, 71. See also Rafael Heliodoro Valle, *Cartas de Bentham a José del Valle* (Mexico, 1942).
[8] *Gazeta de Guatemala*, 18 Sept. 1832.

1830,[1] and there is a charming story told by William Bridges Adams in 1832.

It was my fortune [he writes] to sojourn some months in a small and obscure town, on the Eastern base of the Andes. The public peace was frequently disturbed by revolutions and party changes; but there existed in that town a small knot of young men, who grieved over the disasters with which ignorance had afflicted their native land. ... A collection of the works of Bentham, translated into the Spanish language, was their acknowledged choicest treasure; and each night they met, to become wiser by the wisdom he had spread over the earth. They asked not of kings, or of princes, of conquerors, or of potentates. Their first question of an Englishman was, 'Have you ever seen Bentham?' To their unprejudiced view he was the greatest man on the face of the earth. ... By the hour they would listen to anecdotes of the man whom they venerated, and at each pause in the conversation they would exclaim, 'Oh! that he had been born our countryman, to rescue us from the evils of mis-government, and the misery which it has drawn in its train.'[2]

But, alas, I suspect that, like the abortive proposal 'for the Junction of the Two Seas – the Atlantic and the Pacific, by means of a Joint-Stock Company, to be styled the Junctiana Company', Bentham's writings, even in translation, provoked more of admiration than inspiration, and not always admiration. 'Whose work on jurisprudence do you study?' a professor at the University of Córdoba asked of a student from the University of Buenos Aires. 'Bentham's.' 'Whose, Sir, do you say? Little Bentham's? ... There is more sense in one of my writings than in all those windbags. What a university!'[3]

The hopes our founders entertained, their visions of the future, took longer to realize than some at least anticipated. But that their faith was finally to be justified, the foundation of this Chair is in part a witness. The new states of Latin America have grown, or are growing, into nations. The youngest of them is already forty-five, and the majority have behind them more than a century of independent life. Each today is strongly conscious of its own identity. By their own scholars and by those of the United States each phase of their national life is gradually being brought under investigation;

---

[1] *Works*, xi, 33.
[2] *The Tatler,* 9 March 1832.
[3] D. F. Sarmiento, *Civilización y Barbarie* (Buenos Aires, 1889), p. 95.

and the growth of historical literature is already such that it is difficult for the individual scholar to keep abreast of current writings. The latest edition of Mr C. K. Jones's *Bibliography of Latin American Bibliographies* contains more than three thousand items. The current *Handbook of Latin American Studies* contains nearer five thousand than four. The *Hispanic American Historical Review* is in its twenty-eighth year, and both in Latin America and in Spain it has distinguished rivals. In the United States, in Latin America, in Spain, the study of Latin American history has become professionalized. It is time indeed to recognize that here is a branch of historical studies in which English scholarship has been left far behind, and one, I submit, that must increasingly force itself upon our attention.

Let me first define what I mean by Latin American history. I do not mean the history of the discovery, conquest and colonization of the New World, nor the still comparatively neglected study of the Spanish and Portuguese empires in America. We are at last beginning to see that long adventure in better perspective. The mists of prejudice and ignorance are being gradually dispelled. We no longer believe that the Spanish empire in the New World subsisted for more than three hundred years – to borrow Gibbon's famous phrase – 'in a state of premature and perpetual decay', and the 'black legend' has been washed almost white – perhaps, indeed, too white. But these problems lie within a wider field. The history of the empires of Spain and Portugal belongs to the study of colonial or imperial history. Our concern – and I must emphasize what I conceive to be the function of this chair – our concern will be with the history of the independent states of Latin America, with their experience during and since the establishment of their independence, with their impact upon the rest of the world, and with the impact of the rest of the world upon them.

One further preliminary observation must be made. By 'Latin America' I mean no more than the definition of an area, an area larger by far than Europe and the United States combined. The twenty republics, so neatly, but sometimes so misleadingly, labelled 'Latin America', differ from one another in size, in wealth, in population, in race, in history, in culture. They are in different stages of political, economic and social evolution, and they are 'Latin' only in so far as eighteen of them were in part moulded by Spanish colonization, as one, the greatest, was, in origin, the product of Portuguese adventure overseas, and another, the smallest, took its language from France.

To regard the emancipation of the Latin American area from Spanish and Portuguese rule as the starting-point of our studies is, I freely admit, from one point of view, the point of view of a Mexican or a Brazilian, arbitrary enough. That great convulsion was not 'unheralded'. Nor – in the words of Acton, distinguishing modern from medieval history – did it found 'a new order of things, under a law of innovation, sapping the ancient reign of continuity'. The political revolution cradled an economic but not a social revolution. Where such a movement came into being, as in Mexico, it was strangled, or almost strangled, at its birth; and at the end of the wars of liberation the structure of colonial society remained essentially unchanged.[1] The three centuries of colonial experience, as Dr Silvio Zavala has rightly observed, are not to be dismissed as a mere prelude to the historical drama initiated by the liberators. And whatever the conscious reaction against this colonial heritage in parts of Latin America today, the roots of Spanish American society 'lie deep in the colonial past'.[2]

From another point of view, also, that of a European, it is not to be supposed that the liberation of Latin America awakened Europe to the sudden consciousness of what it had not known before. Since that early morning of 12 October 1492, with the moon past full,[3] when the little fleet of Columbus first sighted land, the ocean had linked, not divided the continents. First the pirate, then the smuggler, sailed to destroy in America the power of Spain in Europe. In eighteenth-century England in particular, from the days of the Asiento to those of the invasions of Buenos Aires, from Anson and Vernon to Popham and Baird, interest in Latin America had been steadily growing. Its secrets, long hid, were gradually being revealed. Its trade enriched Spain's rivals, not Spain herself. And it may well be argued that the emancipation of Spanish America was as much a phase in the commercial expansion of Europe and England as it was, more obviously, the critical period in the development of new American nationalities. In that expansion Spain failed to participate; and it was this, not the

[1] [But see above, *Tradition and Revolt in Latin America*, pp. 8–11.]

[2] Silvio Zavala, *New Viewpoints on the Spanish Colonization of America* (Philadelphia, 1943), p. 2.

[3] S. E. Morison, *Admiral of the Ocean Sea, A Life of Christopher Columbus* (Boston, 1942), p. 225.

American or the French Revolutions, though these too played their part, which worked the silent destruction of Spain's imperial system. Spain's colonies were lost before the revolution began, though it needed the Napoleonic invasions of the Peninsula first, apparently, to contradict, and then to demonstrate that fact.[1]

Yet though the lines of demarcation between the colonial and the subsequent history of the Latin American peoples are today less sharply defined than once they were, the lines are there. If, as Sir Charles Webster has said, the emancipation of Latin America from European control ranks 'with the American and French Revolutions as one of the determining political forces which brought into existence the world in which we still live',[2] for the Latin American peoples it meant more than the establishment of a new political order. It was the awakening to a new life, the entry into a world of new experience; and it is that experience which must be, more particularly, the object of our study.

European control, political control, was ended. This, in itself, was a fact of primary importance. The freedom which the Latin American states had won they were left to organize in their own way. There was to be no partition of Latin America, no exercise of suzerainty, no division of territory. In this respect the policy laid down by Castlereagh and Canning, the policy of non-intervention, was, in its essentials, maintained throughout the nineteenth century, and in this respect at least the Monroe Doctrine received the silent support of British naval power. But, henceforth, the door was open, as it had never been before, to trade, investment, immigration; and for the next hundred years not the United States alone but Latin America also acted like a magnet upon the hopes and ambitions of the European peoples.

The emigrant stream to Latin America began in the decade after Waterloo, with the migration of Germans to Brazil and of Scotsmen to Argentina. But disillusion quickly followed. 'I am convinced,' wrote Sir Francis Head in 1826, 'that those who have hitherto emigrated to this country [Argentina] ... have passed their days in disappointment and regret – that the constitution of every individual has been more or less impaired – that their religious principles have altogether been destroyed – and I there-

[1] [See above, 'The Fall of the Spanish American Empire', pp. 87–91.]
[2] C. K. Webster, *Britain and the Independence of Latin America, 1812–1830* (2 vols., London, 1938), i, 3.

fore would sincerely advise poor people, particularly those who
have families, not to migrate to such hot latitudes. . . .'[1] Not till
the middle of the century was the flow renewed, with the founding
of agricultural colonies on the Argentine pampa and of German
settlements in southern Brazil, and not till near the end, with the
mounting figures of Italian immigrants, did it swell to any considerable volume. But though the emigrant stream to Latin
America was far smaller and less widely diffused than the great
migration to the United States, in the transformation of the
Argentine pampa, in the equally startling transformation of São
Paulo, in the colonization of southern Brazil and of south-central
Chile, the immigrant played as decisive a part as ever he played in
the Mississippi Valley.

Foreign investment also began in the decade after Waterloo. The
story is familiar. So eager was the desire to lend that, when the
Peruvian loan was marketed in 1822, the extreme pressure of the
brokers pushed the contractor and his agents from one corner of
the Royal Exchange to the other and finally through its doors.[2]
But the loans went into default, the mining companies, or a large
number of them, failed, and, after the experience of the eighteen-
twenties, as with immigration, so with investment, it was not till
the middle of the century that the stream freshened (though it had
never entirely ceased), to flow with increasing momentum in its
closing decades. Spread over a great range of enterprises, in the
transport and public untility companies, in the export and extrac-
tive industries, as well as in government securities, it reached its
height in the nineteen-twenties, when American capital had reinforced the diminished supply from Europe.

It is a fashion, these days, to look upon this record as one of
exploitation, in the derogatory sense of that word. This is not
clear thinking, nor a help to understanding. If the export of capital
to Latin America had a different effect from the export of capital to
the United States, if it prolonged the dependence of the Latin
American countries for their trade and revenue on the export of a
few staple products, this was due as much to internal circumstances as to causes over which the creditors had control. And
whatever the other results of this particular form of economic

---

[1] F. B. Head, *Rough Notes taken during some rapid Journeys across the Pampas and
among the Andes* (2nd ed., London, 1826), pp. 305–6.
[2] *The Times*, 14 Oct. 1822.

activity, the fact remains that it was foreign investment which endowed the Latin American countries with what Professor Hancock has described, in another connexion, as 'the "permanent outfit" which was the economic foundation of their nationhood'.[1]

This story of the migration of people and capital from Europe to the Americas is the story of the closer linking of the continents. And it is obvious that between the economic development of the Latin American area (like that of the United States) and the growth of modern England there is a vital connexion. The twenty-five millions or so of British capital invested there by 1830 had grown to £180 millions by 1876 and to nearly £1,000 millions by 1913.[2] From the middle decade of the century, moreover, until the first World War, Latin America supplied about one-tenth of British imports and received a tenth of British exports. These figures, for Latin America as a whole, conceal, no doubt, as much as they reveal; but they serve at least to show the fact of interdependence. Yet even where the linkage has been closest, it has remained for American scholars to write the history of such matters as the rise and decline of British pre-eminence in Brazil, and the intimate relations between the Argentine meat industry and the British market.[3] And for the rest the field is almost virgin soil.[4] In that delightful book, *Desert Trails of Atacama*, Isaiah Bowman has described how, at Copiapó, he found a mass of buried treasure in the form of records extending over almost a hundred years and dealing with the affairs of the Copiapó Valley, and particularly with those of the principal copper mining company there. The originals, he adds, 'have recently been destroyed by the home company in London on account of lack of space'.[5] That was in 1924, and the fates, since then, have not been kind. Yet the records of those companies and business houses whose connexions with Latin

[1] W. K. Hancock, *Survey of British Commonwealth Affairs* (London, 1940), ii, 290.

[2] According to the calculations, based mainly on the *South American Journal*, of J. F. Rippy, 'British Investments in Latin America, End of 1913', *Journal of Modern History*, xix (Sept. 1947), p. 231.

[3] A. K. Manchester, *British Preëminence in Brazil, its Rise and Decline* (Chapel Hill, 1933); S. G. Hanson, *Argentine Meat and the British Market* (Stanford Univ. Press, [1938]).

[4] [But see now also H. S. Ferns, *Britain and Argentina in the Nineteenth Century* (Oxford, 1960), and David Joslin, *A Century of Banking in Latin America, to commemorate the centenary in 1962 of the Bank of London and South America Limited* (London, 1963).]

[5] Isaiah Bowman, *Desert Trails of Atacama* (American Geographical Society, 1924), p. 182.

America have been so long and so close are materials for the history not only of Latin America but of England: the destruction of any part of them is an irreparable loss, and the study of what survives is urgent.

The predominant position which Britain enjoyed in Latin America for most of the nineteenth century was founded on the solid facts of British trade and British capital, as well as on those of British diplomacy and British naval power. Yet as the century closed that position was already being undermined. 'Spanish America,' Canning had declared in 1824, 'is free; and if we do not mismanage our affairs sadly, she is English.' 'Today,' retorted the American secretary of state, Olney, in 1895, 'the United States is practically sovereign on this continent, and its fiat is law upon the subjects to which it confines its interposition.' Olney was as wide of the mark as Canning. Nevertheless, a profound change had begun. Its causes are familiar. Here, it suffices to note that henceforth American trade, American capital, American diplomacy, began to win for the United States that special position in Latin America hitherto occupied by Great Britain;[1] and, within the next twenty-five years, the first World War, which completed the revolution in the position of the United States as a world power, completed also the revolution in the respective positions of Great Britain and the United States in Latin America, except, perhaps, in southern South America.

But if a period in the history of Anglo-American relations in Latin America thus ended – and those relations deserve the closer attention of the economic as well as of the diplomatic historian – there were, between the two World Wars, developments more momentous still. The immigration frontier in Latin America closed. The stream of investment ceased. Bolts and bars were clamped upon the doors of trade. And as government policy was increasingly directed towards the development of domestic industries and the widening of the basis of primary production, the old familiar economic structure of the principal Latin American countries, and their old external economic relations, began slowly but surely to change. Latin America entered the beginnings of its industrial age. It entered the age of nationalism. It entered the wider sphere of world affairs. We are witnessing, I think, the close

[1] [See above, 'Anglo-American Rivalries and the Venezuelan Crisis of 1895', pp. 214–5.]

of an era, and a new Latin America is growing before our eyes.

If, however, the historian of modern England or modern Europe can no longer afford to ignore the history of Latin America, we must, also, enter on the study of Latin American history for its own sake, for its own intrinsic interest, as well as for the wider light that it may cast. For Latin America was, in the nineteenth century, and it still is, a vast laboratory of political, social, racial and economic experiment. Here the very old and the very new dwell side by side, the mule track and the aeroplane, the primitive plantation and the steel mill, the Indian tribe and the complex urban society. Here the frontier, the zone between civilization and the wilderness, is still a political, a social, and an economic fact. If, as Frederick Jackson Turner said, in the most famous of his essays, 'the United States lies like a huge page in the history of society',[1] so also does Latin America. Nowhere has the struggle between man and his environment been sterner, or the relation between land and people more intimate. Nowhere has the conflict between the individual and society been more passionate, and nowhere has the reconciliation of freedom with order been more difficult to achieve.

Pioneer lands, European frontiers, the Latin American countries may have been. But they were, also, old societies, moulded by the intimate contact of European with Indian and, in some cases, with African culture, and set, by European inheritance as well as by American experience, into distinctive forms. The heritage and the experience were alike very different from those of the English colonists in North America, and they conformed less easily to the ideas and forces which dominated the nineteenth century. Yet, with their declarations of independence, the Spanish American communities, medieval in quality and cast, were called upon, at one bound, to assume the form and functions of the modern democratic state. They rejected what was old and familiar for what was new and untried. They engrafted alien political philosophies on to old established ways of life. Only in Brazil was political and administrative continuity preserved; and it is significant that the political history of Brazil in the nineteenth century is in singular contrast to that of her Spanish American neighbours.

What followed is in part familiar. As Bolívar had feared and prophesied, the Spanish American states were plunged into con-

[1] *The Frontier in American History* (New York, 1921), p. 11.

fusion. Their course seemed set in a monotonous rhythm of revolution and dictatorship, of anarchy and despotism. To Sarmiento, writing one of the classics of nineteenth-century literature, the early history of his country, Argentina, revealed itself as that of the warfare between civilization and barbarism, with barbarism for a time the victor. It is well, however, to recall that early warning of Acton, which Professor Butterfield has recently quoted: 'we must distrust our knowledge of every period which appears to us barbarous. It appears so as long as we have not found the key to its real character.'[1] And while the early annals of the Spanish American republics, and some of the later ones as well, may seem to provide a notebook for illustrating afresh a modern version of the *Politics,* they are not to be neatly and outrageously docketed as the simple annals of dictatorship tempered by assassination and revolution. That would be to mistake the surface currents for the deeper tides beneath. The struggle between Buenos Aires and the provinces in Argentina, the quest for land and liberty in Mexico, the rival conceptions of church and state in Colombia, these are not trivial themes, and they give meaning and form to much which is, at first sight, bewildering and confused.

Political life in Spanish America, moreover, had a flavour all its own. Our conventional terminology is misleading. Dictatorship meant autocracy, sometimes tyranny. But it was a Tudor despotism, not the systematic regimentation that informs the totalitarian state. Democracy, in a political sense, meant scarcely more than republicanism. It was a pattern of government laid up in heaven but not, perhaps wisely, to be practised on earth. Yet what shall we make of Hudson's description of Uruguay during one of the most turbulent periods of its history? 'It is,' he wrote, 'the perfect republic: the sense of emancipation experienced in it by the wanderer from the Old World is indescribably sweet and novel . . . the knot of ambitious rulers all striving to pluck each other down have no power to make the people miserable. The unwritten constitution, mightier than the written one, is in the heart of every man to make him still a republican and free with a freedom it would be hard to match anywhere else on the globe.'[2] As for revolutions, those established extra-legal habits of changing a government, a revolution, Isaiah Bowman once wrote, 'affects but

---

[1] H. Butterfield, *Lord Acton* (Historical Association, London, 1948), p. 11.

[2] W. H. Hudson, *The Purple Land* (London, 1904), pp. 334–5.

a few centres, a limited number of persons, a very thin layer of the people. . . . For the rest, the life of the communities of Hispanic America goes on unaltered by revolutionary changes. The seasons, the crops, trade, social gatherings, the community organization – these are the things of outstanding importance.'[1]

That is not true of every Latin American revolution. It is certainly not true of the greatest of them all, the Mexican Revolution of our own times. But it was true of a great many. Politics was a way of life and of making a living, remote from the control and interests of the masses. The majority were, and were content to be, spectators of events, indifferent to the form of government provided that government did not too arrogantly trespass on the interests of the governed.

In some of the Spanish America countries, where the Indian and mestizo masses, the native and mixed stocks, oppressed by poverty, ignorance and disease, still remain outside the national life, and where, in Acton's pregnant phrase, there is not 'propelling power . . . equal to the heavy burden of a half-barbarous population', dictatorship may still be a necessary stage in the long struggle to establish order, unity, and social coherence. The shadows of the centuries lie heavy on those ancient lands where Man and Nature still struggle for mastery. Their experience is outside our own. And here indeed, as Sir Maurice Powicke reminds us, the value of history may be 'precisely that it can enlarge our faculties of curiosity, understanding and compassion and take us into the company of people whose experience eludes our categories'.[2]

Yet even in those countries whose political, economic and social development seems, in western eyes, to have been most retarded, time does not stand still nor are men's minds inactive; and in Latin America as a whole the transformation which has occurred in the last hundred years is sufficiently remarkable. Brazil, so long an empire amid republics, was always in a class apart, monarchical, aristocratic, a land where, as Gilberto Freyre says, 'the plantation system acted as a powerful republican opposition to any autocratic excess on the part of the Crown and where the Crown served as a permanent limit to autocratic excesses on the part of plantation lords'.[3] In Chile the reign of the caudillos virtually ceased in the

[1] *Desert Trails of Atacama*, pp. 109–10.
[2] F. M. Powicke, *Three Lectures* (London, 1947), p. 43.
[3] *Brazil: an Interpretation* (New York, 1945), p. 52.

eighteen-thirties, and Chile, aristocratic but republican, evolved, in the security of her mountain barrier, a parliamentary system which, whatever its faults and failures, was as remarkable an experiment in pure politics as the nineteenth century knew. Argentina waited longer. It was only after the great struggle between the port and the provinces had been resolved that the country could enter, in the 'sixties, on its full and natural economic life. Thereafter, with a rapidity unexampled save in the United States, a backward frontier area was transformed into a highly urbanized commercial society.

In the later development of these countries, though to a lesser extent in Chile than in the other two, the immigrant and immigrant capital played a decisive part. In each, economic expansion was accompanied by a widening of the basis of society and politics. In each there arose a new class, or classes, to bridge the gap between the opulent and the impoverished. But these countries do not stand alone. Three other states, Uruguay, Colombia and Costa Rica, have experienced, in the present century, peaceful processes of reformation and reconstruction, and a fourth, Mexico, has undergone a profound social revolution, a movement of passion, hope and hate, unleashing violent forces, producing its own art and literature, now apparently spent, now again in full spate.[1]

No single explanation is adequate to these phenomena, and certainly not a racial one. That, at least, is one lesson to be learnt. There are, in this age of nationalism, false gods in Latin America, as everywhere else. But racialism is not among them. This is the continent of a new man, and it is a continent of hope. New life is stirring, new forces are arising, political, social, economic. And while the conquest of the wilderness still goes on, new civilizations, neither Latin nor American, are in process of evolution. At our loss and at our peril we ignore them.

[1] [This essay was written in 1948. See also above, 'The Caudillo Tradition' (1957), pp. 224–6, and 'Tradition and Revolt in Latin America' (1964), pp. 15–17.]

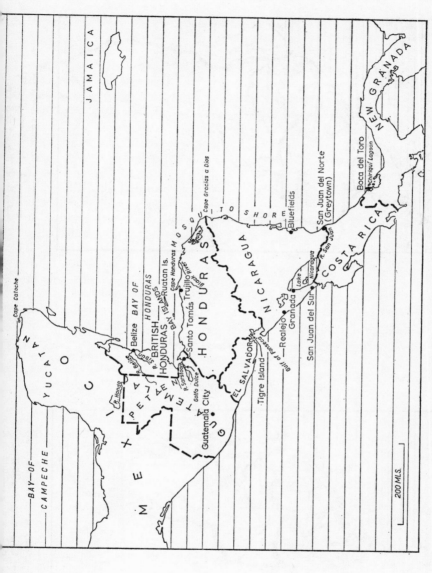

Map 1. Map to illustrate the Central American dispute.

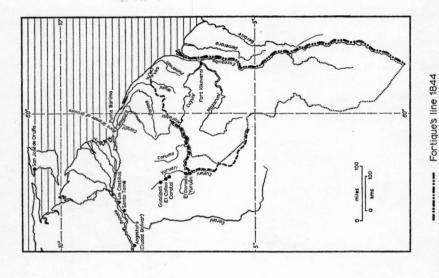

Fortique's line 1844 ▪▪▪▪▪▪▪

Aberdeen's line 1844 ▬ ▬ ▬

Present boundary ▬▬▬▬

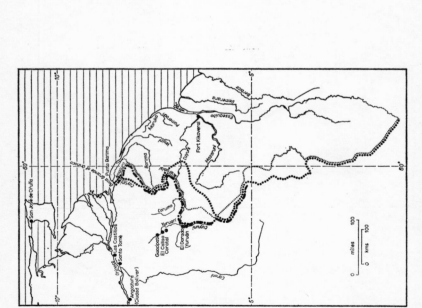

1840 sketch line (after Arrowsmith) ▪▪▪▪▪▪▪

Schomburgk line 1841-42 ▬▪▬▪▬

Present boundary

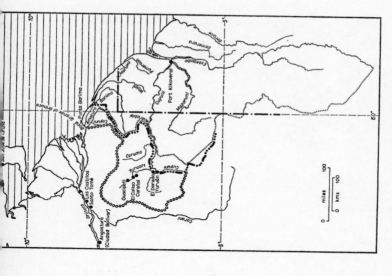

Map 2. Boundaries between British Guiana and Venezuela.
Interpreted on the base of the American Geographical
Society's 'Map of Hispanic America', scale 1:1 million.

· — · — Rojas line 1881

■■■■■ Granville's line 1881

ooooooo Extreme British Claim

············ Present boundary

Index

I

Index

Index

Index

Index

Index

Index

Index

Index

Index

Index

Index

Index

Index

Doc
F
1410
H88
1969